The Last Wild Places of Kansas

The Last Wild Places
of Kansas
Journeys into Hidden Landscapes

George Frazier

UNIVERSITY PRESS OF KANSAS

"Daniel Boone" by Stephen Vincent Benet. From A BOOK OF AMERICANS by Rosemary
and Stephen Vincent Benet. Henry Holt & Company. Copyright © 1933 by Rosemary
and Stephen Vincent Benet. Copyright renewed © 1961 Rosemary Carr Benet.
Reprinted by permission of Brandt & Hochman Literary Agents, Inc.

"Journey West" by Victor Contoski. Published in 1977, in ARK RIVER REVIEW. Copyright
© 1977 by Victor Contoski. Reprinted by permission of Victor Contoski.

All photos by George Frazier.

Published by the University Press of Kansas (Lawrence, Kansas 66045), which was
organized by the Kansas Board of Regents and is operated and funded by Emporia
State University, Fort Hays State University, Kansas State University, Pittsburg State
University, the University of Kansas, and Wichita State University

Library of Congress Cataloging-in-Publication Data
Names: Frazier, George, 1966– author.
Title: The last wild places of Kansas : journeys into hidden landscapes /
George Frazier.
Description: Lawrence, Kansas : University Press of Kansas, [2016] |
Includes bibliographical references and index.
Identifiers: LCCN 2015043968
ISBN 9780700622207 (pbk. : alk. paper) | ISBN 9780700622207 (ebook)
Subjects: LCSH: Natural history—Kansas. | Wilderness areas—Kansas.
Classification: LCC QH76.5.K2 F73 2016 | DDC 508.781—dc23
LC record available at http://lccn.loc.gov/2015043968.

British Library Cataloguing-in-Publication Data is available.

Printed in the United States of America

10 9 8 7 6 5 4 3 2

The paper used in this publication is recycled and contains 30 percent postconsumer
waste. It is acid free and meets the minimum requirements of the American National
Standard for Permanence of Paper for Printed Library Materials Z39.48-1992.

For Christina Frazier, Alan Ziegler,
Jay Bredwell, Gary Shea, and Lee Bissinger,
my latter-day Kansas coureurs de bois.

And Chloe.

Whoever travels in Kansas . . . feels buffalo hooves in his heartbeats.
Victor Contoski

Contents

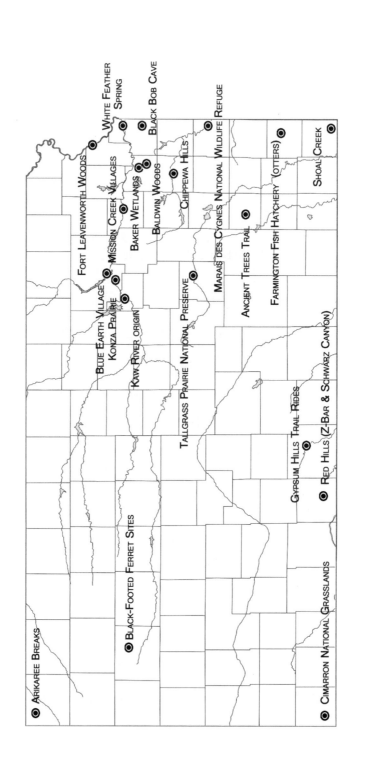

Prologue

It was like something that fell from outer space. Rising up forty feet above an otherwise featureless prairie near modern Cawker City—better known today for its gigantic ball of twine—a mysterious artesian well called Waconda Spring bubbled up from deep underground. The sea-green water filled a perfectly circular pool fifty feet across set in a gray limestone mound on the north bank of the Solomon River. It looked like a volcanic crater. Generations of plains Indians trekked to the spring for ceremonies. In later years, curiosity seekers fished up beads, arrow points, French and Spanish medallions, and human bones. A deep-sea diver, hired in 1908 to ascertain its depth, failed to find the bottom (though geologists from the University of Kansas using sonar later pinpointed it at thirty-five meters).

In 1767, William Johnson, Britain's Superintendent of Indian Affairs who once paid the Iroquois a bounty on the scalps of French children, became the first European to see the spring. The explorer Zebulon Pike, following advice from Pawnees at Guide Rock village, detoured from his unsuccessful trip to climb the peak named for him and toured the spring in 1806. Following Kansas statehood, Cawker City Mineral Company extracted salt from the mineral basin. A bottling company distributed the medicinal water "Waconda Flier" nationally, winning a medal at the 1904 St. Louis World's Fair. In the first years of the twentieth century, a series of resort hotels and a sanatorium were built so patients could bathe in pure Waconda water and drink the briny solution as a "mild and gentle laxative but a sure laxative."

Wild landmarks infused with personal and cultural meaning like Waconda Spring have always been rare. Natural places you can fall in love with, places of passion, of pilgrimage—I have always just called them wild places. Undisturbed remnants of ancient ecosystems, habitats for rare or threatened species, pristine stretches of river, unusual geologic features, exclamations of topography—wild places aren't merely beautiful landscapes; they possess a totemic lure, a power or presence that attracts people, sometimes across generational and cultural chasms spanning centuries. As modest as Waconda Spring or as continental as Antarctica, the power of a wild place doesn't derive from sheer scale or visual grandeur, nor does it translate necessarily into tourism dollars.

Today, the Waconda Spring site is located in Glen Elder State Park. Steeped in Native American, pioneer, and geological lore, the spring seems like the perfect focal point for a park celebrating natural Kansas. But don't look for it if you visit Glen Elder, not unless you plan to scuba dive. Despite a desperate battle in the 1950s and early 1960s, the Waconda Spring was buried under the waters of a reservoir in 1965, sacrificed to mitigate flooding a hundred miles downstream in the Kansas River valley. In keeping with the all-things-wild-and-beautiful-must-be-destroyed theme, the builders of Glen Elder dam bulldozed ruins from the sanatorium into the sacred spring just before the waters of Waconda Lake buried it forever.

Let's be honest. Kansas is not known for its wild places. The state seems to have an inferiority complex of landscape, always trying to be something it isn't. The most prominent natural feature on the state seal isn't a tallgrass prairie or a cottonwood forest, it's a *mountain range*. Since the last wild bison sought refuge on the back of a nickel, the public image of natural Kansas has progressed from great American desert, to dust bowl, to flyover country, to coffee table book of sunflower fields, fenced buffalo herds, and rainbows above winter wheat—a placeless farm-country landscape. Or so it would seem.

While attending graduate school at the University of Kansas in Lawrence, I once stood on the south side of US Highway 40 and watched the intentional destruction of a biologically diverse half section of virgin tallgrass locally referred to as the Elkins Prairie. The site provided habitat for two federally threatened plant species—Meade's milkweed and western prairie fringed orchid—but more than that it was just *cool*, a virgin prairie on the outskirts of Lawrence that I could ride my bike to. Pioneers on the California and Oregon Trails probably stopped there to take on water from a small seep spring feeding Baldwin Creek. Elkins Prairie was a wild place in every sense.

Seeing the tubes of fresh black earth churning out like sausage from the discs of the tractor lit a fire in my heart for the wild places of Kansas. It crystallized a feeling I'd had growing up in the suburbs west of Kansas City, that wild Kansas was a unique crossroads of ecosystems, the place where the last lip of eastern deciduous forest dissolves into a kingdom of grasses, where rivers of birdlife flow along timeworn flight channels in May, where memories of a great biomass equal to the Serengeti still echo across the vast emptiness of the western plains.

Unlike friends who took their passion for wild places to cities like Boulder, Laramie, and Anchorage, I dug my heels in and began exploring my own backyard. With few exceptions, the places I found, or rather, that revealed themselves to me once I expunged my prejudices about Kansas, are little known to most people who have spent their whole lives in the state.

They are places where relatively undisturbed prairie, forest, wetland, and river ecosystems cheat death and incubate the DNA of lost wild America; where extirpated mammalian species are making comebacks; where flying squirrels leap between centuries-old trees illuminated by the unearthly green glow of foxfire; where rings marking the sites of Kansa earth lodges rise up on the prairie in March; where cold springs feed watercress pools that once held the reflections of Indian traditionalists; where soapweed canyons home to great colonies of prairie dogs are ground zero in a war over the rights of private landowners to protect wildlife and hasten the return of the most endangered mammal in North America; where the ice moon paints the Smoky Hill with memories of the buffalo wolf and the lonesome rattle of false indigo; where a single visit can trigger dreams that leave you drenched in sweat from killing bull elk with stone-tipped arrows; where the blue lid of sky forms a vacuum seal over treeless pastel hills, orange in winter, where bluestem rises.

A few are impossible to find on maps, hidden behind barbed wire on private property. Most are magnificently bereft of anything beneficial to 99.9 percent of modern America. True wildernesses, they are not, but we are all sinners. At the correct angle of light, when the south wind blows pollen carrying biological memories of the glaciers, these places are a crack between the worlds, portals to the lost buffalo wilderness, the *Last Wild Places of Kansas*.

Land Ho!

What you are about to read is not a guide book, but the early working subtitle, "A Trespasser's Guide," helped inspire me during the nine years it took to write and edit *The Last Wild Places of Kansas*. Does this mean I encourage you or anybody else to trespass on private property? Hardly. If you don't believe me, skip ahead to "The Renegade Streams of Eastern Kansas" (chapter 6). Some incredible public properties appear on our itinerary—the Cimarron National Grasslands, Kansas River, Fort Leavenworth Woods, Ancient Trees Trail, Marais Des Cygnes National

Wildlife Refuge, Haskell-Baker Wetlands, and more—the list is sturdy and substantive. But Kansas has the smallest percentage of public land in America—only 2 percent of total acreage—so it's inevitable that many wild places are under private stewardship. Probably more than any other recent work on the geography of wild Kansas, this book will take you behind the barbed wire and beyond the small collection of easily accessible, well-known spots that others have covered in great detail.

But before embarking, I'd like to say a little more about trespassing, which can be as much a complicity of heart as of hoof. To the extent that you can trespass on your own preconceived notions of wild places, private versus public land rights, the ethics of accessibility, forgotten Native American history, and the existential value of America's rapidly disappearing wilderness legacy, I will ask you to climb carefully but forcefully over metaphorical strands of barbed wire that impede a better understanding of wild places in a state like Kansas. Along the way I won't gloss over the difficult and confusing issues faced by anybody trying to create a wild lands ethos and personal connection to a place that is mostly off limits to the public. Toward those ends, I hope to be not only your guide, but also your shameless enabler.

But let me also state clearly and directly that trespassing—in the literal legal sense—is against the law in Kansas. Federal, state, and local antitrespassing statutes exist to protect landowners and provide for exclusivity of use. This includes wild lands owned by private organizations like the Nature Conservancy and the Kansas Land Trust, railroads, scouting and religious organizations, Indian reservations, corporate farms and ranches, and certain restricted tracts managed by the military and universities. Whether your intent is to hike, scout for morel mushrooms, get a close-up view of a bald eagle nest, dance with prairie chickens, shoot prairie chickens, hunt for artifacts, fossils, buried treasure, or to bury treasure—do so only *after* you acquire permission from the land's owner. It doesn't matter whether you see a "no trespassing" sign or not. When in doubt, get permission. Ninety-eight percent of Kansas is privately owned, so do the math. If you suspect that guns or large dogs might be involved, get it in writing.

The era of Google Maps and GPS-enabled smartphones has radically simplified the process of finding out who owns a parcel of land. Given an address or a set of GPS coordinates, your local county appraiser's office can help out and in some cases online Geographical Information Systems provide self-service via the Internet. You might not get an email address, but it's a place to start.

There are good ways and better ways to ask for permission to explore private property. When possible, I start by sending an email that explains who I am, why I want to visit, and a range of dates and times that could work. Whether or not the first contact is by email, phone, or a knock on the door, I almost always meet the landowner or property manager in person before my visit. When meeting for the first time, it helps if you've done your research. If you mention that you've heard that the deep pools made by glacial boulders where Little Illinois Creek runs into Illinois Creek make a great place to fish for flatheads, you might transform a skeptical stare into a welcoming handshake. Smile early, smile often. If you have cute kids, bring them with you, if not, consider borrowing some. If you have ATVs or a pit bull with a penchant for irony and gallows humor, consider leaving them at home.

There are many sound reasons why landowners wouldn't want strangers tromping across their prairies, climbing around in their caves, or gallivanting through their bottomland forests during rifle deer season. Be ready to take no for an answer, but I've found that you won't often have to. I've made lifelong friendships with people I originally met while seeking permission to explore wild places. They've given me private tours; fed me breakfast, lunch, and dinner; and sent me home with gifts of homemade wine, wild honey, rutabagas, giant turnips, watercress, and funny mismatched eggs from chickens that look far too exotic, to my chicken-challenged eyes, to live in Kansas. Never underestimate the allure of wild places. They attract an exceptional group of stewards and caretakers. Without them, this book would be an obituary.

Lay of the Land

Chapter 1, "Blackbob and the Prophet," looks at two virtually forgotten wild places on private property in the densely populated suburbs of Kansas City, a reminder that wild places can persist *anywhere*. More remarkable are the stories of two Native American traditionalist leaders associated with these places and some reasons why their histories barely register as footnotes in the larger history of Kansas.

Next we move completely across the state to far southwestern Kansas, where in chapter 2, "La Jornada," we bask in the lonely emptiness of Cimarron National Grasslands and the stories of Jedidiah Smith, George Sibley, an unconventional family of modern-day prairie dog hunters, and a rare population of high plains black bears on the largest piece of public property in the state.

The quest to reach an ancient pecan grove where James Audubon and Chief Joseph of the Nez Perce both camped leads into the heart of Kansas "Old Growth," the subject of chapter 3. Post oaks born before George Washington, flying squirrels, the eerie glow of foxfire, warblers, and crow-sized pileated woodpeckers—the wild places of Kansas aren't just the domain of big grass.

Ten species of mammals that once roamed Kansas were officially extirpated in the state at some point since the 1800s. One by one, chapter 4, "The Alpha and the Omega," traces the details that led to their disappearances. Much of the chronicle comes from J. R. Meade, the audacious explorer and founder of Wichita and the Kansas Academy of Sciences. But extirpation is not the same as extinction, and the triumphant return of many of these species is the subject of the remainder of the chapter. Included is a trip to far western Kansas to see firsthand how the bizarre calculus of landowner rights led to an all-out war between the Logan County Commission and Larry Haverfield, a rancher determined to reintroduce the most endangered mammal in North America back into the wild on his property.

Efforts to reintroduce the northern river otter in Kansas and the first documented evidence of a wild otter in Douglas County since the 1800s are explored in chapter 5, "Ottering."

Chapter 6, "The Renegade Streams of Eastern Kansas," follows Cherokee County attorney Chris Meek's supreme court battle to determine whether Kansans have the right to float the streams of their state. The results of the case are nothing less than shocking. Woven into the narrative is the saga of Mokohoko, the traditionalist Sac and Fox leader who refused to surrender lands along the Marais Des Cygnes, saying it "would be like putting our heads in the mouth of the great Bear's to be eaten off."

Echoes of Native American history and spirituality are still palpable in the Kansas "Badlands," which includes the Red Hills and Arikaree Breaks. Chapter 7 looks into badlands geology, Rocky Mountain oysters, Carrie Nation, the Gant-Larson ranch in Medicine Lodge, Schwarz Canyon and cave bats, the largest bison herd in Kansas, and the story of the Cheyenne's Cherry Creek encampment.

Chapter 8, "Big Springs Go-Go," takes a deep look at the relationships between family farms, private property, and wild places from a Greenwood County farm on the Verdigris River that has been inhabited for centuries.

The book culminates with chapter 9, "Bardo on the Kaw," as flooding threatens an attempt to float the entire length of the Kansas River, the best known and most accessible wild place in Kansas, and to retrace the steps of rogue eccentric Étienne de Veniard Sieur de Bourgmont, who led a remarkable expedition deep into the homeland of the Kansa in 1724. The history of the river is inseparable from the history of the Kansa people. An encroaching wave of tragedy and chaos followed them from their Grand Village des Canzes on the Missouri; to the Blue Earth Village near Manhattan; and finally to the last settlements of Fool Chief, American Chief, and Hard Chief on Mission Creek outside of Topeka.

Lastly . . .

This book is not an academic text aimed at a small audience of aficionados and grad students—it's my love letter to the unique landscapes and eccentric characters that have enriched my life and helped mold my unwavering belief in the sanctity of wild Kansas. More than anything, I hope it inspires *you* to get up and go! You don't have to own land or grow up on a farm to have a strong connection to wild places. Get outside and hoof it, comb the backcountry, push aside the garbage and delve deep, discover your own places. If there's a prairie mound, or a pawpaw patch, or a great blue heron rookery that you've always wanted to check out, get permission and explore it. Now is the time, while you're still a kid, while your kids are still kids, while your knees still have a few chunks of good cartilage, while your artificial hip still has a few good years left on it. No excuses, OK?

Just know that to build a deep connection to wild places in a state like Kansas, you might have to cultivate a specific frame of mind, spend more time alone than you're accustomed to, read books that you can't buy on Amazon, ask open-ended questions, purify yourself, maybe pray, invest in a dorky multi-color LED headlamp and some expensive binoculars, purge your mind of prejudices. Then maybe your spot will call you. At the very least you might meet some crazy characters and discover a side of Kansas—and of yourself—that you'll never find browsing coffee table books about the Sunflower State in gift shops along I-70.

George Frazier
Lawrence, Kansas
July 26, 2015

Author's Note

This is a work of nonfiction, reported as events happened and without embellishment. In a few cases the names of private landowners have been changed to protect their identities, but otherwise their stories are extant. Any mistakes, omissions, or inaccuracies are completely the fault of the author.

CHAPTER ONE

Black Bob and the Prophet

After three grueling days stuck on the most intractable software bug of my professional career, I felt like a man trying to roast a turkey with a birthday candle. This much was certain: I'd caused the problem and only I could fix it. But as our customer in California lost patience, I hunkered down with valgrind, callgrind, lint, electric fence, purify, gdb—an arsenal of debugging weapons that programmers reach for when they're desperate. Nothing helped. At night, I dreamed of shopping for my burial plot.

I'm fortunate though, my wife, Christina, knows me. To clear my mind and set the stage for code satori (and because early August in northeast Kansas had been a hot humid mess) she thought a change of venue might help, so at sunset we drove out to Bloomington—the state park—to feel the wind from the lake and watch a free presentation on Kansas caves.

Bloomington—the town—once was an abolitionist farming community. Most of its residents simply tried to scrape enough off the land to survive winter, but a few were eccentrics and dreamers, and two years after settlement the town found its way onto the radar of pro-slavery activists.

In 1856, Bleeding Kansas struck like a panic attack. A pro-slavery Indian agent murdered town militiaman Thomas Barber near Lawrence, which made him an instant martyr for the Free State cause and subject of a poem by John Greenleaf Whittier, a famous poet in an era when famous poets attracted nutty followings like alt-country bands do today. Following the Emancipation Proclamation, freed slaves poured north, and by the end of the 1870s Bloomington had one of the largest African American farming populations in the state. In Steele Grove—one of hundreds of Kansas walnut groves that used to have names—Bloomingtonians imbibed in spirited Baptist revivals and, sometimes, in spirits. The killer tornado of 1917 thrust hard to the right at the last second, sparing the tiny village almost certain annihilation.

But Bloomington's luck didn't last. When Clinton Reservoir was proposed, planners penciled the entire town into the flood control pool. In the 1960s the Army Corps of Engineers started buying farms, a few by force of eminent domain. Piece by piece the town was taken apart and bulldozed. Eventually Bloomington lay fallow for a decade, waiting for the Wakarusa River to back up against the massive earth-fill dam near Lawrence and deliver the extremities of the new lake to the heart of the old town.

Thus was born Bloomington—the state park—where the abolitionists and the named groves and the nineteenth-century martyrs who inspired rock star poets have been replaced by sunburned dads banging on jet ski motors, popup-trailer base camps where nobody drags themselves out of bed to fish before noon, and college kids playing Ultimate and grilling Hilary's Black Rice Burgers. We walked down to Bloomington Beach and found a half-buried bottle of Grape Malt Duck (an extinct species of near beer) that might have been dumped out of a wormhole connected to 1981. A green Chevrolet Celebrity drove by with a bumper sticker that read, "Everybody looks Republican when you're high."

When it comes to caves, I like being an outsider. I've never been caving, nor karsting, nor spelunking, and though I'd love to take an Icelandic cruise to Vatnajokull Glacier Cave if someone else paid for it, the Horton-Strahler Number is a complete mystery to me, I don't honk for hematite, and I'll never impress a woman with my knowledge of speleogenesis. But as the sun slipped beneath the horizon, I settled deeper into my chair and listened as a ranger from Clinton Lake showed slides and reminded me how little I knew about the caves of my home state.

To date, more than eight hundred caves have been discovered and explored in Kansas, and any cave hunter worth his stalactites has a decent chance of finding new ones by driving around the countryside looking for piles of junk—preferably massive ones—because piles of junk sometimes divulge sinkholes, and sinkholes sometimes divulge new caves. Sinkholes have insatiable appetites, so people feed them crushed grain silos, rusted Ford Fairlanes, storm rung windmills, bee boxes, Johnny Mathis record collections, bricks and stones from old foundations, bedsprings. Inevitably, though, the land does a little jiggle and the sinkhole returns, not much different from before. Beneath a sinkhole, bedrock is subject to slow erosion from acidic groundwaters and artesian springs. Patiently, this hydrochemical drill can bore pockets in bedrock—pockets called caves.

Kansas caves, often completely submerged by the spring that formed them, are not for the squeamish. A grown adult can rarely stand upright in all but the most vaulted caverns. Expect bat guano, colonies of slime molds, blind spiders, hellgrammites, varieties of salamander known only from a single cave, even nesting broods of rattlesnakes.

The presentation continued with field notes scribbled on a hand-drawn map: "Enter balcony room after passing second stone terrace once you leave bathtub. Watch out for nose scraper 15 feet past last strawtite. Lots of stalactites. Punch through narrow two-foot throat hole near mud cairn. Don't worry. Slime and muck, but plenty of good air."

Christina nudged me, pointing out a pair of big brown bats—*Eptesicus fuscus*—dive-bombing katydids mesmerized by the lights of the projector. If either bat noticed the slides and felt a pang for some lost home, it didn't let on. These prairie bats probably spent their days under the bridge over Rock Creek.

After the presentation ended and the crowd began to leave, a man walked up to the ranger and asked, "Have you ever been to Blackbob Cave?"

"The Blackbob Cave slide. I skipped it, didn't I? Give me a sec," the ranger answered, and brought up an old grainy image, probably a scanned forty-year-old Polaroid. Skinny oaks and walnuts lined a draw that panned up to a ridge in the back of the shot. Shingles weathered back to bare wood hung mutely on a few of the trees—zombie no-trespassing signs.

But that cave! Even through the digital distortion of the scanned slide it wasn't merely dark, but black-hole black, a featureless oval in the vertical limestone seam below the forest, and it was enormous. A man with a cheesy grin knelt in the foreground of the photo (a mental image flashed in my mind of seventies singer Sammy Johns—"I'm gonna love you in my Chevy van and that's alright with me"—from the cover of one of my dad's records). A spring gushed from the cave like it might sweep him away.

The man asked the ranger if he knew where Blackbob Cave was or if it even still existed. "I've only been to caves back home in southeast Kansas, by the strip pits," the ranger said, "but I think Blackbob Cave is around here somewhere. Closer to Kansas City in Johnson County. On private land."

I'd never heard of any place like Blackbob Cave in eastern Kansas, much less in Johnson County. I suddenly felt anxious; a core belief that I'd internalized decades ago rose up and threatened to breach. I shook my head and looked out across the dark lake. The ranger had to be wrong.

I grew up in Johnson County. We lived on the outskirts of suburbia, where the city grew right up to the edge of the corn. It was safe, secure, and idyllic in so many ways. I played Little League baseball, ran cross county, watched game four of the 1980 World Series twenty-three rows back from home plate, and received a top-notch public school education that included classes in computer programming, which eventually became my career.

But I also bought a banged-up black Les Paul Custom guitar and taught my-self to play, started bands, and got involved in the burgeoning Midwest punk rock scene. I discovered the literature of the road and books on environmental advocacy by Gary Snyder, Aldo Leopold, William Least-Heat Moon, Paul Gruchow, Annie Dillard, Rick Bass, and Edward Abbey. By the time adolescent rebellion became harder to ignore, Johnson County started to feel as straightlaced and banal as 1860s Bloomington was abolitionist and eccentric, especially when it came to my increas-ing fascination with wild places.

As Kansas Citians began migrating to the suburbs in the late 1960s, developers planted shopping centers and housing developments in cornfields that a few gener-ations before had been buffalo pastures. Decades after the greater prairie chicken was thought to be extirpated in the county, birders located a relict population on the prairie outskirts of Johnson County Executive Airport. Prairie chickens en-gage in a wild mating dance each spring. Airport leaders, worried that a sex-crazed bird might bring down a jet, convinced the county to repeatedly mow the boom-ing grounds (effectively "clear-cutting" their prairie). Nobody ever saw the prairie chickens again.

But the world felt different forty miles to the west in Lawrence, where I went to college. Like Bloomington, Lawrence was founded by abolitionists. The gorgeous Elkins Prairie flanked remnants of the California and Oregon Trails west of the city. The Wakarusa and Kansas Rivers cradled the lower reaches of Mount Oread, the limestone cuesta that the University of Kansas sat atop. It was in Lawrence—in Douglas County, not Johnson County—that my obsession with the wild places of Kansas was born. Provisioned with field guides to trees, shrubs, woody vines, prairie flowers, mushrooms, reptiles, amphibians, and birds, I set out to learn the country. I discovered spikes of turkey-clawed big bluestem poking up through the brome, mistook quail for prairie chickens and prairie chickens for pheasants, got completely covered in ticks—even in the corners of my eyes—followed red fox tracks in the snow, and once was sprayed by a skunk when I went looking, drunk, for the ruins of a nineteenth-century hermit's camp. My friends and I screen printed "Out of my Bog!" T-shirts to protest a road that threatened Baker Wetlands. I wrote a corny song about the ghost of a Bear Shaman.

Eventually most of those friends left Kansas for places like Boulder, Moab, Asheville, Seattle—places closer to *real* wilderness. I too was searching, but proportional to my friends' wanderlust, I dug my heels into the rich "prairyerths" and stayed put. My pilgrimage was leading me nowhere, that is, to *here*. If I could find the lost wild essence of America in Kansas, I could find it anywhere.

In 1541, when Francisco Vasquez de Coronado became the first European to set foot in present-day Kansas, its eastern portions were dominated by the tallgrass prairie, an infinity of sky and wind stretching from the Wabash River west 750 miles to the Flint Hills. Sprinkled among the vast prairies, ancient stands of deciduous forest inhabited by black bears, cougars, red wolves, luminous fungi, and flying squirrels clung to north-facing flanks of limestone hills. Rivers like the Missouri, the Kaw, the Marais des Cygnes, the Neosho, the Verdigris and countless smaller streams were shrouded in cathedral groves of cottonwood, sycamore, and pecan. In western Kansas, clouds of bison by the tens of millions thundered across the Smoky Hill country, creating a robust economy for predators such as the grizzly bear, gray wolf, and man. The arid rain shadow of the Rocky Mountains stole taller grasses from the mix, giving rise to the shortgrass prairies of the Great Plains. In spring and fall, a great biomass of birds rested from their timeworn migrations at prairie potholes, playas, and expansive saline wetlands along the Arkansas River.

The story of the prairie and plains wilderness, of course, does not have a happy ending. As Kansas transformed itself into the breadbasket of the nation, more than 80 percent of the original tallgrass prairie was destroyed. Bears, cougars, wolves, black-footed ferrets, deer, river otter, elk, and most beaver and pronghorn antelope vanished from the state. The bison were systematically slaughtered in a holocaust of sport and gluttony. Wilderness retreated to the true West, to the public lands of the national parks, national forests, and Bureau of Land Management (BLM).

By the late twentieth century, Kansas had no national park, no true national forest, no lonely tracts of BLM land—in fact, little public land of any sort. At 2 percent of total acreage, Kansas ranked dead last among states in public land holdings. Most state parks, wildlife refuges, and public hunting areas were created adjacent to federal and state reservoirs. Selected for flood control, not to protect native ecosystems, sensitive species, or natural landmarks, many were just thorny brambles on the wayside of declining rural America.

It cannot be overstated that access—the lack of it—profoundly shaped the psychology of Kansas wild places. While it is true that Kansas had no pristine cathedral landscape enshrined by the National Park Service, the remaining wild places we *did* have were systemically forgotten, like a repressed memory, a wound. Lack of access came to mean nonexistence.

But I knew, or at least I wanted to believe, that this wasn't the whole story. Kansas still had the Flint Hills, the largest native tallgrass prairie left on the planet, and hundreds of relict prairies survived in the counties bordering Missouri. Kansas still had old-growth forests and wetlands frequented by whooping cranes, one of the most endangered birds in the world. Extirpated species were returning to the state. Kansas still had the vast emptiness of the western plains.

I believed that the truth about Kansas wild places was somewhere between the indifferent yawns of wilderness purists and the quaint clichés of coffee table books with pretty sunsets, little boys fishing in farm ponds, small kept herds of bison, and rainbows Photoshopped over winter wheat. I didn't want to feel like an outsider in my own state, so I made a pact with myself to seek out the last wild places of Kansas, to find the truth behind the barbed wire. When I saw that Polaroid image of Blackbob Cave nestled in its sleepy hollow, however, something snapped, exposing a prejudice that had festered inside me since I was a teenager. I was forced to consider the possibility that there might still be wild places in Johnson County.

Back home from Bloomington, I brewed jasmine tea, moved out to the back porch, lit citronella for the mosquito gods, and grabbed my laptop. The journey of a thousand miles starts with a single search (Book of Google: 6:14). How hard could it be to find a gigantic limestone cave in Johnson County, world headquarters of Garmin?

First I dug into the "Kansas Springs Inventory," an online report by the Kansas Geological Survey. A table of stream flow measurements buried in an appendix showed that even in late July the spring was a gusher. Blackbob Cave was in Johnson County—the report confirmed it—but the rest was smoke and mirrors.

I kept going, but "Blackbob" and "Cave" made useless search terms. Google thought I wanted to shop and proffered every conceivable megastore with a Blackbob Road address. I'm even privy to a teenager's perfectly preserved bulletin board post from the days before Facebook: "If my dad didn't cave and sell the Subaru I would drive myself. . . . Don't make it weird, just pick me up at the Ulta off of Blackbob."

But when I sliced Black from Bob ("Black Bob") and decorated the search with a few more terms, Google gave up a hint. The cave was named after Black Bob, a remarkable but forgotten Shawnee tribal leader who once governed much of what is now modern Johnson County.

The boundary before and after "settlement" reciprocates the BC/AD timescale of Western history in most Midwestern states. The word is as imprecise and deceiving as it is pejorative. Kansas history didn't begin with *settlement* in the summer of 1854 when the Kansas-Nebraska Act opened the floodgates for white pioneers. At the time of the American Revolution, more than a half-dozen Native American tribes lived in present-day Kansas, including the Kansa, Osage, Pawnee, Arapaho, Kiowa, Cheyenne, and Comanche. The Indian Removal Act of 1830 (and other treaties) radically changed Indian Kansas when thousands of Delaware, Kickapoo, Wyandot, Potawatomie, Miami, Chippewa, Sac and Fox, Iowa, Ottawa, and others were deported from their eastern homelands to reservations carved from the lands of the original Kansas tribes. Among them were the Shawnee.

From 1832 until just after the Civil War, the Shawnee lived on a large reservation in Johnson County. Missionaries and government agents pressured them to assimilate, and about half the tribe complied in some measure.

The other half didn't.

These traditionalists still mostly adhered to the old ways, shunned Christianity, danced the old tribal dances, and observed equinox celebrations. They stayed up until sunrise under the silky radiance of the corn-picking-moon telling stories. They hunted white-tailed deer and buffalo, bathed in the cold waters of ancient springs, and rubbed themselves with fresh sage and wild mountain mint.

Black Bob was one of these traditionalists, but his legacy has faded compared to the undisputed superstar of Shawnee traditionalism, in fact one of the craziest characters of the entire nineteenth century: Tenskwatawa, the Shawnee Prophet.

His ears pierced through with feathers three per side, his neck draped with some kind of mustelid—either a weasel or a mink that seems almost ready to reanimate and sink its teeth into his neck—Tenskwatawa can be seen in a portrait that hangs in the Smithsonian, missing one eye and smiling like Mona Lisa. Black sheep brother of the beloved Tecumseh, Tenskwatawa would live to see his people exiled, first to Illinois, and then to Missouri, Arkansas, and Kansas. But in his youth he started a remarkable pan-Indian spiritual movement. US presidents kept tabs on him. Eventually Tenskwatawa would come to Kansas on a mission he wasn't prepared for, and like most things in his life, it would not go well.

Black Bob. Tenskwatawa. These men once lived within hiking distance of my boyhood home. Why had I never heard of them? The first robin tested her voice in the darkness and dawn was near, but I was too pumped up to sleep. I felt on the edge of something vaguely historic.

My discovery took a final twist: The White Feather Spring—not in Johnson County, but close. This spring, according to a brief newspaper article archived from a now defunct Kansas City, Kansas, newspaper, was the site of Prophetstown, the last home and burial site of Tenskwatawa.

I shut my laptop. This rambling August night was finally threatening to end, but not before I'd found the stories of two Shawnee traditionalists, two wild springs, two mysteries lurking somewhere in the backyard of my childhood. Had I stumbled onto a lost fossil record of wild Kansas? If two Shawnee traditionalists from the 1800s knew these places—loved these places—and if, as I believed, the traditionalists sought out wild landmarks with spiritual gravitas—the kind that are rediscovered century after century by careful students of the land—then this might be a rare chance to experience a living history, an electrifying sense of place where past and future collide in deep time.

I didn't know if either site had survived Kansas City's dogged suburban expansion, but I was determined to find out. That night, instead of burial visions I dreamed in code, and by mid-morning the next day I'd fixed my bug. Now I had to find those two wild places.

White Feather Spring, at least, hid in plain sight. The next day I called the Wyandotte County Museum in Bonner Springs, and the second volunteer I spoke with gave me an address in Kansas City, Kansas, a few miles north of the Johnson County line.

Saturday looked good for a trip, and I thought about calling my friend August. Not because the woods were full of peril, even though this could be a sketchy neighborhood at night. But, hey, it was a *neighborhood* at least, not a wilderness, one hundred miles plus from the closest scrawny Ozark black bear, probably three miles from the nearest guy decked out in camo pants and night vision goggles. No, because he kind of *looks* like Tenskwatawa. In a badass way. And I knew I could count on August to get properly stoked up about a historic spring. He once walked across America in total silence—as in *vow* of silence—and met a woman so taken with him, that in spite of the fact they had never properly spoken (or maybe because of it), she agreed to marry him. He lived and breathed magnetism, and I hoped the spring might still harbor some remnant of Tenskwatawa's magnetism.

On Saturday, August showed up around noon. We hopped in my car, tuned in college radio, and drove off toward a future site of urban renewal in search of the last wild places of Kansas. August forgot shoes and I didn't dress properly for the woods, but we had everything we needed.

Tenskwatawa, the Shawnee Prophet, died in November of 1836. There are several theories about the precise location of his grave, but many say it lies beneath an unceremonious heap of rocks and chunks of concrete above White Feather Spring, which doesn't even receive a mention in the *WPA Guide to 1930's Kansas*, the Depression-era government-funded travelogue describing dozens of intermittent springs, lost Indian camps, buffalo wallows, ghost towns, even insect mounds: "On the left at mile 13.5 are GIANT ANT HILLS, two feet high and six to eight feet in diameter, made by blank ants."

Sixty years after Tenskwatawa's death, Charles Bluejacket, one-time leader of the Shawnee, came back to Kansas from Oklahoma at the request of historians to relocate the grave since nobody still living in Kansas remembered where it was.

He walked.

Two weeks after the trip Bluejacket died from exposure.

The Shawnee Prophet has been called the strangest of strange Indian characters. The details of his life are shrouded in controversy, beginning with the translation of his birth name Lalawethika, which probably meant "rattle," and not "loud mouth" or "noise maker" as claimed by some eighteenth-century ethnographers.

Some of what we know about the Prophet comes from a series of bizarre encounters with explorer Charles Trowbridge. Trowbridge called them "interviews," but the Prophet spoke no English and Trowbridge spoke no Shawnee. Their interpreter, most likely Ottawa, probably spoke little of either. Trowbridge was obsessed with ice age mammals, and had a theory that the Indians either saw them directly or had a cultural memory of them. He asked the Prophet question after question about woolly mammoths. Tenskwatawa had no idea what he was talking about, but countered the puritanical Trowbridge with raunchy, X-rated versions of Shawnee creation myths that spared no details of mankind's first lusty attempts at procreation. The two men left the interviews utterly bewildered.

We drove about an hour east from Lawrence and finally came to a dead-end road in Kansas City's Argentine district. I was certain we were lost, but August found a bronze historical marker hidden in a tangle of weeds. Prophetstown. In the 1830s, Tenskwatawa lived on a high bluff above White Feather Spring called Prophetstown. He named *every* place he lived Prophetstown.

I asked three women sitting on the porch of a white Victorian farmhouse if they knew where the spring was. They spoke to each other in Spanish and one went inside. Eventually a middle-aged guy came out pulling a T-shirt over his head. Ernesto Arvizu pointed to a mound of limestone slabs in the backyard and told us he thought it was the grave of Tenskwatawa. A big German shepherd slept on the pile and occasionally opened one eye to check us out. White Feather Spring was somewhere down in the woods below.

Ernesto and his wife, Lupe, originally from Mexico, had been volunteer caretakers of the spring since moving into the neighborhood in the early 1990s. They included images of Tenskwatawa in their *Día de los Muertos* altar alongside their own ancestors and Lupe even made a walking stick with hawk feathers and "Tenskwatawa" etched into the wood.

We sat on the porch and talked about the deep history below us down in the ravine. In the Depression, when the Kansas River dried up and flowed backward, White Feather Spring never stopped running and served as a community water source. Shawnee tribal leaders and visitors from as far away as Canada came on a regular basis. A few years ago the Shawnee Tribe and Eastern Shawnee Tribe bought the small parcel of land with the grave and spring. The library down the street kept a permanent display on Tenskwatawa's prophecy about the zero-year curse: Every US president elected in a "zero year" would die in office. Indeed, the next seven zero-year presidents died in office: Harrison, Lincoln, Garfield, McKinley, Harding, Roosevelt, and Kennedy, ending with Ronald Reagan, who survived an assassination attempt.

Ernesto pointed us to a steep trail with a white clothesline anchored like a fixed rope to trees that traced a cat run straight down to the spring. The woods were choked with redbud and dogwood, no doubt beautiful in April. One of the women wagged a finger at August's bare feet and called out, "*Hiedra venenosa!*" (poison ivy).

Tenskwatawa, the Shawnee Prophet, was born Lalawethika in 1775. Orphaned and raised by his sister Tecumapese. Lalawethika was sickly and weak as a child. When refused to teach him how to use the bow and arrow, he blinded himself in the right eye trying to teach himself. He was a serial failure at hunting, scouting, studying with a Shaman. He planted pitiful corn gardens. After marrying, he drank himself into a whiskey stupor every night.

It didn't help that his brother was Tecumseh, future Native American and Canadian folk hero, military genius, and cultural icon. As the eighteenth century closed, Tecumseh led a small band of warriors trying to stop a white invasion of Shawnee lands. After Daniel Boone pushed his Wilderness Road through the Cumberland Gap, the Shawnee's fertile Ohio River country was vulnerable to American expansion. Skirmishes between settlers and Indians became more frequent and deadly. Since 1789, when he traveled to the south to fight alongside the Chickamauga, Tecumseh believed that only a pan-Indian confederacy—a kind of NATO of midwestern tribes—could keep Americans from taking every square inch of the Indian homeland. But creating such a confederacy was complex. Tribal societies were decentralized, individual warriors often made military decisions at a very local level. They had wide-ranging social customs and spoke many different languages. Some were mortal enemies. But Tecumseh knew time was running out. He needed a breakthrough.

One day in 1805, Lalawethika collapsed in his lodge. His wife ran for help, but it was too late, he was pronounced dead. His body lay in a dark chamber for hours as the family started making plans for burial. Lalawethika, however, wasn't dead. He had been in a trance. Eventually he stood up and walked away from the death pallet, babbling unintelligibly, his brain firing like popcorn in a microwave bag. Within a week the details of his vision had gelled and he started telling the story to anyone who would listen. Lalawethika changed his name: He was now Tenskwatawa, the Shawnee Prophet.

In his trance, two warrior-guides showed him a lost world with clouds of game animals, forests with no end, pristine water, and no settlers. Tenskwatawa said the Master of Life spoke to him directly, giving him precise instructions—precepts. If enough people kept the precepts and joined together, their good mojo would cascade, growing exponentially, pulverizing their enemies and ushering in the utopian era of his vision.

Some of the precepts sound familiar today. Steer clear of booze (alcoholics would be forced to drink molten lead in the afterlife). Eat traditional indigenous foods, no bread. Wear clothes sparingly. Because the old dances had become corrupt, learn new dances. In all, it amounted to a grand reboot.

Keeping precepts turned out to be one thing the former Lalawethika was really good at. He never took another drink the rest of his life. Soon, everybody was talking about this strange vision from the brother of Tecumseh.

Tenskwatawa's popularity was about to increase exponentially, and not only within the Shawnee nation. In 1805, Indiana territorial governor William Henry Harrison—the future US president—was charged with keeping an eye on the Indians. When he heard about the Shawnee Prophet, Harrison dared Tenskwatawa to provide some sort of proof he had direct contact with the so-called Master of Life. Harrison kept the pressure on the Prophet and made the dare public. The word even got out to other tribes.

The timing was perfect. In less than a month, a total solar eclipse would cross the arc of the Midwest. Whether he was tipped off by British allies—eclipses were well understood by 1800—or by the Master of Life, Tenskwatawa nailed it. On the big day he gathered a throng of fresh followers and, for effect, emerged from his medicine tent at the precise moment of complete darkness, imploring everyone to renounce the ways of the settlers or face the wrath of the Master of Life.

It worked. Hundreds who witnessed the spectacle were convinced of Tenskwatawa's authenticity. Harrison cried foul, saying the Prophet's muse was scientific and not divine, but nobody listened. After the eclipse Tenskwatawa's new religion spread like prairie fire through the tribes of the Midwest.

Tecumseh seized the opportunity. In 1807 the Prophet and his followers abandoned their settlement near Greenville, Ohio, and established the first Prophetstown at the juncture of the Wabash and Tippecanoe Rivers in Indiana Territory. Tenskwatawa was everywhere, imploring the people to stay vigilant; he continued to reveal more details of his visions as they came to him. Tecumseh galvanized the movement, rallying support, adamant that the Shawnee and other tribes would never sign another treaty that touched the current boundaries of their lands, and that Indian forces would fight together if provoked. They warned settlers not to trespass on Indian lands.

In November 1811, Harrison took action. With Tecumseh away in the south rallying more Indian support, Harrison sent troops to Prophetstown. Tenskwatawa panicked and sent for Tecumseh. He told Harrison to take a time out, to count slowly up to ten. The Indians wanted no trouble. The two forces dug in on either side of the Tippecanoe River.

Eventually, fighting broke out. The battle went on for days with numerous casualties on both sides. Tenskwatawa retreated into his prayer tent, pacing around, imploring the Master of Life to give the Indians invincibility to American bullets. Wave after wave of warriors hurled themselves into the ruckus, believing the precepts kept them safe, but the army repulsed the Indians and burned Prophetstown. Afterward, incensed by the needless loss of life, the anguished survivors threatened to kill Tenskwatawa. When they demanded to know why his medicine failed, the Prophet blamed it on his wife's *period*! She didn't tell him she was menstruating, so the Master of Life ignored his prayers.

When Tecumseh made it back to Prophetstown, his Indian confederacy was in tatters. He died a year later on Canadian soil, fighting alongside his British and Canadian allies in the War of 1812. Without Tecumseh, and on the wrong side of history, the Shawnee had no other choice but to accept a treaty with the Americans, leading to their removal from the Ohio country. Disgraced, Tenskwatawa escaped to Canada, where he remained for the next twenty years, living quietly among a small group of followers.

The US War Department didn't forget about Tenskwatawa, though. His dealings in Canada were carefully monitored. In the 1820s, when plans were under way for the "final" Shawnee removal to Kansas Indian Territory, Tenskwatawa was homesick for his people. He negotiated his return in exchange for agreeing to help US Indian agents transition the Shawnee to a new life of planting and agriculture on their Kansas reservation.

But Tenskwatawa was a trickster to the very end. Once he was safely in Kansas, he refused to assist the corrupt government chiefs, quietly assembling his small entourage at the final Prophetstown. He lived apart from the tribe on a small government allowance, enough to support four small huts at the end of a winding path through the woods, secluded from the outside world above the ancient White Feather Spring.

The hills of the Argentine lead west and join forces with a greater line of bluffs between Turkey Creek and the Kansas River. The stream below White Feather Spring carves a bowl-shaped valley that thwarts development, a quarter-mile gash in the limestone softened by sycamores and elms. The spring has created a calm, quiet retreat within the city.

As August and I stumbled down the steep path, rappelling along the clothesline, there were small rock cairns at every juncture. But the serenity of the place was fouled too often with junk and refuse, Mountain Dew cans scattered everywhere and car batteries sunk into the dirt of the cliff.

What struck me most about the spring was its potency: That day it was a torrent, bursting from a two-foot hole in the limestone, fifty feet below the top of the bluff. Long rectangular stones, almost like post rocks, were inlaid back into the chute. A mist rose even though it was almost one hundred degrees outside and otherwise dry.

Today, White Feather Spring is far from pristine; there are no blind cavefish wiggling in the wet darkness of the limestone. A culvert east of the site is covered with gang graffiti, and watercress grows in bald tires and an old refrigerator. Without the spring the valley would be just another vacant lot braided by a polluted creek. This decline punctuates the incredible change that has taken place here in the last 180 years. A scant five generations ago, chants of the traditionalists filled the valley. Tenskwatawa personally selected this wild place for his hermit camp, the last Prophetstown, a direct connection to a lost time that survives almost forgotten today, just north of the Johnson County line. August and I sat beside the spring for a long while. I was right, he *was* stoked, and it was good to have him with me. Eventually we heard a faint buzzing in the woods, the drone of cicadas gearing up for the night.

In 1832, frontier artist George Catlin spent months trekking across the West painting Indian portraits. This was two years after the Indian Removal Act of 1830, and Catlin knew there were famous old characters like Tenskwatawa living in the new Indian country. Catlin didn't care in the least about the new government chiefs who ran the reservations; in Kansas he painted only three Shawnee. The Prophet sat for his portrait in his hut at White Feather Spring. Catlin wrote that he was aloof from the rest of the tribe, resigned to a hermit's existence by the spring, spending his days meditating.

The Shawnee Prophet was a complex figure. In his youth he built a traditionalist movement that swelled beyond the borders of his tribe before unraveling in bloodshed and heartache. Never completely accepted by the Shawnee, especially after Tippecanoe, his final years in Kansas raise many interesting questions that will never be answered. Did he spend his last days beside the ancient spring keeping the precepts that the Master of Life gave him in his youth? Did he find a morality in landscape where human and spiritual realms come together in balance?

Tenskwatawa died while engaged in three days of fasting and prayer. As he grew sicker, his attendants sent for a white doctor. Surprisingly, the Prophet agreed to treatment, but only after his meditations were complete—he was concerned the drugs would interrupt his concentration. The doctor didn't think much of

Tenskwatawa, or Indians in general, calling him "a broken man dying on a crude pallet next to a poor 'excuse' for a fireplace, away from his tribe." I think the Prophet was exactly where he wanted to be, comfortably alone in the yet wild prairie, a lone wolf surrendered to his destiny, no longer beholden to Tecumseh, the tribe, the British, or Canada. The doctor returned three days later with medicine but Tenskwatawa slipped into a coma. He died later that day.

A month later I went to the library near the spring, the one that supposedly maintained a permanent exhibit on Tenskwatawa. I looked around but couldn't find it. One by one, I spoke with the entire staff, but none of them had ever heard of the Shawnee Prophet.

Finding Blackbob Cave—or any biographical nuggets on Black Bob—involved significantly more sleuthing than my search for White Feather Spring. Tenskwatawa was a major footnote in the history of manifest destiny, linked to the rise of an American president. *He left tracks.* Black Bob and his band of unreconstructed Shawnee, on the other hand, shared none of Tenskwatawa's lust for notoriety. I took this as a hopeful sign. Maybe Blackbob Cave was a more exquisitely preserved vestige of wild Kansas.

I searched for six months, on and off, for the cave, tapping the usuals, cold calling experts, emailing elderly volunteers at arboretums, bugging mail carriers. I wrote to the Absentee Shawnee tribe in Oklahoma. I drove the back roads of southern Johnson County with topographic maps sprawled out on the passenger's seat. I got paranoid and began to suspect that people were holding out on me.

Late in September, a friend of a friend at the Kansas Geological Survey said that he didn't feel comfortable telling me or anyone else where the cave was, but that I was "getting warmer" and to visit the Kansas Speleological Society website. Maybe he was messing with me—or clueing me in—because the website was basically a digital no trespassing sign: "The Kansas Speleological Society does not disseminate information on the location of Kansas Caves."

Fall came and went. I gained four pounds over the holidays then lost the four pounds starving myself on brown rice, cottage cheese, and Bud Light. On the night of the first cold pounding rain of late February, the kind of rain that once each year motivates smallmouth salamanders to migrate across the Baker Wetlands in Lawrence, I emailed Lee Bissinger, the only spelunker I knew, and asked what he'd do. Lee said I should go to the library and look for old copies of "This Month's Guano," the newsletter of the Kansas City Area Grotto, a caving club. I shuddered. What's the deal with cavers and nasty stuff like bat poop?

I found the newsletters and later that week a Grotto guy got back to me. He read my email and called friends at the Kansas Speleological Society—they who do not disseminate information on the location of Kansas Caves—and I guess since cavers trust cavers somebody passed along my email to the Sammy Johns ringer from the cave lecture Polaroid. Though he hadn't been to the cave since 1980, the day the picture was taken, he remembered the address and landowner's name from memory and emailed it to me. He also attached a scanned image of his hand-drawn field notes. I was beginning to dig the simultaneously pedantic and folksy lingo of speleology: "Enter below a well-defined dripline, after which you'll pass the flowstone. Further in you'll notice some rim stone dams before coming to a bathtub. After 94 feet the traversable portion of the cave abruptly ends at a travertine waterfall."

That night I had a crazy dream about raccoons dressed up like soccer players sneaking into an all-you-can-eat buffet and ravaging the salad bar. Just before I woke, a cook came storming out of the kitchen holding a caged canary, running right past the raccoons, collapsing in the seat beside me and shouting, "I say we take us a couple of sledgehammers and bust through that travertine waterfall ledge so we can go deeper in. You with me?"

Wawahchepaehai, or Black Bob, was born into a thoroughly traditional secretive clan of the Shawnee that never joined the pan-Indian coalition of Tenskwatawa and Tecumseh. By 1793, the "Black Bobs" left the Shawnee homeland, settling first in the Missouri Boot Heel near Cape Girardeau on a reserve given to them by the Spanish governor, Francisco Luis Hector, baron de Carondolet (a name that still rolls off the tongue), then later in the Kansas Indian Country on a 24,000-acre spread near the headwaters of the Blue River near modern Olathe. According to tribal rolls, almost none of the "Blue Indians" took Anglicized names (unlike 95 percent of the rest of the tribe), although there were a few exceptions like Wolf Dodge, Old Possum, Doctor Rib, and Coffee.

Black Bob was fiercely traditional and politically shrewd, abstaining from Shawnee government deals that involved individual land allotment. He did, however, take one very public stand that would have severe repercussions. The Kansas-Nebraska Act, which opened Kansas to settlement in 1854, decreed that a public vote would determine the right to own slaves in new states. The Black Bobs weren't allowed to vote, but that didn't stop them from taking sides. Their reserve was pinned between the Free State enclave of Lawrence and John Brown to the west and pro-slavery–leaning counties of western Missouri to the east. The Black Bobs threw their support to the anti-slavery faction, even though Native Americans were deprived of basic freedoms the abolitionist movement stood for until the twentieth century.

For Black Bob, who carefully picked his battles, compromising when necessary to preserve as much of his people's traditional culture as possible, this stand came with a price. Somehow, the crazed Confederate guerrilla William Clark Quantrill noticed the Black Bobs, and in 1860, it was a very, very bad thing if William Clark Quantrill noticed you.

On the last Saturday of February my friends Jay Bredwell and Daniel Mellott rode south with me from Kansas City toward the Blue River and Blackbob Cave. We had the windows down, a warm prelude to spring. As we neared the valley of the Blue River, suburban Johnson County receded into a patchwork of limestone-studded brome pastures sprinkled with disinterested cattle.

The Blue River flows only a short distance from its origins in the pastures of southern Johnson County before yielding to the Missouri, winding east across the Red Bridge neighborhood before veering north through a shallow limestone canyon that crosses under I-435 east of Grandview Triangle. Near its headwaters, clusters of enormous homes near Overland Park's arboretum reminded us that the glacier of Johnson County suburbia still continued its slow southward march, global warming be damned.

The last mile we cruised slowly from mailbox to mailbox until we found the right address and then drove up a long private road that led to a house over the ridge. A golden retriever sashayed down and escorted us along the driveway like a sentry. A trim woman with auburn hair was working in the garden with a man in khaki coveralls. They were trying to straighten a tiller for the next furrow. I saw the deep-forested ravine east of the house. The trim woman walked toward us smiling, like she expected us, even though I hadn't called in advance.

Martha Radke Long shook hands with me using her left hand. Once she learned we'd come to see the cave, she tossed her leather work gloves in the wheel-barrow, left the spinach rows to her friend, and asked us to wait while she ran up to the house to get her kids. We hung out on the porch, next to a rock garden with freshly sheared clumps of singed Indian grass. The window shutters were singed too.

Martha came back out carrying a brown paper attaché tucked under her left arm. She had changed into a T-shirt and without the coat I noticed her right hand was wrapped up in a wad of gauze. "My attempt at prairie management," she said. "I thought I'd save time by burning the Indian Grass instead of chopping it down. After I lit the first bunch my daughter yelled, 'Mama the house is on fire!' Before I could think I grabbed the handle of a shovel in the fire and burned my hand."

Martha showed pictures from her collection. "Here's a shot of the cave and a map that a KU geologist made when he came out in 1980." I recognized it. I had a digital version on my laptop in the car.

She also showed us some pictures of a trace running along a ridgeline that she believed was an old Indian road that stopped at the cave. We passed the pictures around and started walking toward the woods. Jay opened the gate for Martha and we crossed a cattle grate that separated the garden from the forest. Downy woodpeckers chased each other between the trees, their diminutive trills, like tiny kingfishers, echoing through the woods. Juncos were everywhere. A brown creeper bumbled up a shaggy hickory. We descended the steep trail, through deep-seeming woods, dropping probably fifty feet as it switched back once or twice. I pulled my sweater back on. The dog disappeared around a bend. Farther ahead we stopped at the edge of the draw above a steep limestone cliff. I peeked over the ledge and then turned to Jay and Dan. I could hardly believe what I saw down there in those February woods.

The kids ran down to the spring splashing their way toward a larger creek below. Martha's daughter brought a paper bag to catch frogs. I looked over at Dan. "Dr. G," he said, "I believe this is the real thing." Below us along a ridgeline that curved out of sight to the north, a brilliant green channel slithered from the base of the ledge around the root wad of a thick sycamore, skeletal in its winter nudity, parting a brown veil of hickory leaves and dead grass. It was green not from the clear freezing-cold water but from a lush carpet of watercress unlike anything I'd ever seen in the state of Kansas, much less in Johnson County. The gurgling of the spring as it poured from the cave made the little hollow sound enchanted. No pristine Ozark watercress garden could trump this.

I walked down the trail, gingerly stepped into the creek, and turned toward the cave. It wasn't as big as I expected, but the surge of water bursting from the

Sam Hindman emerging from Black Bob Cave, Johnson County, Kansas.

blackness was astonishing. The site would have been a perfect commons for the Black Bobs and easily the most valuable water source on their reserve.

Piles of yellow limestone were heaped around the entrance. Blackbob Cave tunnels ninety-four feet back into the Argentine limestone formation, which is the common limestone of Johnson County. Martha said, "If you don't mind getting soaked you can climb back a few yards and sit in a little pool. We keep a board across two rocks to sit on. It's *really* dark."

Jay put on his miner's lamp and ducked under the overhang, doing a sweet little limbo to get farther back into the darkness. The dog happily followed. I wondered if Black Bob himself had bathed in the pitch-black spa.

Dan and the kids followed the trail of watercress around a bend and Martha led us down to a flat gravel bar. She said, "If you look along the edge of the ridge you'll see a trail. That's the trail we believe the Indians used."

At first I couldn't make it out. She motioned me to squat lower. I squinted, and she said, "It's hard to see, but there, look against the ridge, it twists left and then straightens out."

I could just barely recognize a faint path in the limestone and a wider swale that led up to the road. It occurred to me that Quantrill might have used this trace

when he ransacked the Black Bob settlement in September 1862. By then, the border skirmishes of Bleeding Kansas had died down, with most of western Missouri
under heavy Union patrol as the Civil War gripped the nation. Missouri didn't join
the Confederacy, but it harbored sympathizers. The quasi-Confederate Quantrill
led a band of criminals and terrorists who had a bone to pick with almost everyone
in Kansas, including the Black Bobs. His gang included Frank and Jesse James
and a sadistic lunatic named Bloody Bill Anderson. When they raided Lawrence
in 1863, killing more than 150 men and boys, Quantrill took great effort to spare
women and children. But his men had no qualms assaulting Black Bob women as
they destroyed the settlement and, more calamitously, burned the communal crop.

Unlike Tecumseh, Black Bob didn't want to die for a cause; he valued survival
over annihilation. The tribe regrouped after the attack and spent part of a winter
starving in the ruins of their village. By spring most left Kansas to wait out the Civil
War with the Cherokee and Absentee Shawnee in Oklahoma.

On cue, settlers poured in and claimed every parcel of the Shawnee's Kansas
reserve. Black Bob died either in 1864 or 1868. Nobody knows where he is buried;
there was no obituary. But his unwavering traditionalist stance on land ownership
provided a lasting legacy for his people. Because the Black Bobs still owned the
land in common, a few survivors eventually received payment for their stolen reservation during the 1870s and 1880s.

As we got ready to leave, Martha confided that after a quarry was built north
of her land the spring seemed to run a little less vigorously. The forest too had
changed. It used to have ancient oaks, but the F5 Ruskin Heights tornado of 1956
scoured the hollow and knocked rocks from the cave into the opening of the spring
run.

"We really probably shouldn't have done this, but a few years ago we had a guy
run a pipe from the middle of the cave up to our house," Martha admitted. "We
drank that water until the city added us to the line." I could tell this troubled her.
She questioned whether a harmless (and actually very green) use of the spring
would somehow jeopardize it. Carefully, very carefully, I had been trying out the
idea that I might have misjudged my erstwhile Johnson County brethren and sis-
teren—at least some of them. Now I was sure of it. Not only was Blackbob Cave
remarkably well preserved, a hallowed tribute to the Black Bobs and proof that
wild places can survive profound environmental and societal change, but a preser-
vation ethic thrived in the suburbs of Kansas City, embodied beside me in the form
of Martha Radke Long.

Martha wanted to drive up the road and show us her neighbor's house, which was banked up into the side of a hill like stacked enchiladas; hippie-rigged spigots and PVC pipes siphoned off a different natural spring into a basement bathtub. But her husband called and needed help; his truck was mired up in the pasture. We said we'd dig him out, but Martha would have none of it—and I think she thought her truck could eat my car for breakfast—so she loaded us up with bags of fresh watercress and a dozen chicken eggs for my daughter. As we drove away Jay said, "It's good to know there are still people on earth like Martha Long."

I have never determined with any certainty Black Bob's exact relationship to the spring—there is no written document that definitely places him at the site—but the late Herb Shuey, a Johnson County historian, told me he believed it was the central meeting place for the tribe. The old trace and the clearing below the cave seem to support the theory.

The biography of Black Bob is little more than a weathered fossil. There are notes from a few speeches he gave at the Shawnee Mission and an account of a trip aboard the stern-wheeler *Polar Star* from Kansas City to Saint Louis to sign the treaty of 1854 in Washington. But Black Bob's real biography is written in the land near the Blue River. Splashing through the spring and catching frogs with Martha's kids, we could feel a tangible presence in the little hollow by the cave.

Government control of private property is a charged topic in Kansas. So is dispossession. Some believe the government shouldn't own land at all. Others believe the government shouldn't control what a private landowner does with his property. Black Bob believed the government didn't have the authority to say that land could be owned by private individuals at all. Native Americans aren't the only people who have been forcibly removed from Kansas lands.

This brings us back to the story of Bloomington—the town and the state park. Back when I was in graduate school, I watched helplessly as a man plowed furrows into Elkins Prairie, effectively destroying ten thousand years of natural history in the best remaining tract of virgin prairie left in eastern Kansas. He said he did it to make his property "more productive." The Nature Conservancy had offered to buy the prairie a year earlier for 50 percent of what developers had recently paid for similar land.

As I was standing on the south side of US 40, the old California Trail, a farmer named Verne drove by and stopped to talk. His grandparents homesteaded in Bloomington. He was a third-generation farmer. But when plans for Clinton Lake materialized he received a registered letter from the Army Corps of Engineers. The new lake would soon submerge every last acre of his grandparents' homestead, which he and an uncle still owned.

His uncle refused to leave. Eventually the Corps condemned the property and forced him out. Verne sold—he even hired an attorney to negotiate a better price—but the money he made could never replace a landscape that was forever braided into the DNA of his family.

What happened to Verne was wrong. But was the plowing of Elkins Prairie an effective civil disobedience or a murder-suicide in the face of divorce?

The road beside Martha's property doubled back to the east. We passed the cave one last time on our way home. I lowered my window and slowed down as we neared the swale that led down to the cave. For an instant the sound of gurgling water was faintly audible, and I could hear the frogs trying out their creaky voices, proving that winter would soon be over. One by one, each tiny chirp seemed to turn the new violets of the forest a shade greener.

CHAPTER TWO

La Jornada

Driving north from Elkhart, I could see thunderheads as sinuous as porcelain pitchers that were visible in three different states—Oklahoma, New Mexico, and Colorado—all slowly moving toward a place in southwest Kansas that's lucky to get eighteen inches of rain a year. I'd been holed up in the refrigerated El Rancho Motel waiting for late July's still heat to loosen its grip on the flat plains of Morton County. Highway 27 paralleled Happy Ditch at the entrance to Cimarron National Grassland, 184,000 desolate dust bowl acres restored to high plains prairie and now managed by the US Forest Service. Pronghorn antelope, elk, mule deer, and even bears wander its lonely sand sage arroyos and salt cedar gulches. It might be the wildest place left in Kansas.

Heeding forest service advice to keep alert for porcupines while driving, I crossed the dry ravine of the Cimarron River and turned onto a dirt road, passing three grave-shaped pits packed elbow-to-elbow with entire families, mostly Hispanic, fishing on a Friday night (per acre the ponds receive more angling pressure than any other waters in the state). Every wagon that took the Cimarron Cutoff route of the Santa Fe Trail had to stop at Middle Spring, the ancient water source where I was headed. The Cimarron Desert—also called *La Jornada del Muerte* or Journey of Death—was a treacherous, arid stretch of trail forty miles from the next water at Lower Spring near present Ulysses.

A party of Comanche killed Jedediah Smith here in 1831 (or at least nearby—he might have died at Lower Spring or at another spring in Seward County; the exact location is disputed). He was only thirty-two, but already a legend. Smith discovered and popularized the South Pass route through the Rockies (you'll get there if you drive west from Cheyenne, Wyoming, on I-80; look for the gigantic sculpture of Abraham Lincoln's head). He was the first white explorer to walk into California from the east and cross the high Sierra. He basked in the cool fog of Northern California's coastal redwood groves more than forty years before John Muir lyricized them. He survived a grizzly bear attack by calmly instructing his terrified crew how to sew his scalp and part of his face back onto his skull as he nearly bled to death.

A ukulele crooned a sweet Hawaiian melody on *Woodsongs Old Time Radio Hour* as I pulled into the parking lot at Middle Spring. The slight breeze was hot as a foundry; I checked my cooler protecting the lone beer I planned to drink when the sun set over Point of Rocks. The air smelled of sweet sage and feedlot. Western and eastern kingbirds bickered above the public outhouse.

An elderly man worked the blue metal handle of a water pump with both hands. His wife waited in the shade, keeping a wary eye on me while I grabbed my camera from the car. The man's name was Elgar and he wore Levis tucked into suede boots with a light blue cardigan sweater. Covered in sweat, he mopped his face with a white handkerchief, which wasn't surprising since he was wearing a light blue cardigan sweater in the *middle of summer*. When I said I was looking for the site where Jedediah Smith was killed, his wife left her shady spot and started walking back toward the car, a mood in her step.

Elgar followed me along the short path down to Middle Spring—several small rush-choked pools of murky goo outlined by willows and cottonwood. The ooze fed a little creek that didn't run for long before disappearing beneath the sand. Broad mud stomps hidden in the willows smelled like wet bologna. Mosquitoes swarmed above the pools, and after it was too late I noticed about two dozen no-see-ums attached to my legs like demon poppy seeds stuck on two skinny white bagels. A Kansa creation myth has it that after men emerged from the earth they became boastful of their long tails, so Wakanda chopped them off, turned them into nagging women, and sent swarms of mosquitoes to remind men that modesty is a virtue. If that's true, maybe when men subsequently ignored the nagging of the women, Wakanda said, "screw it," and finished her job with swarms of no-see-ums. These worthless sand midges had sucker-punched me before, but only in the American South. Their microscopic beaks inject an anticoagulant that causes itchy red welts that can last for days. Canoeing once in a swamp south of New Orleans, my friend got so many no-see-um bites he had to beg the night manager of our motel to let him soak in the filthy green algae-filled motel pool for relief.

Elgar and I took our time wandering around the mud hole. I tried not to obsess about the no-see-ums, but every few seconds I gave my legs a good swat and smacked the back of my head to make sure they knew that the smorgasbord formerly known as my neck wasn't an open buffet. I'd visited the Cimarron Grasslands at least a dozen times in the last six years with nary a no-see-um, but I'd never been to one of these springs near sunset, and certainly never in shorts and a T-shirt. Elgar was sweating hard in his light blue cardigan sweater, but the no-see-ums had it out for me, not him. Modesty, it seems, is indeed a virtue.

Elgar told me what he had read about Smith's demise:

The summer he died was really dry, as bad as the dust bowl one hundred years later. He was leading up a train of wagons, and when they ran out of water, he split up from the others and nobody ever saw him again. They never found his body, so they don't really know if he died here or at one of the other water holes scattered along the river. When the rest of them got to Santa Fe they found some of his clothes for sale in the Mexican market. In the market they said the Comanches got 'em off a white man they killed on the Cimarron.

In the American West, people have been making impetuous decisions over water, the most precious commodity left of the 100th meridian, for millennia. Even people like Smith, who fatally let down his guard near Middle Spring, a place where he must have known the Comanche would be waiting for him.

Jedediah Smith was born in New York in 1799, but he moved to Saint Louis as a young man when Saint Louis was a frontier jumping-off point for big adventure. General William Ashley had grown outlandishly rich trading liquor to Native American fur trappers in exchange for beaver pelts, but in 1822 when the government banned alcohol sales to Indians, Ashley's Rocky Mountain Fur Company converted to more of a Mary Kay business model, sending hordes of young, inexperienced white fur trappers into the drainages of the intermountain west in search of their fortunes, and on a strictly commission basis. Instead of pink Cadillacs, trappers were rewarded with a riotous gathering called the Rocky Mountain Rendezvous—a sort of nineteenth-century Burning Man without the stoned billionaires—where they could cash in a season's worth of pelts, down rivers of whiskey packed in by mule train, and commune with fellow trappers, Indians, explorers, and even a few curious European tourists who must have looked like Tour de France riders at a Sturgis motorcycle rally.

Smith was part of this inaugural class—Ashley's Hundred—and immediately distinguished himself. When the keelboat transporting him from Saint Louis to the Yellowstone country capsized on the upper Missouri, Smith fought back an attack by Arikara and Blackfeet Indians. He delivered pelts by the wagonload and rose to full partner in the business. Over the next eight years he knocked item after item off his bucket list. Besides surviving the grizzly bear mauling and co-"discovering" South Pass (Robert Stuart got there first but the Crow had been using it for centuries), Smith blazed vast swaths through the American West, more than doubling the distance covered by Lewis and Clark. He built solid relationships with the Crow Indians, spending the winter with them in 1823. He walked across Utah along the route I-15 takes today between Saint George and Ogden. Mexican authorities imprisoned him when he first set foot in California (then part of Mexico). At the end of the 1820s he was famous, if not handsome. The grizzly sewing lesson saved his life but left him with a brutish facial scar, so he grew his hair long on one side like a 1980s forelock.

He didn't do this for the ladies. Smith was pious; he carried a Bible around with him everywhere, never married, didn't drink or smoke, and didn't sexually assault native women although he had no qualms preemptively executing one or two male members of any tribe he felt was a threat to set the tone. In Oregon, Smith tracked down a Kelawatset man who stole an ax, dragged him out of his tent, and had him whipped in front of an entire village. The next day the Kelawatset took revenge on Smith's camp, killing all but one man. Smith survived this time—he was away hunting—but his luck wouldn't last much longer.

In April 1831, he led twenty-two wagons with eighty-five men west from Saint Louis toward Santa Fe (having returned home to Saint Louis the previous year to enter the mercantile business with his brothers). In May they crossed the Arkansas and entered the Cimarron country, the most dangerous part of the trek. It had few navigational landmarks and even less potable water. Two days out from the Arkansas the wagons got mired in sand. They followed buffalo trails and wandered in circles. Things got desperate, horses began dying of thirst, and so Smith and another man, Tom Fitz Patrick, set off to find water. Eventually the two separated.

There is no firsthand account of what happened next. Some believe Smith was downed by arrows or killed with a lance by a band of Comanche who tracked him down at Lower or Middle Spring. His body was never recovered.

Smith once wrote, "I am well satisfied if I can gather a few roots, a few snails, . . . , or a piece of horse flesh, or a fine roasted dog."

Luxury, he could do without, but water was a different story. In the Cimarron, this theme would recapitulate in years to come.

Elgar's grasp of local history was a deep taproot; we talked until the cicadas began their Tibetan drone in the cottonwoods. Four buzzards that wasted an hour circling finally got brave or hungry enough to swoop down forty feet away and start carving out the entrails of a dead rattlesnake along the road above the spring. There was sullen heat; parched tumbleweeds; sand, salt, and dirt; and the mummified carcass of a jackrabbit at the scummy edge of the spring—but very little comfort here. It must have been a godforsaken place to take a lance through the gut.

"On the weekends, plenty of hell raisin' goes on," Elgar said, knocking a smashed Coors Light can out of the soapweed with his craggy cane carved from a hedge branch that he bought off a guy at a VFW hall in Amarillo. "But I come out for the air and the quiet. I used to run cattle down by Boise City (Oklahoma). Spent a lot of time by myself."

We walked back up to the parking lot where Elgar's wife was reading a book in the back seat, engine idling, air conditioner at full throttle. I met her gaze this time, and after a second she smiled. Elgar noticed and said, "We don't come up to Elkhart very often anymore. When we do, I like to come out to the grassland, even when it's too hot. She's a good sport. She hates no-see-ums worse than you do."

After they left, I drove a mile west to Point of Rocks, the Ogallala sandstone bluff where I like to watch sunset on the grassland. Point of Rocks might be the first Kansas landmark ever described in writing—Spanish explorer Francisco Coronado noted it in his 1541 journal. It was the principal landmark of the Cimarron Cutoff rising above a monotony of sage, yucca, and buffalo grass, the first hint to parched wagon teams that the cool mountains and their icy rivers of pure water were getting closer. Grain elevators in Elkhart—the size of children's toys barely visible on the horizon—magnified the scale of the prairie emptiness and how it trumped modern civilization here. The river, a sandy ghost, parted sets of spare hills. A single female mule deer flicked her tail in the shadows watching me.

Walt Whitman wrote, "While I know the standard claim is that Yosemite, Niagara Falls, the Upper Yellowstone and the like afford the greatest natural shows, I am not so sure but that the Prairies and Plains last longer, fill the esthetic sense fuller, precede all the rest and make North America's characteristic landscape."

I popped open my beer and raised a toast to Whitman, Jedediah Smith, and Elgar.

And Elgar's wife.

The US National Grasslands are managed by the US Forest Service but feel more like BLM lands, those unfenced, unlabeled, unbaptized western expanses where anything goes—uranium prospecting, wild burro wrangling, wind farming, nude

Point of Rocks at Cimarron National Grasslands, Morton County, Kansas.

trail running, polygamy, varmint shooting, Rainbow Family Gatherings, Indian War re-enactments. BLM lands are mostly unclaimed remnants of western expansion—the leftover turkey of Manifest Destiny—but the National Grasslands were established for a specific purpose—to keep the Great Plains on American soil, or more accurately, to keep American soil on the Great Plains.

The Great Plains transect parts of Texas, Oklahoma, Kansas, Nebraska, South and North Dakota, Montana, Wyoming, Colorado, and New Mexico. Technology, land speculation, and blind faith lured early settlers into what had formerly been called the Great American Desert. Starting as a slow trickle after the Homestead Act of 1862, settlement began to accelerate following the Indian Wars and the decimation of the buffalo. By the mid-1930s the population of the Great Plains topped five million, up from 800,000 in the 1880s. Two-story schoolhouses, garden societies, New Granges, Methodist churches, ladies' temperance societies, and secret speakeasies popped up overnight in dozens of new towns and cities. The great buffalo wilderness was transformed into one virtually contiguous dryland farm in the space of seventy years.

This was crazy, as we know now, and infamously unsustainable. The Rocky Mountains leach moisture from the air as it crosses the Continental Divide, casting a rain shadow across the Great Plains. Every third year on average, the semi-arid prairies of southwest Kansas receive insufficient rain (twenty inches) to sustain row crops and wheat. Center-pivot irrigation with water from the Ogallala aquifer wasn't invented until 1948, and few of the new Great Plains farmers had ever experienced a complete crop failure.

What happened next is a well-known story. The stock market crashed in 1929 and ten years of drought and record heat followed, ravishing already marginal dry croplands and leaving topsoils completely exposed and ready to blow away to New Jersey with sufficient winds. The winds came, along with lethal snusters (storms of snow and dust), black blizzards, Black Sunday, earthquakes (in Kansas!), and an incessant, demoralizing monotony of cloudless blue sky that rained hunger and bankruptcy down on the hardest-hit dust bowl counties of eastern Colorado, western Kansas, and the Texas and Oklahoma panhandles. In the end, hundreds of millions of tons of topsoil and most of the shortgrass prairie were gone.

In response, President Franklin Roosevelt created the Bankhead-Jones Farm Tenant Act of 1937. The act bailed out farm families who never wanted to see another prickly pear cactus or yucca as long as they lived. The federal government bought thousands of dust-stricken, broken farms and ranches in large swatches across the Great Plains and stitched them together into a patchwork of lands that became our system of National Grasslands. Today there are twenty, including Caddo, Comanche, Kiowa, Oglala, Pawnee, and Sheyenne National Grasslands all named after plains Indian tribes; Buffalo Gap National Grassland in South Dakota where black-footed ferrets, North America's most endangered mammal, now thrive after a successful reintroduction; Lyndon B. Johnson National Grassland, which should have been named after Lady Bird, who said in defense of native plants, "I want Vermont to look like Vermont and Texas to look like Texas"; and, in proof that even when the government hunts down and kills you and your entire family it might still someday name federal land in your honor, Black Kettle National Grassland is named for the Cheyenne leader massacred by George Custer's US 7th Cavalry Regiment.

The lone representative from Kansas is Cimarron National Grassland, which spans most of Morton County, the single-most dust bowl–afflicted county in America. The map of the grassland is like a cartographic dust bowl obituary that begins with Point of Rocks Ranch. Established in 1879, the ranch handled thirty thousand cattle at its peak before a flood washed everything away in 1914. Fanning out from the old ranch, today the grassland is largely continuous, although gaps of private property still exist, and largely contiguous with the Cimarron River.

The Cimarron shares a mystique with other western rivers that flow east across the plains like the Canadian, Smoky Hill, Platte, and the Red. Born on Johnson Mesa near Folsom, New Mexico, the river quickly dives under a three-foot pool of sand—subterranean except during spring snowmelt—and then flows almost seven hundred miles across four states before joining the Arkansas. The 1931 film adaptation of Edna Ferber's book *Cimarron* won the Academy Award for best picture. It featured a famous re-enactment of the Oklahoma Land Rush (and racial stereotyping that's hard to watch today). Travelers on the Santa Fe Trail avoided drinking water directly from the river. H. B. Mollhausen wrote in 1858, "[in the main channel] . . . it has only a slight taste of magnesium; but it becomes almost undrinkable in the pools because of its alkali contents. It is also accompanied by a bad, must odor, . . . , wagon wheels, as well as the hoofs of animals, stirred up an evil-smelling, blue-black mold." Mollhausen found a mummified buffalo on a sandbar. Another of its names means River of Mountain Sheep.

The first task of the US Soil Conservation Service, in charge of the grasslands until the US Forest Service took over in 1954, was to clamp down and hold hard on to what topsoil remained.

Two ecosystems dominate the Cimarron: sandsage prairie and shortgrass prairie. Distinct ecologies, sandsage prairie evolved on sandy rolling dunes and shortgrass prairie evolved on deeper loamy soils. During the early years of restoration, the Soil Conservation Service sowed any seed it could get its hands on, but with experience began to target sowings by ecosystem using sand sagebrush, sand dropseed, sand lovegrass, sand bluestem, blue grama, and switchgrass on sandsage prairies and buffalo grass and blue grama on shortgrass prairies. Today a mix of restored prairie and riparian habitat has emerged that is both wild and diverse.

The return of large prairie dog colonies is one testimony to the success of the restoration. Along with the bison, the black-tailed prairie dog is the quintessential Great Plains mammal. Prairie dog colonies are veritable buffets for a host of obligate species—up to one hundred at various times of year—that rely on them for food and shelter. Some of these species couldn't survive without prairie dogs.

Six weeks before my visit to Middle Spring I'd made another trip to the grassland to learn more about one such obligate: the varmint hunter.

A few hours after sunrise on a dirt road that ran along the rim of the Hugoton natural gas field north of Rolla, I slowed down next to a broad tableland of yucca and sage. The harsh cyclical whine of a windmill intruded on the rueful cooing of mourning doves. I turned off the engine and listened carefully while scanning the fields with binoculars. Nothing. I started the car again and turned off of the main road onto a set of jeep ruts that climbed up into the prairie. At the top of the next hill I stopped again to listen. This time, in between gusts of wind, I heard high-pitched chirps and whistles, the unmistakable chatter of prairie dogs. Scanning the horizon, I began to see small brown blemishes on the pastel face of gentle hills—the mounds of a prairie dog colony.

Black-tailed prairie dogs are small chubby ground squirrels that live in complex social groups on the shortgrass prairie. They have a rich vocabulary of chips and whistles that some scientists believe is a full-fledged language. As much a part of the Great Plains as tumbleweeds and dust storms, the prairie dog's habitat has been declining for decades.

An outbreak of *Yersinia pestis*—bubonic plague—was slowly working through the grassland. The possibility that a serious plague event could wipe out most of the remaining wild prairie dogs led to an unsuccessful push for federal protection under the Endangered Species Act. Plague, which killed off a third of Europe during the Middle Ages, can spread from rodents to humans through the bites of infected fleas. Forest service literature from the Cimarron district office advised visitors to avoid contact with prairie dogs and use insect repellent (if only they had deet back in the Dark Ages).

To manage prairie dog colonies and keep them out of adjoining properties, the forest service encourages black-tailed prairie dog "hunting" on the grassland, even though populations have plummeted across the Great Plains. Today prairie dogs are found on less than 2 percent of their historic range. Their demise hasn't dampened enthusiasm for prairie dog shooting or, as it's sometimes called, prairie dog hunting. In North Dakota the number of out-of-state recreational prairie dog hunters increased from 163 in 1999 to 1,326 in 2012. Although I found a hand-written recipe for "prairie dogs wings" on a 2002 post to a bulletin board (www.hotspotoutdoors.com)—mix together a dozen quartered prairie dogs, two bottles of Tabasco, one bottle of blue cheese dressing, and a bottle of the "kind of vinegar that makes your wife mad when you use it"—almost nobody eats them; the order Rodentia has yet to endear itself with American foodies. To me, if the kill ain't cuisine, the hunt's not a hunt, it's a sport.

Shooting prairie dogs might be preferable to killing them with rat poison. The rodenticide chemical Rozol, preferred for prairie dog eradication, in theory kills only rodents, but another chemical agent sometimes used instead, Phostoxin, will kill everything that lives in the burrows. Given the choice between shooting and

poisoning I admit that shooting is the better alternative. But I'm no fan of more
Ted Nugent–like aspects of the hunt such as organized prairie dog killing contests
that award extra points, like in figure skating, when wounded prairie dogs fly up
through the air from the force of getting popped. I'm also not amused by terms
like "Montana mist," "Dakota droplets," "red mist," or "popped dogs" that describe
exploding prairie dogs eviscerated by high-caliber bullets. Sport shooting prairie
dogs on public lands is illegal in Colorado, but not in Kansas.

The trail was either getting rougher or someone replaced my wheels with pogo
sticks; I banged my head on the roof and spilled tea all over my maps trying to stay
within the ruts. Lately my auto karma was seriously out of alignment; hell, it was
in full-blown retrograde. In Hugoton the previous afternoon I found out why some
semis fasten cartoon signs to their haunches that illustrate a huge truck about to
pulverize a tiny sub-compact. Apparently they do make wide right turns. I escaped
unpulverized but with one less headlight. The same night, near sunset at Point of
Rocks, a rogue wind yanked my driver side door out of alignment and now I had
to act like my own valet attendant and let myself in and out through the passenger
door.

Prairie dogs scattered in every direction as I swerved to avoid a roadside ordnance of prickly pear and cholla cactus. I passed two pickups parked in the prairie
but didn't see any people. Cursing my attempt to follow the loop back to the main
road, I noticed a small compact car parked on a flat expanse of buffalo grass. A boy
and a man dressed like ranchers sat close together on a portable wooden bench taking turns peering through the scope of a heavy barreled bolt-action rifle. Nearby,
two little girls were helping a man with shoulder-length blond hair arrange a picnic
on a blanket. They smiled and waved me over.

Don and Allen—accountants who called each other Starsky and Hutch—lived
together in Manitou Springs, Colorado, and were visiting Allen's sister and her
kids in Garden City about two hours northeast of the grassland. Don and the girls,
who had no interest in killing prairie dogs, were making their own entertainment.

Fumbling with my car keys as I crawled out of the passenger door, I almost
fell down catching a bottled water Don tossed at me. We shook hands and he said,
"Sorry we don't have anything stronger. Allen decided to drink all the gin in Cow-
town last night. Western Kansas brings out the martini shaker in him."

Bam! Allen fired. I almost crushed my bottle of Aquafina. The girls snickered.

While Allen was growing up, his father worked in Garden City feedlots but his
grandfather had a small ranch where Allen spent all the time he could. Now only

his sister was left and she was raising three children alone. Allen and Don visited every chance they could. The kids worshipped them. The girls both had iPhones. I asked what they were listening to and they answered in unison, "M.I.A." Revolutionary Sri Lankan girl rap.

This was not what I expected of prairie dog hunters. Allen's seaside pearl Toyota Prius hybrid wasn't much of a hunting rig (though Don told me if he didn't commute an hour each way Allen would have a white Caddy with bull horns on the hood). As we ate saltines and grapes, I asked Don more about prairie dogs and Garden City and if he ever hunted. "*This* isn't hunting," he said, "it's the day shift at coyote café." Coyotes are lured to gunfire on the grassland since it usually means an easy meal. "And besides, they never hit anything but cactus and tumbleweeds."

Bam! They fired again. Bam! Bam!

"I'm from Denver," Don said, "the city. Allen grew up on the ranch shooting prairie dogs and polecats. It's just what they do." He invited me to drive down to Amarillo with them later and eat at Big Texas Steak Ranch. "It's better than anything in Elkhart."

I didn't doubt this. The night before I had dinner at a place that had just run out of something the menu called "Hot Awesome": ham, bacon, cheese, and mashed potatoes between two chunks of "Oklahoma" toast. Big Texas Steak Ranch sounded great, but I had more stops to make at Cimarron.

"If they kill any, you're welcome to as many prairie dogs as you can fillet," Allen offered and yelled over at Don, "Can he have some of your prairie dogs?" Don gave us thumbs up. I decided to stick with Hot Awesome.

As an excuse for three kids to hang out with their eccentric uncles in a wild place, this "hunt" had some merit, but killing prairie dogs for sport still doesn't sit right with me. In places like suburban Denver with fewer natural predators, prairie dog populations have skyrocketed, but across their entire range, prairie dog numbers are still declining (a recent proposal to list black-tailed prairie dogs under the Endangered Species Act failed, but is sure to come up again). I'm all for hunting and fishing, but I think there should be at least a few places where prairie dogs can just be prairie dogs, where they can kick back and fulfill their niches in the grand scheme of the shortgrass prairie, work on their whistles, try to dig to China or at least to Amarillo. Sooner or later a hungry mother kit fox or sharp-eyed ferruginous hawk will strike blood, but until then there should be a few places where prairie dogs don't have to worry about two guys someday bumping chests behind a truck one hundred feet away after a single exploding bullet launches them heavenward for an extra eleven points. "Montana Mist!" If not on public lands like Cimarron National Grassland, then where?

Elkhart, Kansas, is the county seat of Morton County. It wasn't named after elk, the animal (a surveyor from Elkhart, Indiana, thought one good turn deserved another), but it should have been. Also called wapiti, a Creek word that means pale rump, elk once ranged throughout Kansas. On a high Flint Hills vista in 1806, Zebulon Pike watched hundreds of elk scattered across the prairie in a single panoramic view. Mature bulls can weigh half a ton. In autumn, during the rut, males bugle a mournful wail that evokes the heart of wild America perhaps like no other sound. Nobody knows who killed the last indigenous Kansas elk, but they were extirpated a century after Pike described his panorama.

In 1981, elk raised in Kansas at the Maxwell Game Preserve were released on the Cimarron. By the early 1990s the herd had grown to two hundred individuals. Unfenced, they wander as they see fit between the grassland and nearby prairies in Oklahoma and Colorado. The wapiti is the largest mammalian species ever successfully reintroduced to the wild in Kansas.

I thought finding at least one wild elk would be easy if I was patient and willing to cover a lot of ground. Elk are *big*. They should stand out, or so I thought, on a flat treeless plain. I hiked four miles of ideal river habitat but only saw a few deer and a badger digging in the soft sand of a gulch. Closer to sunset I drove slowly along the river for thirty miles scanning with binoculars. I saw no elk at the Artesian Miracle Well, the fishing ponds, or even west of the grassland in Colorado. This was my sixth half-concerted effort in the last two years to scout elk in the Cimarron; I thought I must be doing something wrong.

I wasn't the only one. Andy Chappell, wildlife biologist for Cimarron National Grassland, hadn't seen an elk in five years at the grassland. Chappell is out on the range almost every day. These elk are tricksters. Chappell finds tracks and other sign. He believes the herd is down to about fifty individuals. They would do well to stay in Kansas. Chappell said, "Colorado and Oklahoma don't want to deal with them because they're not in the mountains. When they cross the state line they get shot."

The hills and plains surrounding the valley of the Cimarron are a harsh environment. Elk and prairie dogs weren't really newcomers when they repopulated the grassland, but nonnative plants have a much harder time adapting to the dry plains. Cimarron is plagued with a few nonnative imposters—some cheatgrass, Japanese brome, Russian tumbleweed, alkali weed, and horseweed—but native species more than hold their own on the dry upland plains where they evolved.

The bottomland is a different story. Tamarisk, or salt cedar, is the kudzu of the desert southwest and a serious threat to riparian ecology at the Cimarron. Since hitching a ride across the Pacific as an ornamental shrub in the 1880s, tamarisk has invaded hundreds of thousands of acres of river bottoms and springs, choking out native willow and cottonwood by exuding a salt lick perimeter that works like a force field against native plants. The wispy shrub sinks deep roots and looks like a cross between red cedar and giant ragweed.

In Egyptian mythology, Set—god of individuality—created a trap made from tamarisk for Osiris, god of the underworld. In America, tamarisk makes a highly effective trap for groundwater, a god of the western states where no "non-beneficial" use goes without a fight. Conferences and professional associations are dedicated to eradicating the shrub. Government agencies use helicopters to map seasonal dispersal patterns. Graduate students spend summers backpacking through wild lands doing tamarisk fieldwork.

Removing the plant is tricky. Like invasive red cedar in eastern Kansas, tamarisk is a cancer you have to hit hard from different angles and is notorious for coming out of remission because removal creates a disturbed environment ideal for—you guessed it—the growth of more tamarisk. You can't just bulldoze the stuff, you also have to restore what remains.

Andy Chappell told me the forest service has tried several protocols:

First we tried burning, but it just grew back. Then we tried spraying, but it cost a fortune; you had to coat each stem. We started getting somewhere when we attached a brush saw to a Bobcat and cut the bushes off at the base. The problem with that was it left lots of slash. Today we start with the Bobcat and then burn everything out. This reduces slash and adds some nutrients back into the soil. A few months later we'll spray the regrowth. To keep it from coming back we plant native shrubs. We've used cottonwood, willow, fragrant sumac, and sandhill plum.

Even without tamarisk, the valley of the Cimarron has fundamentally changed since the time of Jedediah Smith. Trail journals describe the Cimarron Cutoff as treeless, even in the river bottoms. Today you can map the river from an airplane by connecting the dots between cottonwood and willow groves that line the valley. Fire suppression is the most likely cause for the trees' advance.

After more than sixty years of restoration, Cimarron National Grassland is a dry patchwork of replanted prairie, nonnative shrubs and forbs, prairie dog towns, antelope meadows, hide-and-seek-loving elk, varmint hunters, oil and gas prospectors, and motorcycle cowboys and their cattle. Will it continue to cheat the modern world, gradually softening back into a landscape that the Comanche who killed Jedediah Smith would recognize? Would we ever tolerate taking the restoration to its natural conclusion?

I called Andy Chappell and asked if the forest service would consider reintroducing the bison or black-footed ferret. He knew where I was headed. "All the environmental groups want us to get rid of the cows and replace them with buffalo," he answered.

Hell yeah, I thought. Many times I'd camped in shallow canyons near the river and burned cow patty fires to keep warm, pretending they were buffalo chips. But it wasn't that simple. The National Grasslands aren't managed primarily as incubators for original ecosystems. Chappell said, "If we decided to reintroduce bison, then who would feed them? Who would take care of them? Much of the grassland is fenced into grazing units. The Morton County Grazing Association holds the grazing permit on the grassland. How would bison affect them? How could we separate buffalo from cattle? There really is no middle ground; we can't just start adding a few bison here or there. It's all or nothing, bison or cows."

Bison or cows. The buffalo question might be binary, but what about black-footed ferrets? They aren't enormous ungulates already supplanted with IQ-challenged replacements that play a crucial role in the bottom line of modern agribusiness. I could stuff half a dozen into my daughter's Christmas stocking. Better yet, they *eat* prairie dogs, a species the grassland brings in sport shooters to control. After cheating extinction, there are enough captive ferrets in existence to supply an experimental population at the Cimarron.

Chappell believes that neither Cimarron nor Comanche National Grassland in Colorado is suitable for the black-footed ferret. The forest service could limit prairie dog hunting, but the real problem, Chappell said, is plague. Plague wiped out the entire prairie dog population on Comanche National Grassland in the late 1990s. Chappell expected the same at Cimarron, but so far there has been no similar catastrophe on the Kansas side. "We recognize plague by what happens to the towns," he explained. "You don't see bodies; predators and raptors take the dead prairie dogs. But weeds start to grow and you get spider webs in the burrows. We have ongoing plague, but some of the colonies are holding on."

Chappell is right: The grassland is not a nature preserve; it is a "land of many uses," as the forest service motto goes. Congruent with the mandate of the national forests and grasslands, today the largest publicly owned wild place in Kansas is managed largely to protect the private interests of the few individuals and businesses that graze cattle and mine fossil fuels at the grassland, a familiar status quo across western public lands since the days before tamarisk. But this is Kansas, where 98 percent of *all* lands are privately owned. We have plenty of nicely equipped private rooms for cattle. Maybe these questions are *all* binary—it's either prairie dogs, black-footed ferrets, wapiti, and buffalo, or cows, varmint hunting, gas mining, and a sliver of tourism.

But the wild heart of Cimarron is a trickster with a long tradition of thwarting the intentions, be they best or worst, of men. A few years ago during a field trip several members of the Kansas Association of Biology Teachers watched a young cinnamon-colored black bear cross the Oklahoma state line one mile south of Elkhart and wander north onto the grassland. The bear spent the next several months hanging out near the river. Finally it moved north to the Richfield area in Morton County. From there it zigged and zagged along the North Fork of the river to Ulysses before crossing back west and wandering through Kearny, Wichita, and Greeley counties on its way to Colorado.

Black bears once ranged throughout Kansas, but habitat loss and human persecution led to their disappearance from the state by the 1880s. A lone bear was killed near the Baldwin Woods in 1967. Occasionally there are reports of bears in southeast Kansas, probably dispersing from the Ozarks.

In the 1980s, a population of cinnamon-colored black bears began colonizing the upper reaches of the Cimarron River valley in Oklahoma and New Mexico. They were forced from the mountains of southeastern Colorado or northeastern New Mexico as those bear populations increased. In Cimarron County, Oklahoma, farmers started reporting bears when they cut corn in the fall. Antelope and deer hunters began seeing them in the most rugged terrain. Northwestern Cimarron County is remote, and as many as twenty Great Plains bears are thought to inhabit the shortgrass prairie there. The recent sighting was not the first at Cimarron; at least three verified bear sightings are known from the grassland. Who knows how many bears pass through on the sly?

Is there a future for black bears at Cimarron National Grassland? Without the intervention of wildlife managers will we soon be able to remove black bears from the list of extirpated Kansas species? Bears are protected in Oklahoma and Kansas,

and individuals will probably continue to disperse as this group repopulates its historic range. Perhaps there is no better validation of how successful the restoration
at Cimarron National Grassland has been than the fact wild bears are checking out
the digs, perhaps plotting their return.

One fall on a short stop at the grassland on my way back from Colorado, I
pitched my tent in the middle of a wagon circle of yucca and prickly pear cactus
that grew beneath an eroded dirt stratum packed with river gravel and chalky bits
of bones, probably bison. Before trying to steal a few hours of sleep, I hiked along
a path of monuments placed by Daughters of the American Revolution marking
the route of the Santa Fe Trail in the Cimarron River bottom. Near the river, a tiny
fenced-off square of land with plastic memorial bouquets held the graves of two
young girls, daughters of a pioneer family that lived at Point of Rocks Ranch. Their
bodies were found in the river directly below the graves after a freak flood in 1914
washed the entire ranch away. Intermingled among the graves were a few volunteer
corn plants, shriveled from the summer now past. Their ancestors could have been
planted by the girls' father.

Some of the hardship on the Cimarron Cutoff might have been avoided if the
advice in George C. Sibley's journals had been published back in the 1820s. In his
youth, Sibley explored the salt plains of the Arkansas River and learned to speak
Osage and Kansa. But in 1808, he settled into life as a government manager at Fort
Osage east of present-day Kansas City on the Missouri River. There he facilitated
trade between Americans and the Kansa and Osage Tribes, watched other people
get rich and time pass him by.

In 1821, when US Senator Thomas Hart Benton of Missouri proposed an expedition to mark a permanent road along the Santa Fe Trail, he asked Sibley to
serve as one of three project commissioners, in part because of his relationships
with the Osage and Kansa. Sibley took the job. The chance to recapture his youth
revitalized him.

Sibley left Fort Osage in 1821 to measure the distance from Westport to Santa
Fe and to establish campsites along the route. At a spot along the Neosho River he
named Council Grove, Sibley secured "eternal passage" from the Osage and Kansa
for about eight hundred dollars. He tried the Kansa cure for rattlesnake bite ("take
the inner part of a turkey buzzard's maw, dry it to powder, apply to the wound").
In western Kansas he dug for water rather than drink from creeks ("the water was
strongly seasoned with Buffalo urine"). He cooked coffee, bacon, and biscuits over
buffalo chip fires. Green flies assaulted him on the tallgrass prairie and sand flies

Hiking trail at Cimarron National Grasslands, Morton County, Kansas.

crawled into his filthy clothes on the High Plains. He almost fried when lightning struck his tent. The two other commissioners deserted, but Sibley was happy to finish the project alone.

After the fieldwork was complete, Sibley holed up at a Saint Charles, Missouri, tavern to transcribe his journals. His meticulous notes detailed every spring and water source in the driest part of the route. He spared no detail; Sibley wasn't writing ad copy. He clearly emphasized how difficult conditions would be in the future land of the dust bowl. After he mailed the final draft to Washington, he didn't hear anything back for a year. Eventually somebody telegraphed that they never received the report. Irritated but resilient, Sibley transcribed another copy and sent it to Washington again. Another telegraph came, again about a year later, telling him they'd lost the *second copy*. A lesser man might have found another hobby, but Sibley was no quitter. He made two more copies, again by hand, but this time delivered the manuscript in person.

It didn't help. The journal was never published in his lifetime. No road was ever constructed from the survey. Sibley's efforts—and Sibley himself—were forgotten. When his notes were rediscovered in Washington and published in the 1950s, it was too late to help Jedediah Smith or serve as a cautionary tale for pioneers. The

Santa Fe Trail remained a braid of wagon ruts and buffalo trails that were eventually absorbed back into the wild.

That night I lay in my tent and listened to cicadas in the tamarisk—both recent Cimarron pioneers. Through the transparent tent mesh I saw a shooting star. I thought about Jedediah Smith and the Comanche and the sad graves of the little girls. Sibley's official mission might have been to survey a road across the Great Plains, but his real contribution was his failure. Dust bowl pioneers soon got their own taste. The lesson still resonates. This land should not be settled; it belongs to the wild.

Public wildlife areas and parks in Kansas suffer a credibility issue. When the leftover acres of federal flood control buyouts were allowed to grow up in jungles of scrub forest, poison ivy, and giant ragweed, and then thrust forward as the face of "nature" in Kansas, no wonder the Kansas landscape elicits well-meaning yawns. Yes, there is merit in all land devoted to wildlife, but when possible we should build parks and refuges around true wild places, not arbitrary abandoned parcels. Kansas still has wild places where the primordial landscape has touched generations, creating cultural and historical connections. Cimarron National Grassland is a little of both, an abandoned graveyard of farms and ranches that through a national calamity were returned to the wild. Their stark plains mutely attest to what happens when people ignore simple lessons of nature.

It's a classic western story. The real journey here—*La Jornada*—is one of renewal. Hopefully this renewal will continue and with each passing year Cimarron National Grassland will get closer to the real meaning of the word Cimarron: *wild*.

CHAPTER THREE

Old Growth

Before the first European explorers pushed west of the Cumberland Gap and reached the treeless grasslands of the midwestern interior, the word *nature*, in America, meant forest. This created a cognitive dissonance. To express his "love of nature," Detroit native J. Sterling Morton, founder of Arbor Day (a buttoned-up affair as tree worship goes, Yule frenzied pagans hooking up in the sacred groves probably would have wondered, why bother?), plowed the native prairie of his adopted Nebraska to plant forests and gardens. Homesick pioneers soothed their agoraphobia by planting groves and shelterbelts, wrapping themselves in the known, and taking advantage of the Timber Culture Act of 1873 that provided up to 160 acres for those willing to "improve" the prairie by planting trees. They viewed the prairie as a canvas, not a work, albeit minimalist, in itself.

"To make a prairie it takes a clover and one bee," wrote Emily Dickinson. But to maintain a prairie, it takes regular doses of chaos, preferably in the form of fire, alone or in combination with grazing by large ungulates or hay mowing—anything to cull woody species intent on turning the wheel of ecological succession, the process that eventually converts open grassy areas to woodlands. In pre-settlement Kansas, Native Americans burned the prairies to create fire belts around their villages and improve habitat for hunting. But when homesteaders came and created crop fields that served as fire breaks, successional species began to take hold, and eventually large parts of the state became forested.

On a typical quarter section of Kansas upland prairie, the successional process went something like this: First, a homesteader plowed the native prairie to create cropland. Then for several years or generations, a farmer grew crops, which gradually depleted soil nutrients. At some point, raising livestock became more profitable or desirable than farming, so the farmer planted the field in brome. If the farmer failed to consistently burn, mow, or graze cattle on the brome field, succession took root. First, volunteers of sumac, red cedar, or cottonwood started growing in the field. Eventually a "scrub woods" developed—a forest with low biodiversity dominated by black locust, honey locust, Osage orange, black walnut, buckbrush, and poison ivy.

By the end of the twentieth century, 99.3 percent of the original American tallgrass prairie had vanished. Most of the 0.7 percent that remained was in the Kansas Flint Hills. Farther east in Douglas County, which was 94 percent prairie at the time of settlement, only 0.5 percent remained. In Wyandotte County, which was 75 percent prairie at the time of settlement, 0 percent remained. Between 1988 and 2010, 20 percent of the remaining virgin prairie in Douglas County was lost to housing developments, road projects, and agriculture. Much of the original prairie had become a scrub woods. This was what settlement *did* to prairie.

I used to think that *all* Kansas forests were scrub woods, but the original wilderness of eastern Kansas wasn't all prairie, and amazingly, on certain north-facing hill slopes and rare stretches of flood-prone river bottoms, an overlooked collection of heirloom forests quietly survives to this day, virtually unknown.

Virgin forest. It sounds as out of place in Kansas as voting Democrat. I first considered the possibility that native forests still survived while studying old maps of the Marais des Cygnes River. Originally home to the Osage Indians, the river was explored by French fur traders before 1800. Later, several emigrant tribes exiled to the Kansas Indian territory lived near its banks in the early 1800s. French for "Marsh of Swans," the Marais des Cygnes flowed gently from its headwaters in the Flint Hills through prairies and forests as elegant as its name before merging with the Little Osage to form the Osage River, the longest river contained entirely in Missouri.

It was also haunted.

I had heard from several people who deeply knew rural Franklin and Miami Counties that feral squash and corn gardens descended from plots planted by Native Americans still sprung up every year in the humidity of early summer along Tauy Creek close to where it empties into the Marais des Cygnes. I never found one of these spirit gardens, but once while walking a plowed field along Eight Mile Creek, another of the river's tributaries, I found a perfect arrowhead on the mud delta of an intermittent stream swollen from morning rain. Rinsed clean, it stood out like a pearl bracelet in a black velvet box. Reaching down to pick it up, I suddenly stopped. Water flowed everywhere in the field, dripping from trees, pulsing through wheat fields turned rice paddies, breaching debris jams, gathering in a torrent of roiled mud and tree trunks floating down Eight Mile Creek, which only a week before had been less than a foot deep. The arrowhead sparkled in the sun, an alien in the storm-strewn field, like somebody had set it down only moments before and might soon come back to retrieve it. I looked around and saw no one, but drums pounded in my imagination as I stood among footprints of people dressed in soft deerskin and beaver tooth necklaces, footprints washed away by thunderstorms that dissipated centuries before.

Even the heron rookeries in giant sycamores along the river seem haunted. Generations of birds have reared their young in groups of large nests that possibly date back one hundred years or more.

Early settlers wrote that the riverbanks teemed with wild foods: pawpaws, persimmons, chokecherries, gooseberries, nettles, mayapples, morels. The Marais des Cygnes was also thick with native pecan groves, and that really intrigued me. I never knew pecans were native to Kansas, and while pawpaws and persimmons were substantial fruits, nobody ate them (or even knew what they were) in the suburbs where I grew up. Even though pecans were commonly available, the thought of wild pecan groves seemed exotic, like sunken steamboats buried in farm fields along the Missouri River. More incredibly, I learned that some existing groves might predate settlement; in other words, trees growing today along the Marais des Cygnes might have provided shade for the Osage and French fur trappers plying the River of the Swans in sweet gum pirogues. The thought was electrifying.

Ironically, wild land inventories show that outside of the Flint Hills, native forests have fared better than native prairies in Kansas (though the distinction is relative at best, extant high-quality prairies and forests are all mournfully rare). Forests fared better for a number of reasons. Both the emigrant Native American tribes and early European settlers sought forested tracts for their homes. Forests were important social gathering places. Old groves along rivers and streams—many were given names—hosted weddings, chautauquas, Fourth of July celebrations, and the like. Biologically, forests were more regenerative than prairies. Though individual grass plants have much shorter life spans than trees, the ecological diversity of prairies isn't as hardy as woodland plant communities. Forests tolerate disturbance and bounce back better than tallgrass prairies (scientists don't agree on how long a restored prairie needs to reach a maturity equivalent to a climax forest, if that is indeed even possible).

But with so many tens of thousands of acres of scrub woods, I wondered how I would recognize the rare virgin forests that remained. I knew there were two main types: the western outliers of the once vast eastern oak-hickory deciduous forest complex and the riparian river bottom forests dominated by huge cottonwoods. Generally speaking, old-growth forests have a high degree of biological diversity, not just a few dominant species. They contain gigantic trees, whether by girth or height. "Gigantic" is species-specific, but in old-growth forests the most successful trees can attain their full potential. They contain still-standing corpses of giant dead trees. Old-growth forests are cluttered with decay—in this case dead wood is a good thing. They also support a rich collection of shade-loving "understory" species like pawpaw, ironwood, and box elder—a kind of forest "minor league" that the scrub woods can't afford. In England, forests that pre-date 1600 are deemed "ancient," but in America the term "old growth" has become synonymous with "climax," a condition where all of the principal forest species are present and functioning in symbiotic harmony.

As in prairies, indicator species are a good tool for locating old-growth forests. Hitchcock's sedge, Canadian wild ginger, New Jersey tea, yellow lady's slipper, large-flower bellwort, northern maidenhair fern, green violet, Michigan lily: Find a large assortment of these herbaceous plants in Kansas and you are likely in an ancient place. Biologists classify natural communities by their most abundant and dominant species. Some have wistful names: Ozark limestone glade, pecan-hackberry floodplain forest, pondweed aquatic wetland, buttonbush swamp. In eastern Kansas the three most common forests are oak-hickory, cottonwood-sycamore, and blackjack–post oak cross timbers.

I soon discovered that undisturbed pecan-hackberry forest communities were particularly rare. Although we have no "pecan culture" in Kansas—no praline stands, no billboards that bark out "only 250 miles to the biggest pecan roll outside of Dixie"—commercial Kansas pecan groves produce roughly 1 percent of the nation's pecans, mostly from wild trees. The Kansas Forest Service and various agriculture agencies offer advice for "improving" pecan stands. Methods include thinning trees, controlling animals that feed on pecans, clearing undergrowth, and removing dead trees—practices at odds with allowing a forest to approach climax. I failed to find an old-growth pecan grove along the Marais des Cygnes; it became clear that only the biggest rivers in the state—possibly only the Kansas and Missouri—could still foster the kind of habitat necessary to harbor an ancient remnant of native pecans.

Though finding such a grove was a long shot, the possibility was riveting; pecan trees can live longer than three hundred years. Walking into an ancient pecan grove would be like walking back into a lost era. But I put my zeal for these wild places on hold for several years after I discovered a different but no less unique forest close to my home in Lawrence. It all started when I got interested in a species I never dreamed lived in the woods of eastern Kansas: the southern flying squirrel.

Flying squirrels are forest specialists so removed from the rhythm of modern American society that few people know they exist. Although the flying squirrel is a state threatened species in Kansas, even more rare are people that have seen them in the wild—since 1990 fewer than twenty-five reports were filed with the Kansas Biological Survey, the agency that tracks such things. The existence of nearby flying squirrel colonies seemed so bygone I scoffed at their inclusion on a checklist of Kansas mammals. The species' entire history in the state probably consisted of at most a handful of early specimens—despite its status I was sure the species must be extirpated.

It wasn't.

The smallest Kansas squirrel, flying squirrels live in the upper canopy of large oak-hickory forests in the eastern third of the state. The size of a chipmunk, as quiet as their most serious predators—owls—and utterly nocturnal, flying squirrels are like ghosts of the forest—nobody ever sees them. Incredibly acrobatic, they don't actually fly, but glide up to three hundred feet at a time from a kite of loose skin that connects their front and hind legs. Their sad, disproportionately large eyes are straight out of a Keane painting. They nest almost exclusively in woodpecker holes. Because the uppermost forest canopy is their gymnasium, flying squirrels are terrific indicators of forest health since only high-quality oak-hickory woodlands support the large closed canopies necessary to support their foraging.

They sometimes make nocturnal appearances at bird feeders, but the best way to actually see a flying squirrel is to walk deep into a forest on a still night and listen for their bird-like coos or the thud they make while landing. Brave souls have yanked flying squirrels out of flicker holes with their bare hands. Regardless of the technique, your chances of seeing a flying squirrel in Kansas are slim to none, even if you know what you're doing.

When I told my friend Gary Shea that we might have flying squirrels nearby, he wanted to drop everything and search for them immediately. Gary moved to Lawrence for graduate school (driving into town for the first time precisely as the moon went into full lunar eclipse), but he called the entire American West his home. Gary baked sourdough bread in a homemade brick oven behind his girlfriend's house, brewed his own beer, and played standup bass. He once rode his mountain bike from Boulder, Colorado, to Juneau, Alaska, and back. Soon after we met he started giving me old used camping gear—a white gas stove, a Eureka tent, Coleman fuel bottles, sleeping pads. We lured fellow grad students out on almost weekly camping trips. The Midwest was uncharted territory for Gary, so he didn't complain that almost all of our destinations were treeless; he was one pioneer who understood that wild places in a grassland state tended to be, well, grassy. I showed him my favorite prairie relicts and the best windswept sandbars to camp on along the Kaw.

But Gary was a woodsman at heart. He'd spent a decade discovering a collection of secret spots in the western Rockies, rich alpine microhabitats, wilderness trails connected by cross-country ski huts, deep aspen glens. Now we finally had a good reason to hit the woods. This probably explained why he was so enthused about flying squirrels. But first we had to find them. Gary beat me to the pertinent information before I even started. His friends in the KU environmental studies program all told him the same thing: Go to the Breidenthal Forest.

North of Baldwin City a steep limestone cuesta plunges into the valley of Coal Creek, creating a complex of hollows and ridgelines that feels more like North Carolina than Kansas. The Baldwin Woods is the name of the oak-hickory forest that drapes this escarpment. It may be the westernmost true eastern deciduous forest remnant in America, the port of exit where a squirrel crossing by treetop from the Atlantic Ocean to the Great Plains would finally have to debark. The largely contiguous woodland includes Douglas County State Lake and three preserves managed by the University of Kansas—the Rice Woodland, the Wall Woods, and the Breidenthal Biological Reserve. Baldwin Woods is on the roster of the National Park Service's collection of National Natural Landmarks.

Covering only ninety acres, Breidenthal is the pristine heart of the woodland. Even people who will never appreciate the subtle intricacy of five-acre prairie remnants and swampy wetlands love the place. Descending the steep trail toward the headwater stream that runs through the forest, first-time visitors are always surprised by the elegant grandeur of the huge trees. White oak, chinquapin, bitterroot hickory, shagbark hickory, and sycamore dominate. Blackjack oak glades—mixed savannahs of grass and trees—cover the drier hillsides.

Gary, Alan Ziegler, and I made it to Breidenthal for the first time just after midnight on a night in late April. As we drove south from Lawrence on Route 1055, the road climbed the first ridge south of Vinland and then cut through the deep woods. The swooning darkness of the forest rubbed out the few dim cabin lights—at least one kerosene—on the edges of the preserve. I buttoned my jacket against the cool of the hollow as we pulled off the road in front of a wooden gate.

A screech owl trilled in the distance. Alan shined his flashlight at the sign on the gate: "Research area, no hunting or picnicking." Gary had obtained prior permission to visit the forest. We didn't bring a picnic.

The trail led into pitch-blackness. Before Alan and I could chicken out, the thin light of Gary's lamp took off into the forest as he crushed through leaves on the trail ahead of us. Alan followed and made a mourning dove call. I hurried after them both—I didn't bring a light.

Our mission was to find flying squirrels, so we needed a strategy. We decided to walk thirty feet, stop and let the forest quiet down, then hold perfectly still until we either heard a flying squirrel or counted to 180 (three minutes). Then we would repeat the process. I had no idea what a real flying squirrel was supposed to sound like, but I imaged something similar to a fox squirrel scraping acorns or my Uncle Joe chomping Brazil nuts at Thanksgiving. The spring foliage was behind schedule; we wouldn't hear flying squirrels plunging through thick branches of leaves; that is, *if* flying squirrels actually plunged through thick branches of leaves at all.

A snipe hunt.

We walked/stopped/counted our way slowly through the woods, the spooky outlines of sycamores and giant oaks outlined by pale yellow moonlight. Hundreds of tiny midnight blue lanterns decorating a pawpaw grove actually were small blooms, garnet-red by day. We worked slowly like this up a steep hill until we stood on top of a ridge that led down to the creek. No flying squirrels. We lay down on a cushion of moss and leaves to rest, the chamber music of owls and coyotes not too far away. Gary and Alan switched off their lights. We let the darkness hold us. Gradually our eyes adjusted and stars began to sparkle though gaps in the treetops.

Then I noticed something strange. A very faint glow, so faint I didn't completely trust my eyes, but a glow, bluish-green, on the mossy hillside above us. It was easier to see if I didn't focus on it. "Ectoplasm," Alan said quietly. Even more quietly, Gary said, "Phosphorescent fungus. Must be growing on the deadfalls."

The forest was enchanted with foxfire. In folklore, woodland fairies flitting through the woods leave behind these "fairy sparks." Foxfire only grows on rotting wood, which meant the preserve had at least one important characteristic of an old-growth forest. Breidenthal was unlike any place I'd ever been in eastern Kansas. I couldn't wait to see it in the sunlight.

I returned alone the next day and retraced our steps of the night before. The front woods by the road had been completely logged within the last fifty years, but farther back, beyond the steep mossy embankment where we saw the foxfire, the trail twisted up to a summit that overlooked a picturesque valley of old-growth sycamore and oak-hickory. The valley, I thought, would be the perfect place to build a log cabin, but luckily no one ever did. An intermittent spring-fed tributary of Coal Creek wound through the valley. The water remained fairly clear even in the muck of August when other eastern Kansas waterways were brown and covered with a skim of yeast and agricultural yuck.

West of the creek, the trail turned south onto the grade of the Atchison, Topeka, Santa Fe, and Galveston railroad, abandoned around 1890 and since closed over by a tunnel of tree limbs. Carved limestone bricks painstakingly lined a spring run that led down a steep wooded escarpment to the bed. The fallen timbers of a bridge marked where the trail paralleled a remarkable sandstone formation topped by a fifty-foot ledge with a small indentation cave. Graffiti, some of it historical, vandalized the sandstone: "J. D. was here in 1886." Gary came back later and transcribed everything he could decipher. Below the cliff, light echoed off the water like a chandelier. The creek cut richly textured patterns in the rock and exposed a thin seam of bituminous coal, the sooty kind once mined from shallow pits whose tailings were still visible in fields near the forest.

In late summer, fallen logs in a dry oak-hickory forest like Breidenthal feed a colorful community of mushrooms, fungus, mosses, lichens, and flowers that pop up on or near the decaying wood, but strangely these old forests feel "fresher" than scrub woods. Breidenthal is surprisingly pleasant in August when the scrub woods are an itchy jungle of ticks, mosquitoes, and poison ivy. These forests, unlike ancient homes, come equipped with natural air conditioning that improves with age.

For many years I remained faithful to Breidenthal. Then warblers changed everything.

Because my daughter Chloe was young, I had decided to teach her (and myself) how to identify wood warblers. Warblers are the costume jewelry of the bird world, vividly colored insect specialists barely larger than bugs themselves, the "O" in the OCD of raving spring birders obsessed with the magic of the annual migration. Birders speak lustily of warbler "fallouts" and the difficulties of identifying "confusing fall warblers." Their call notes and field marks are clues in an annual grail-like quest.

When our warbler list numbered exactly six—yellow warbler, black and white warbler, yellow-rumped warbler, Nashville warbler, common yellowthroat, and orange-crowned warbler—I realized that searching better habitat might improve our chances and help build our list. Most wood warblers are at the edge of their range in eastern Kansas, they prefer high forest canopies, not sprawling open grasslands. Old-growth riparian forests with towering cottonwoods like the trees at Burcham Park along the Kansas River in Lawrence are like a warbler truck stop where birds can rest during the day and bulk up on mayflies and mosquitoes to help fuel the next night's journey, which could span one hundred miles or more.

One April morning after the first hard spring rain, I joined a dozen birders at Burcham Park, squinting and craning our necks for fleeting glimpses of the tiny birds. Those in the know claimed warblers were behind schedule. We saw only yellow-rumpeds, a hardy species that sometimes winters in Kansas. The king of Burcham Park ornithology, Bob Antonia, dispersed warbler gospel on grateful newbies like myself: "We don't get the same numbers of eastern wood warblers here at Burcham. The groves along the Missouri are closer to the main body of the migration." Weston Bend State Park in Missouri was the place to go, according to Bob.

That night I got the maps out and traced the Missouri River's purple line north from Kansas City's Lewis and Clark point through Fairfax, Quindaro Bend, Little Platte Bend, Pomeroy Bend, Pope Bend, Stigers Island, Delaware Bend, and Mad Lake until it banked sharply right, then left, to form Weston Bend northeast of Leavenworth. What really caught my eye though was a featureless blue polygon on the Kansas side of the river across from Weston Bend—apparently a huge expanse of bottomland forest on the Fort Leavenworth Military Reservation. The map showed an airstrip but no other signs of man-made structures. How big was this forest, I wondered, if indeed it was still a forest? This was the kind of open bottomland expanse along a major river that I'd searched for years back during my quest for a Kansas old-growth pecan forest. Forget warblers. Remembering back more than fifteen years to my searches along the Marais des Cygnes, I wondered whether I was really onto something this time.

Google quickly took me to a Kansas Biological Survey report on the natural resources of Fort Leavenworth that answered all of my questions. Not only was the land across from Weston Bend still wooded, there were concentric rings within the forest, each progressively older, and the jewel at the center took my breath away. A pecan forest. An old-growth pecan forest, completely surrounded by five thousand acres of ancient cottonwoods and sycamores, in the lowlands along the Missouri River itself. I read and reread the description. It was the *last* old-growth pecan forest in Kansas and the northernmost in the country.

The forest had a rich cultural history. Lewis and Clark collected plant specimens there, James Audubon visited during a trip across the West, and it was a prison for Chief Joseph and the Nez Perce Indians after their final surrender during the Indian wars. Like many of the last wild places of Kansas, this place was almost completely unknown; I'd lived my entire life in the state and never heard of it. The pecan grove was only "discovered" again by researchers in the last decade. My fifteen-year-old question had a three-hundred-year-old answer.

Thanks to warblers, my search for Kansas old growth was on again. There were details I needed to sort out, like whether the military let people like me tromp through the woods on the base. Then, in a stroke of serendipity, Jay Bredwell emailed to invite me to a public walk the next Saturday led by plant specialist Caleb Morse of the Kansas Native Plant Society at Fort Leavenworth Woods. The timing was incredible. As long as we could clear security at the fort, the Holy Grail of Kansas forests was in sight!

We pulled up to the security checkpoint at Fort Leavenworth at 10:00 a.m. sharp. The week before, a stalled storm front spawned a mile-and-a-half-wide tornado that completely destroyed Greensburg, Kansas. Farther east, the same storms sent the Kansas and Missouri Rivers over their banks in flood-prone areas, including parts of Fort Leavenworth. I'd been monitoring the deluge. A friend saw grass carp wallowing in a drowned cornfield near where I-435 crosses the Missouri. The pecan grove grew basically at river level; if Weston Bend was as prone to flooding as I thought it was, the chances of getting back there on foot didn't seem promising.

Fort Leavenworth was founded in 1827 along a series of limestone outcrops that overlooked the Missouri River, but the loess hills and wooded lowlands surrounding Weston Bend had attracted people for centuries. To the north of the modern fort, French fur traders built Fort de Cavagnial in 1744. Their trading partners, the Kansa, lived there before there was any written name for the buffalo. In 1804 Lewis and Clark found ruins of a major Kansa village and the old French fort, both abandoned by the time France ceded the Louisiana territory to Spain in the 1760s.

Across the river from the pecan grove, Weston, Missouri, hides in a protected hollow, a living link to the Border Wars. Weston is a quaint river town that feels haunted. Victorian homes, antebellum homes, steeply pitched streets, brick sidewalks, narrow alleyways, and a downtown brimming with antique stores and niche shops make Weston unlike any community in western Missouri. It's scary as hell on Halloween.

Only two land miles from Kansas, Weston symbolizes the historic differences between the two states. Before the Civil War, hotheads who wanted to make Kansas a slave state caused ceaseless trouble for the little town. At the time, Weston was the second-largest port on the Missouri behind Saint Louis. Wealthy slave-holding families moved into the area and established hemp and tobacco farms (roughly 2.8 million pounds of tobacco is still grown in Platte County, Missouri). Karma didn't seem to be on Weston's side. A fire demolished the central business district in 1855 and a cholera epidemic swept through and killed hundreds. After a major flood in 1881, the Missouri River got cold feet and changed course, slipping into an old channel two miles west of the city. Literally overnight the port of Weston disappeared along with the town's principal reason for existence. Weston's residents remained, however, preening over their antebellum homes and keeping company with the ghosts of the Kansa, fugitive slaves, and cholera victims. Today you can drink a hand-made beer three stories underground in a bar that smells like a dank coffin.

After clearing security we parked under shade trees outside of the Fort Leavenworth commissary to wait for the plant crowd. Some old guys from the Abdullah Shrine Temple did a brisk business hawking ten-dollar bags of Vidalia onions outside the Army credit union. Officers in comfy weekend fatigues streamed out of the commissary, two or three carts per family, loaded with tax-free stashes of double-case toilet tissue (forty-eight rolls), tubs of baby wipes, buy-two-get-one-free Cool Ranch Doritos (one gram of fat per two chips; do the math), boxes of Valvoline 5W30 motor oil, frozen pizzas, five-gallon tubs of rainbow sherbet—everything in bulk.

It was easy to identify the plant crowd as they drove up in hybrid cars dwarfed by the beefed up rides at the commissary (I'll admit I envied two twin RVs retrofitted like minivans). Between the giant loads of groceries and the super-sized vehicles it felt like *Land of the Lost*. Once gathered, we got back in our cars for the short drive to Fort Leavenworth Woods.

I was surprised that a dozen people had enough zeal for native plants to haul themselves up to the base on the first sunny Saturday morning in weeks. We donned blaze orange vests (turkey season had just opened) and gathered under an American elm tree. Most of us wore shorts and wide-brimmed hats. We looked like a bunch of dorks. Morse, a young KU botanist with a passion for sedges ("showy spring ephemerals are not my thing"), explained that US military bases had been in federal hands for a long time, and most were never developed, so they were great places to look for relatively undisturbed natural areas. The base was home to three basic plant communities, two of which were maple-basswood forest on steep bluffs along the river and oak-hickory forest on the remaining uplands. He said the upland understory was particularly rich—and a great place for a plant walk—because it had many interesting state rare plants, including the putty root orchid, sometimes called the Adam and Eve orchid, which puts out one big basal leaf in October that dies in the spring when it flowers. It's hard to see because it doesn't have any actual leaves.

From their reaction, I could tell that orchids were the warblers of the plant crowd. Another KNPS member got into a long discussion with Caleb over the correct way to classify them. After more than five minutes of listening to their back-and-forth conversation, Jay interrupted them before they really reached a consensus: "Hey Caleb, George says there's a pecan grove somewhere back in the woods. Do you know anything about it? Are we headed back there?"

Caleb said, "Yes, yes, the pecan grove. More than any one species or plant or orchid here at the reserve, the pecan grove is the coolest, most significant natural resource in the bottomland."

Shirley Braunlich, who organized the trip, rounded up the crowd to get every-one's attention. She knew this was what many of the non-KNPS members were here for. Caleb said, "This pecan grove is something really unique. It is believed to be the only native old-growth pecan forest in Kansas. The huge trees may have been planted by Native Americans; there is a 'grovey' aspect to them. Somehow, they have managed to survive the river's dynamism for many centuries now. Near the core of the pecan grove, in some sycamores, a heron rookery has been there for probably over a hundred years at least."

I was totally jived, for about a second. "Unfortunately," Caleb said, "we won't be able to get back there today because of the flood."

I looked over at Jay, who didn't flinch. Jay had come prepared to march through flooded terrain. He wore knee-high rubber boots and had gloves and a rain slicker tucked into his knapsack along with maps and binoculars.

Collections manager of the Bridwell Botany Research Lab at the KU Museum of Natural History, Caleb was not shy about heading into the backwoods. We forded a rain-swollen stream that topped everyone's boots and found a gravel trail leading up into the forest. Maybe we *would* make it back to the pecans. I'd been on bird outings where nobody wanted to get their feet wet looking for ovenbirds or prothonotary warblers, but this wasn't such a group. I thought everybody would be a professional biologist, serious people who sieved creeks. But with one exception, nobody except Caleb worked in the life sciences; our group included two librarians, an engineer, a store manager, and three retirees. Jeff Hansen, in particular, had the Latin names for plants etched on the back of his eyelids. He could stay with Caleb blow by blow.

We stopped to look at a vine that I thought was a raspberry, but it was tricky to say for sure; there weren't any blooms yet, much less fruit. Caleb got his pocket-knife out and cut into the wood of the vine to examine the pith. "I think this one's a blackberry. We have a lot of trouble identifying our native blackberries because they were cultivated intensely here. Until the dust bowl, we were exporting thousands of tons of blackberries."

Somebody asked Caleb, "What's the coefficient on this one. A three?"

She was asking about its "coefficient of conservatism," a number between one and ten that quantifies a plant's ability to tolerate disturbance. Ones could probably live equally well in a New York sidewalk crack as in an undisturbed forest, but tens are freakishly picky, only found in the most undisturbed natural plant communities—and probably doomed.

"Yeah, the blackberry is probably a two or a three. Maybe not a two; twos have loose seed that they spread at the drop of a hat."

From about a hundred feet back on the trail somebody said, "So you're a two, Caleb?"

He just smirked.

The next hour was a hunt for nines and tens. We found several of each. A nine according to the plant experts, Canadian wild ginger is a satiny groundcover with heart-shaped leaves that ants pollinate and deer won't touch. It makes both great bait and seasoning for mud catfish (according to the Ojibwa you just chew up the root and spit on a hook). You can grind up the slightly roasted root and sprinkle it on your clothes for perfume. Some Native American tribes used it for birth control. Caleb assured me that uprooting enough for a taste wouldn't endanger the community, so I jimmied a slice free with my pocketknife and took a small bite. It tasted more like ginseng than ginger. I later read that it contains *Aristolochia*, a human carcinogen.

As we walked farther back into increasingly older groves, Caleb showed us two understory trees, ironwood (the bark looks like a cat used it for a scratching post) and basswood, and several kinds of hickories (bats sometimes slumber under the frayed Rastafarian bark of the shagbark hickory). We found plenty of mustard garlic (an invasive problem in old forests that is just now making it to Kansas after being introduced in New York a century ago) and several species of invader roses. At the end of the walk we found a lone specimen of putty orchid, a ten. Nice, and definitely not showy.

As the plant crowd looked for more orchids, Jay and I looked out across the marsh, or rather, the small lake that we clearly would need a boat to cross. Jay hadn't brought a boat, so the ancient pecans would remain a mystery for now. We couldn't even see the treetops because the understory beyond the marsh was so thick.

On the way back to the cars Caleb said, "If you do end up going to the pecan grove sometime, take a GPS with you." He said the bottomland was completely flat, covered in wood nettles and wild ginger, and everything could look confusingly similar. "Once I was lost for two hours," he recalled. "It was hot, and I was getting itchy from nettle stings. An hour after I realized I was lost and making no progress, I thought I was going to have a nervous breakdown. There's a railroad that goes along the base of the levee, and when the train blew its whistle I started walking towards it. But then I'd hear the whistle from a different direction and start walking the other way. After a while, I realized there was also a train on the Weston side of the river. I had been walking around in circles for two hours."

I was disappointed but armed with new information about the Leavenworth woods and ready for my next trip, which would have to wait until the river dropped. Unfortunately, the rains continued through April and into May—nobody was getting back into that pecan grove. So I turned my renewed gusto for Kansas old growth to the southeast part of the state and another elusive forest. Like the Fort Leavenworth pecan grove, it had recently been "rediscovered" by scientists who were only now beginning to realize that the most ancient undisturbed forests in the entire eastern United States had been hiding in plain sight right here in Kansas.

There's nothing lost and found about the Kansas Cross Timbers. These small disjoint forests are the wallflowers of Kansas old growth. Foresters, loggers, cartographers, and environmentalists failed to notice them for decades—and the Cross Timbers were not just a single forest, but an entire ecosystem of wooded savannahs stretching from the Chautauqua Hills of southeast Kansas to central Texas, a span of more than 350 miles. Only scattered voices hailed these pseudo-wildernesses. Richard Francaviglia, in *The Cast Iron Forest*, detailed the history of scientific research in the Texas Cross Timbers dating back to the early 1900s, but recognition of the smaller Kansas portion came later.

This much is certain: When dendrochronologists at the University of Arkansas studied tree rings from hundreds of red cedars, blackjack oaks, and post oaks, they discovered an ecological gold mine. The Cross Timbers was the last substantial chunk of pre-settlement old growth in the eastern United States, older than the oldest stunted American chestnut groves (routed by chestnut blight), older than the few pitiful swaths of original Mississippi Delta bottomland forest (clear-cut in the early twentieth century), older than virtually any virgin timber still standing east of the Front Range and, if the annals of lost American wilderness had any more room for irony, some of those Cross Timbers forests were in Kansas—the prairie state.

The salvation of the Cross Timbers lay in the tortured arthritic limbs of their hallmark species, the post oak. Because of its crooked grain, post oak lumber had little value other than for fence posts, nor did blackjack oak or red cedar. The forests clung to steep sandstone draws, marginal at best for farming. Because of this, hundreds of intact forests survived unmolested into modernity. These forests weren't towering or deep. There's nothing epic about the Cross Timbers. But they harbored super-centenarian trees between four hundred and five hundred years old— teenagers compared to four-thousand-year-old California sequoias—but ancient for eastern upland species. Thousands of individual trees that sprouted during the 1700s or earlier were still alive, scattered between approximately 380,000 acres of virgin post oak forest, almost all under private stewardship.

Mixtures of timber and grassland, glades are checkerboards of forest and light, the wooded "amphitheatres" of Willa Cather. The Kansas Cross Timbers glades were altogether different from the Baldwin Woods, the last splash of a continuous wave of oak-hickory surging east from the Atlantic coast, or the pecan groves of Fort Leavenworth, once part of a continuous belt of riparian woodland that ran the length of the lower Missouri and eventually spilled out into a jungle of swampland hardwoods in the Mississippi delta. "Archipelagos of forest in a sea of grass" (Richard V. Francaviglia), these trees were obstacles on the open prairie, and although nobody knows for sure, the need to *cross* them might have been the genesis of their name.

The Cross Timbers had a regional identity at least until the late 1800s. They appear on seventeenth-century Spanish maps. Washington Irving, author of *The Legend of Sleepy Hollow* and *Rip Van Winkle*, struggled through the Cross Timbers in the late nineteenth century, recording the following in his diary:

The herbage was parched; the foliage of the scrubby forest was withered; the whole woodland prospect, as far as the eye could reach, had a brown and arid hue. The fires made on the prairies by the Indian hunters, had frequently penetrated these forests, sweeping in light transient flames along the dry grass, scorching and calcining the lower twigs and branches of the trees, and leaving them black and hard, so as to tear the flesh of man and horse that had to scramble through them. I shall not easily forget the mortal toil and vexations of the flesh and spirit that we underwent occasionally, in our wanderings through the Cross Timber. It was like struggling through forests of cast iron.

With the headless horseman in our thoughts, my daughter Chloe and I made the two-hour trip south from Lawrence in late May to walk Ancient Trees Trail in Cross Timbers State Park outside Toronto, Kansas. Driving transects across the valleys of the Wakarusa, Marais des Cygnes, Neosho, and Verdigris Rivers, we watched fields of ankle-deep corn and nearly ripe wheat turn to brome pasture and CRP before blossoming into the full-on emptiness of the Flint and Chautauqua hills (distinguished by their bedrocks: limestone in the Flint Hills and sandstone in the Chautauqua Hills). Dickcissels, scissor-tailed flycatchers, meadowlarks, and upland sandpipers soared above aquamarine fields accented with rose vervain, purple coneflower, and blue false indigo. We drove past the nuclear power plant at Burlington and tried to buy black tea in a brown coffee truck stop at Lebo (with ashtrays in the no-smoking section). Bacteria in the no-flush rest stops on US 75 converted human waste into crop fertilizer. After 140 miles of treeless prairies and cropland, an old-growth forest was the last thing I expected to find at the end of our drive.

When we turned off the highway at Lizard Lips Country Store south of Toronto though, we saw the first solitary stands of oak as we began to descend into the Verdigris River valley. The forest was below the main thrust of the prairie upland. Looking out across the river it was hard to visualize that a deep valley forest interrupted the resonating "om" of the bluestem silence.

Kansas Wildlife and Parks did a good job advertising Ancient Trees Trail, but we still wound up driving circles through various campsites before finding the pathway behind the self-pay station at the park entrance. A summer tanager greeted us at the trailhead—a good sign. It was 10:00 a.m. the Friday before Memorial Day, but there wasn't a single boat on Toronto Reservoir; the torrential rains were obviously cutting into the seasonal economy. The wet spring had set the stage—mushrooms, wildflowers, ticks, mosquitoes, and green in every direction—a perfect day to explore the ancient woods.

I expected broken parkland, but Ancient Trees Trail clung almost exclusively to old forest. With the exception of understory species like spiderwort, flowering dogwood, and sumac, the principal trees of the Cross Timbers dominated the forest: post oak, blackjack oak, and red cedar, the only native Kansas conifer. The hum of pollinators escorted Chloe into the woods; she chased breezy swallowtail butterflies and electric green damselflies. We heard cuckoos secreting about the forest in search of caterpillars, probably just back from their wintering grounds. A painted bunting that we never saw called from the upper canopy.

The post oaks were like a Grandma Layton painting of bonsai trees—they showed their years. The short trees grew close enough together to form a true canopy. Thick mats of spongy emerald moss covered sandstone outcroppings as big as a Walgreen's parking lot. Mustard and gray-blue lichens formed a crust in rain-protected nooks. Chloe crouched under a soot-covered rock overhang, which must have been a good spot for scouting game along the river before the days of Toronto Lake. Chunks of burned red limestone scattered along the trail were possible evidence of fires set by Native Americans.

The trees dripped from days of rain. Moss covered the ground and everything on it—rocks, garbage, logs, oak stumps, cedar roots. In the diffuse light, mushrooms the color of electric coral and salmon popped out from the forest duff. Fog clung to the river and drifted through the canopy. In the heat of summer, the Cross Timbers might be as hot and muggy as any forest in Kansas, but Chloe and I felt like we were walking in a grove more like Muir Woods than Toronto Reservoir, and though the last Spanish missionaries probably left the area soon after Spain sold the future lands of Kansas to France in the late 1700s, the sign of the Maltese cross remained in every deeply lobed post oak leaf.

The oldest trees on the trail were labeled with their birthdays, determined by tree-ring analysis. Chloe darted from tree to tree, literally counting down the years: "1790, 1780, 1773, 1747, 1745, 1740, 1738, 1734, 1727." I later read that there were probably even older trees in the park, trees that were old when the Osage first encountered the Spanish, trees that were alive before George Washington was born. Near its end, the trail looped down toward the lake. The rain and high water had beached piles of nude trunks on the muddy shores, a sharp contrast to the lush green forest.

We finished our hike before the fog burned off, which no doubt reinforced the ancient feel of the place. As we drove out of the park and back onto the prairie, the pastures were vivid green, like the Gaelic hills of Ireland. We spent the night in El Dorado. The next morning the Walnut River was almost over its banks after another night of heavy rains. The Cross Timbers had given us a taste of a truly ancient Kansas forest, and I couldn't wait to try again for the Fort Leavenworth pecan grove.

If it ever stopped raining.

I continued to curse the weather as the deluge continued, but then a break: six days of blue skies and june bugs. With borrowed thigh waders, maps from a Kansas Biological Survey report, a handheld GPS, two bottles of deet, a green camo water flask, my Nikon Monarchs (binoculars), and a pocketful of oatmeal bars, I drove to Fort Leavenworth ready to hack through hackberry, plow through poison ivy, shrug off the Amazonian bloom of mosquitoes and ticks, and do everything in my power to cross two miles of still-flooded jungle and reach the pecan grove. Driving east on I-70, I noted the waters had receded in fields along Stranger Creek. A bakery in Leavenworth touted itself "Home of the World's Most *Exciting* Donut." They served an all-you-can-eat donut bar for a dollar.

The bottomland forests of the Missouri and Kansas Rivers were once a towering kingdom of biota, a midwestern version of Faulkner's "Big Woods," but like all native Kansas ecosystems, old-growth riparian forests along major rivers are extremely rare today. In pre-settlement times, the moods of the fickle river continuously gave birth to, nurtured, and destroyed an array of sloughs, oxbows, and wetlands, creating an environment constantly in flux. But beginning in the early twentieth century, a system of levees and dikes along the Missouri mitigated the chaos of the river, changed its nature, tamed annual floods, and created a deep channel in the middle of the river. It also established a permanent boundary for riparian forests. Agriculture and urban development slowly whittled away what remained. Today few river forests extend more than one hundred feet out from the high-water mark. A deep bottomland forest unmolested by agriculture is exceedingly rare—so rare that biologists now believe the Fort Leavenworth Woods is the single best remaining bottomland forest on the entire lower Missouri River.

The tallest trees in Kansas live in these wild places, and as of 2015, the two tallest individual trees in the state were a sycamore and a pecan, both of riparian stock.

According to the Kansas Forest Service, which tracks Kansas champion trees, an enormous pecan, almost 120 feet high when last measured in 2009, grew stoically somewhere out in the Fort Leavenworth pecan jungle. This pecan, the tallest in the state, was only "discovered" in 2003, even though there's a good chance it was alive before the first Euro-American set foot in the state. Who said the age of discovery was dead?

When I pulled up to the entrance of the base I realized I'd forgotten my blaze orange vest. It was the last day of turkey season, and the MP who searched my car said there were guys back in the woods who'd hunted every day for a month without taking a single shot; this was their last chance. He looked at me and at my outfit—nylon parachute pants and a T-shirt one size too big, both olive green—shrugged, and waved me onto the base. At least I wasn't wearing a turkey costume.

Even on a weekday the commissary parking lot was crammed with shoppers. That place never let up. Guys with toy plastic Zebco reels and buzz cuts—some with children, some without—stood elbow to elbow casting into the pond across from the Buffalo Soldier Memorial. In the distance, behind the stately Victorian duplexes on the main hill of the base, the massive brown sweep of the Missouri River looked like something straight out of *Huckleberry Finn*. With all the rain, I wondered if the casino boats downstream in Kansas City felt an urge to break their moorings and push out into the current. I drove past the main parade and the rookery and finally turned onto a small gravel road that wound down toward Sherman's Airfield, which separated the civilized part of the base from the wilds of the floodplain forest and Chief Joseph Loop, named after the Nez Perce leader and military mastermind of the Nez Perce War who was held prisoner in the floodplain forest for eight months beginning in the winter of 1877.

Crossing the train tracks, the road curved around behind the runway and up onto the levee. I expected to immediately see the river, but instead found a flooded savannah with cruising plovers and red-winged blackbirds, and beyond that the floodplain forest north of the base. I felt lost even before I hit the trail. The big trees were in sight, but to get to them I'd have to cross a half-mile thicket of drowned cottonwood saplings and negotiate several football-field lengths of standing water. Great blue herons plied lazily through the air like pterodactyls. They didn't care if I hiked or swam.

I parked in a lot that grass and sumac were slowly reclaiming. A sign at the edge of the woods said, "Area D: No one allowed in without at least 100 sq inches of blaze orange on front and back and a blaze orange hat during deer season."

Well, it wasn't deer season. Even though the MP told me there were hunters in the woods, I didn't see any cars parked along the levee, although there were pickups a half-mile back at the airfield parking lot. A few pickup trucks and bow hunters weren't going to slow me down. I gathered up my gear. A mother egret circled in on a sycamore in dead silence. She could be as quiet and Zen chill as she liked up in those treetops, but down below in the woods I planned on making noise, plenty of it. Nobody was going to mistake me for a turkey—an elephant or a jackass, maybe—but not a turkey.

At the back of the parking lot I found a pseudo-trail leading toward a smaller levee along a slough, but I could only see about twenty-five yards down the path. Everything else was under water; maybe this trail would keep me out of the muck. I left the waders in the car. I could hike back and get them later if I wanted to.

The pecan grove would be sandwiched between old-growth cottonwood-sycamore stands, which in turn would be surrounded by savannahs of willow and immature cottonwood—perfect fodder for young deer and beaver. I synced my GPS with the satellites and confirmed I was two miles away from the pecans. The GPS would serve as my trail if the footpath failed me. I purified myself in a sweat bath of deet and crammed my pant legs down into my boots. It was only eight o'clock in the morning but already the temperature had topped eighty. The woods steeped in a windless humidity that rose up above the canopy. Summer had begun.

As soon as I started walking, a young white-tailed deer with floppy round ears galloped toward me, biting at a fly on her haunch. When she saw me, she did an about-face and returned to the shadows from where she came. The path petered out after about fifty feet. I decided to see if I could follow her trail; she looked like she knew where she was going.

The deer path led to the first thin grove of pecans. I hoped it was a good sign. I started to lose her trail but then saw a waterlogged field of reeds parted neatly down the middle. There was nothing to do but slosh forward; the water didn't look like it would top my boots. Next to the reeds, in the slow water of an oxbow, grass carp held near the surface like submarines. Cottonwood snacks from the night before littered the edges of a large beaver hole under a sycamore.

I followed the reeds, threading my way through a waist-high field of common milkweed. For a while I thought the path was maintained, but when I crossed a meadow of poison ivy up to my armpits, I knew it was deer's work; no man would willingly walk through this. Though pickled in bug spray, I kept swatting mosquitoes off my neck and ears, finally stopping to dump the rest of the poison on my tender exposed parts. This seemed to work; the mosquitoes retreated to an aura around my head. I cursed myself for wearing short sleeves. I brushed ticks off my arms by the dozens.

Of course these were minor hardships compared to what early explorers must have faced. Caleb had mentioned that the Lewis and Clark expedition stopped at Weston Bend on both legs of their journey, but the visitor who most fascinated me was John James Audubon. Audubon explored this same floodplain forest on an expedition aboard the American Fur Company's *Omega* steamboat en route to the mouth of the Yellowstone River in 1843. Audubon traveled extensively in the American wilderness sketching birds and observing species under actual field conditions. At Fort Leavenworth he encountered two species that soon would be very rare, but whose fates would differ greatly.

Fellow traveler Edward Harris wrote in his journal: "Stopped at Fort Leavenworth. . . . Saw an abundance of Parrokeets [sic]." The Carolina parakeet, a stunning green and yellow parrot, lived in flocks throughout the southeastern United States. In Kansas, the parakeets followed forested drainages out into the prairie. Audubon shot specimens here (though tied to bird conservation perhaps more than any other name, Audubon regularly took specimens for his sketches and enjoyed dining on robin, which he found "plump and juicy"), six of which still exist. The bird had been abundant at the fort for some time before Audubon's visit. Mixed flocks of indigo buntings and parakeets cruised through the bottomland woods, a sight that must have been breathtaking. Unfortunately, the large robin-sized birds were fond of apple seeds and corn. Farmers, ranchers, and "bird hunters" shot them by the thousands. Assaulted further by the feather trade and deforestation, Carolina parakeet populations never recovered. The last captive bird, a male named Incas, died in 1920.

Audubon also spotted a bald eagle nest near the fort, the only verified bald eagle nest in Kansas before 1989. Fortunately, our national bird fared better than the Carolina parakeet (they were removed from the endangered species list in 2007).

The fact that Audubon devoted detailed writings to the floodplain forest proved its merit as a wild place. His journal also noted that after reaching Fort Leavenworth, Audubon and his companions reluctantly gave up their intended "walk across the Bend" after learning that the ground was "overflowed."

More than 170 years later, I could relate.

With more than a mile to go, the deer path vanished. The satellite read on my GPS was spotty, and I wasn't sure I could retrace my steps if it stopped working.

The river had to be directly in front of me; if I could maintain a true heading, I'd make it.

Navigating the reed patches was getting hairier; the tall thickets completely shut me in as I ploughed my way through. Luckily, I kept finding footholds in the bog and didn't plunge in deeper than my knees. I could hear summer tanagers in the trees, their "pit-i-tuck" ringing through the forest. Several female rose-breasted grosbeaks hopped along with their Groucho Marx beaks. Orioles, indigo buntings, gold finches, and redstarts flashed color in the dank murk of the forest.

I'd spent the last half-hour making little forward progress when I came to another backwater. I stopped and wiped sweat from my eyes next to a slough that separated me from a stand of enormous cottonwood, surely the beginning of the first patch of old growth. All was quiet except for the tinnitus of mosquitoes.

I hopped up onto the brace of the dike and looked out over the wetland. The moment froze time. Three spotted fawns, soft as kittens and not much bigger, were lapping water from the sluice. I crept slowly forward and noticed three more, then ten, then twenty, then thirty miniature deer resting in the flooded grass at the edge of the forest. Some lounged in shade. Some glanced warily into the forest. Others napped, using their impossibly lanky legs for pillows. An equal number of great egrets, white as glacial snow, were spaced between the deer like watchful nannies. Installed erectly on their stilts, they observed everything and nothing. In the black watch of the cottonwood grove maybe a dozen mother deer gathered, nervously flicking their tails, instinct gluing them to the safety of the shadows, stopping them from running toward me, their frozen limbs twitching and tugging forward nonetheless to gather their children, muscles mutely screaming, "Run!"

I too was mesmerized and frozen in place, trying to remain hidden beside the fairy tale scene. But great egrets miss nothing, and one by one the birds began to lift. I expected them to circle round and start an airlift operation, something practiced in advance, rescuing the fawns to their mothers in the old growth. Their flight had the same effect; the young deer, startled at the departure of the birds, stood up on clumsy legs, not in any particular hurry, and sauntered off toward their mothers.

When they were gone I began walking along the sluice to a land bridge and crossed to reach the nursery. The fawns left body marks in the fresh grass. I picked up soft clutches of fur that smelled sweetly of honeysuckle and followed their footsteps into the old growth.

In the cottonwood grove the temperature dropped and the understory vanished. It was like ducking from the chaos of the city into the hush of a gallery. Deer trails crisscrossed in every direction like ant tunnels or fault lines or an Etch-A-Sketch. A gentle breeze air-conditioned the forest and brought a tickertape parade of billowing cottonwood seeds. I heard a fox yelp in the distance. The cool temperature didn't lull the mosquitoes; they got bolder and bit me ferociously. I could see how the malarial dolor crushed the spirit of Chief Joseph and his Nez Perce. The spellbinding beauty of the cottonwood seed raining down from the cathedral above, the piercing jab of mosquitoes, the endless variety of unfamiliar birdsong and bugsong and the singsong monologue running in my head about the deep history of the forest lulled and distracted the navigator in me. I kept following paths that seemed to loop back in on themselves, arcing around like the river itself. Surely the pecans were imminent, I kept telling myself. After ten minutes of walking I'd end up back at the opening of the slough, or was it a different slough, or was it an opening at all—perhaps just a thin place in the trees? Like a foolish husband ashamed to ask for directions, I disdained the GPS until I'd been going in circles for nearly an hour. Finally, when I tried to get a reading I became distracted again, this time by the mating call of a wild turkey: "Gobble, gobble."

Damn it! This was the first turkey I'd heard all morning. I crouched down, low. "Gobble, gobble." There it was again, exactly like the first time. I yelled out in a voice that surprised me by its weakness, "I'm here, it's me!"

Damn it again, now I was worried. The two calls sounded identical. Maybe it wasn't a turkey but a hunter making a turkey call. I yelled out again, but no one answered. For several minutes all was quiet. I looked down at my GPS display. The screen was a blank digital gray. Nothing. I pressed all the buttons a dozen times, tried rebooting, but nothing worked. The screen remained a sickening, lost, blank, informationless gray. I retraced the morning in my mind and remembered how, well before sunrise, I had rummaged through our dark kitchen drawers where we kept batteries and pulled out a Ziploc bag of mixed triple- and double-As. I had found Christina's battery stash—but it was her *to-be-recycled* battery stash. The GPS was useless.

Once again I heard it: "Gobble, gobble." I crouched lower and realized I was squatting in a wood nettle patch. The plants stung all the way through my nylon pants.

A train blew its whistle in the near distance. This would be coming from Sherman Army Airfield, due west, not where I expected it. I got ready to follow the whistle but then remembered what Caleb said; there was another train at Weston. I was in the middle of the two tracks. I had no idea which train was which.

I stood up to look for landmarks and a gunshot rifled through the forest. My adrenaline spiked and I stumbled forward, Monty Python–like, into the nettles. Immediately welts rose up on my legs. "Damn it, I'm here," I shouted, "Don't shoot!"

I tried to calm down. I reminded myself that gunshots were like thunder. The sound takes time to reach you. But the shot was loud, like a crack of lightning. What was I doing on a military base in the middle of the woods during a war? Why was somebody shooting a gun during archery season? Didn't people on military bases accidentally get killed by stray fire? I wiped sweat from my neck and upper back. I kept crouched down in the punishing nettle patch with the ghosts of Weston slaves and the Nez Perce and the Native Americans who planted the pecan grove and the Kansa and the French fur trappers and James Audubon and Lewis and Clark and all those shoppers packed into checkout lines at the commissary and the Zebco fisherman by the Buffalo Soldier monument close by, but none able to help.

I was completely and utterly lost.

Then I heard what I thought was barking. It couldn't be foxes because it came from the trees. It wasn't exactly barking, but a guttural complaint, like something was pissed off. I craned my neck toward a stand of sycamore. The barking was actually squawking that was getting louder.

I must have unconsciously offered up a prayer to the forest Manitous because just then an angry mob of great blue herons, carrying on like a pack of old cranky dogs, came into view a hundred yards down the deer trail. The Kansas Biological Survey report described a heron rookery next to the pecan grove. I slowly approached the first tree of the rookery and saw the caricatures of more than a dozen mother birds perched in comically gigantic nests built on huge limbs. Ruddy fuzzballs poked out from beneath the mothers. A few egrets were mixed in among the great blues. I heard a pileated woodpecker cackling crazily somewhere off in the woods. In the distance beyond the sycamores I could see much larger trees.

When I stopped walking, three turkeys flushed from the wood nettle, their wings beating madly like Volkswagens trying to take flight. They landed some distance away, and one made a perfect "gobble, gobble." I relaxed, finally, and took a long deep breath.

Past the rookery a golden light filtered through the branches of tall trees, the tallest trees I had ever seen in Kansas. I was on the edge of the old-growth pecan grove at last. The dream I'd carried with me so many years came rushing forward to meet reality and what waited ahead at the end of the deer path.

Whether it fits our national self-image or not, much of American history is gathered in the grass, strewn haphazardly behind old barns and in fields, cached in undiscovered archeological sites and ghost towns, and harbored in the little clumps of wilderness that still remain. Our American identity is an oil painting on a canvas of wilderness. The Fort Leavenworth Woods is still a remarkable wild place. The paths beneath these pecans were the first to feel the footsteps of Kansas explorers, yet they remain paths, not parking lots. The lives of the oldest trees span a mythic period of cultural and environmental change no less than revolutionary when taken as a whole. The ground under the Fort Leavenworth Woods has harbored many lines that divided clashing forces, lines dividing "civilization" from Indian country; fading cultures like the Nez Perce and Kansa from the onslaught of Manifest Destiny; lost species such as the Carolina parakeet from extinction; the abolitionist fervor of Leavenworth, Lawrence, and Free State Kansas from the stubborn clutches of slavery in Weston; ancient wild ecosystems from the rest of the mowed down, plowed under, farmed out, paved over, railroaded, dry-walled, stonewalled, urbanized, "suburbanated" lands that dominate Kansas today. A few trees at Fort Leavenworth and in the Cross Timbers are older than the entire written history of Kansas, born in a time when people still spoke languages that evolved to describe the landscape of prairie and forest and sky. Unlike the Wailing Wall or the Temple Mount or the Vatican or Stonehenge—iconic monuments made from brick, stone, and timber—this forest is *an actual living thing*, although virtually unknown to most people who live near it. It remains a no-man's-land. For both sides of those dividing lines, I hope it stays that way.

The regal pecans stood before me, a virgin forest spiraling upward in stages, pecan and cottonwood at the ascendancy, then hackberry, then thick clusters of ironwood and pawpaw and dogwood and cherry, then the ancestors themselves in their slumber, enormous deadfalls slowly rotting in the humid summer air, fungi and bacteria and worms and the endless miasma releasing three centuries of stored sunlight back into the churn, spinning the wheel again. This forest was beyond the stage of revelation. It functioned as a self-contained system nourishing plants and animals that kept the ancient processes going, that *were* the ancient processes, filling their own larder, self-creating but for sunlight and time.

With the midday sun percolating through the pecans, almost down to the carpet of wild ginger and jack-in-the-pulpit, I wiped the sweat off my forehead, slung the binoculars over my shoulder, looked ahead at the Missouri River rippling in the gentle breeze, and started walking through the woods toward Weston.

CHAPTER FOUR

The Alpha and the Omega

I am the Alpha and the Omega, the first and the last.
Book of Revelation (1:8)

The question is do we want to have just six things in Kansas: Wheat, soybeans, corn,
cows, horses, and grass, or do we want to share the countryside with wildlife?
Ron Klataske (from a presentation given to Jayhawk Audubon in 2008)

When Daniel Boone goes by at night the phantom deer arise,
and all lost wild America is burning in their eyes.
Steven Vincent Benet

When the Lewis and Clark expedition set out from Saint Charles, Missouri, in May of 1804 pulling a twelve-ton, fifty-five-foot "keeled boat" up the Missouri River, its principal mission—other than to explore and map the Louisiana Territory—was, in Thomas Jefferson's words, "to observe the animals of the country generally, and especially those not known in the U.S. the remains and accounts of any which may be deemed rare or extinct."

Fittingly, they first encountered the American bison (*Bison bison*) in Kansas. On June 28 expedition hunters "killed several Deer and Saw Buffalow" along the Kansas River while the rest of the party hunkered down for three days at Kaw Point—birthplace of Kansas City—behind a redoubt made from cut timber, leery of a possible Indian attack that never came.

In 1804, the buffalo was neither extirpated nor rare west of the Missouri. Later that summer the explorers witnessed "innumerable herds of the Buffalow"—only a small fraction, no doubt, of the thirty to sixty million that roamed across the American plains and prairies at the time. The bison was the last thundering link in Kansas to the era of great Pleistocene mega-fauna—mastodons and wooly rhinoceros and

66

curve-tusked mammoths—that lived on the prairies and plains as the ice sheets slowly melted a northerly retreat to await man-made global warming in the Arctic.

One hundred and seventy years after the expedition's campout at Kaw Point, when I was growing up not far from that first Lewis and Clark sighting, nobody still lived who had witnessed a wild Kansas buffalo. The veins of Kansans may bleed prisms of Jayhawk blue and red, Wildcat purple, or Shocker black and gold, but our identity as a buffalo state unites all Kansans.

By what right, though?

Our iconic state mammal is extirpated in the wild, and for more than 125 years now we have chosen not to share our wild lands with the buffalo. After I learned the story of their eradication in grade school, every time we sang the state song, *Home on the Range*, a sadness soaked into my blood.

What makes a place wild? A wild place in the Kansas sense is not the same as a wilderness, of which Kansas has none larger than a few dozen acres. Wilderness traditionally meant *uninhabited* and *undisturbed* (that is, an unspoiled place where timeless biological processes continued unfettered by human intervention).

A place might be considered wild if it still supports a relatively intact, native ecosystem. In a true wilderness this means unplowed, uncut, undammed, and certainly unfenced, but for a Kansas wild place the standard is fuzzier.

How can we quantify or measure the wildness of a place? Biodiversity is one commonly accepted metric. A tallgrass prairie with four hundred native forbs is wilder than one with only forty. We could create a spreadsheet with two columns—"native" and "exotic"—and start adding rows. On the left: rattlesnake master, Meade's milkweed, compass plant, New Jersey tea, blazing star, purple prairie clover, western prairie fringed orchid, false indigo, big bluestem, Indian grass; on the right: Japanese honeysuckle, garlic-mustard, leafy spurge, crown-vetch, yellow star-thistle, and dandelions. The deeper the left-hand column sags compared to the right, the wilder the place.

Instead of counting everything, we could search for indicator species that tell larger truths about biological diversity. In Kansas, rattlesnake master (*Eryngium yuccifolium*), a spectacular armored member of the carrot family that looks like a cross between a yucca and a one-handed flail, grows almost exclusively in high-quality or virgin prairie meadows. The state threatened Meade's milkweed indicates an even more rarefied prairie pureness, but good luck ID'ing this delicate forb if you're not a trained botanist.

What if we zoom out from relict prairie tracts of several acres to entire parks, counties, or even all of Kansas? Geographers and ecologists use satellite telemetry and computer-based geographic information systems to quantify spatial aspects of landscapes, plotting relationships such as percentage of land under cultivation versus percentage of land in native prairie.

Whether our data is macro or micro in extent, we could choose to employ some combination of census and remote sensing to build up a report card that grades the wildness of a place.

But let's return now to the story of the buffalo for another more accessible measure of wildness. Like rattlesnake master or Meade's milkweed, the American bison is an indicator species. Yellowstone National Park is home to the last wild, free-roaming buffalo herd in the lower forty-eight (although a speckling of smaller wild herds exist in Utah, South Dakota, and Montana). The image of the buffalo exudes pure freedom. There is nothing more wild and free than an unfenced herd of bison, perfect stuff for a Harley-Davidson commercial, but true nonetheless. After the extermination of the buffalo, Kansas was less wild. If someday we decide to create a public haven where our state mammal can once again roam freely across the prairies, Kansas will be wilder.

Healthy populations of native mammals can provide information about the biodiversity of a place. In western states, the presence of the grizzly bear, lynx, or wolverine is an excellent indicator of wildness; a twenty-four-inch grizzly print sunk into the soft earth of a subalpine meadow makes a better commercial for "wild and free" than the gnarliest Harley gang.

Although we could pick from a host of animals, plants, invertebrates, pollens, blue-green algaes, kelp, or blood-sucking liver flukes to test wildness, here I'm going to focus on mammals. Kansans feel a strong connection to the bison because we know the narrative of their demise. That's not the case with many other no less important native mammals. The next stop on our journey to the last wild places of Kansas takes us across the state via a collection of stories—stories of tragic loss, but also stories of restoration and innocence regained.

The buffalo is not our only ghost. The following mammals have disappeared from the state since the mid-1800s: the grizzly bear, black bear, gray wolf, red wolf, cougar, elk, white-tailed deer, mule deer, black-footed ferret, and northern river otter. The populations of beaver and pronghorn antelope, if never reaching zero, came very close. The population of the eastern spotted skunk is close to zero today.

Each loss is a unique story, but in almost every case (other than the buffalo) these extirpations were caused or hastened by habitat destruction and the loss or degradation of tallgrass and shortgrass prairies; oak-hickory, cottonwood-sycamore, pecan-hackberry, cross-timbers forests; and rivers and river wetland systems.

Books about Kansas mammals sometimes handle the topic of extirpated species as a done deal, but extirpation isn't the same as extinction. We can reverse it. Some extirpated mammals have clawed their way back into the wild. Threats to native habitats are still multifaceted, but many of the wild lands of Kansas are on a rebound.

Could we foresee a day when the full roster of native mammals might someday return to the wild in Kansas, at least those species that aren't extinct?

Most Kansans would probably like to see wild bison herds established on remote tracts of public land like Cimarron National Grassland. But could the pale wrinkled paw of a grizzly bear once again leave prints on the soft muddy banks of the Smoky Hill River? Don't laugh. Another fierce extirpated predator has recently returned to the state for the first time in over a century. Although there is currently no suitable grizzly habitat on the plains or prairies, a plausible scenario exists that might someday change that.

About half a dozen extirpated mammalian species are struggling to reestablish themselves today in Kansas. Two in particular are bellwethers. The success or failure of these species could determine whether we ever splice a sound track onto the reel of silent film that is all we have left of our missing mammalian species. The determined work of farsighted Kansans has helped lay this groundwork.

What follows is a collection of stories that all connoisseurs of Kansas wild places should know, gathered together here in a single place, the Alpha and the Omega. Let's begin at the end.

The Omega

The wanton slaughter of the Kansas state mammal, the American bison (*Bison bison*), the great sacred ungulate of North America, is well documented. By the 1860s bison, once ranging statewide, were restricted to the western half of Kansas. Between 1860 and the mid-1880s, hundreds of professional buffalo hunters killed the remaining wild buffalo in an unregulated free-for-all encouraged, in part, to destroy the economy of plains tribes during the Indian wars. Buffalo were shot for sport from the windows of Kansas Pacific railroad trains by European ladies wearing swan feather hats. Grand Duke Alexis, son of Czar Alexander II of Russia, killed buffalo near Hays. Entire hillsides were littered with the rotting corpses of bison slaughtered merely for their tongues. Well into the twentieth century settlers shipped bones collected on the plains east by train where they were piled up in towering boneyards and crushed to make fertilizer and bone char for filtering aquariums.

The last wild Kansas buffalo was probably shot outside Dodge City in 1879, although some might have held on in isolated areas until 1890.

On the plains and western prairies of Kansas, the gray wolf (*Canus lupis*)—also called the buffalo wolf or buffalo lobo—made a living almost exclusively on bison. The Lewis and Clark expedition killed one at the mouth of the Kaw River on June 24, 1804. James Richard Mead, founder of Wichita, documented the behavior of Kansas wolves. Much of what we know today about extirpated Kansas mammals can be traced to his writings. In 1859, stoked with abolitionist fervor and looking for adventure, the twenty-three-year-old Mead traveled to Kansas by covered wagon with two young friends who soon found they weren't rugged enough for the Kansas frontier. When they returned to Iowa, Mead organized an expedition to the Smoky Hill country to hunt buffalo. He spent the next four years living off the land and amassing a small fortune in furs. Mead made friends with the Kansa, was briefly held captive by the Sioux, and witnessed a battle between the Otoe and Cheyenne that lasted two days. He found a cave along the Smoky Hill with petroglyphs and one hundred-year-old graffiti left by a French fur trapper ("TRUDO: 1786"). Later in life, Mead, aware that the wildlife he so loved had been hunted into oblivion, recorded his memories in scientific publications and served as president of the Kansas Academy of Science.

Of wolves, he wrote, "the Lobo, or mountain wolf, locally known on the plains as the 'big gray' were congeners and associates of the buffalo, and lived almost exclusively on them. . . . Hunters with strychnia finally exterminated the wolves, . . . , myself and other men killing some 5,000 of them. They never molested people."

The last wild Kansas gray wolf was poisoned no later than 1920 as part of a government program to eradicate the species.

America's most endangered canid, the red wolf (*Canus niger*), once lived in the Ozarks of extreme southeastern Kansas. In 2015, the worldwide population of red wolves was fewer than three hundred. At one point extinct in the wild nationwide, several pairs have been released in North Carolina's Alligator River National Wildlife Refuge, Mississippi's Horn Island, and Florida's Saint Vincent and Cape Saint George Islands. A reintroduction in Great Smoky Mountains National Park in the early 1990s was unsuccessful. Little is known about habits of red wolves in Kansas. They were probably never common.

A male wolf killed by Clyde Boyd in 1909 near Columbus, in Cherokee County, was probably the last wild red wolf in Kansas.

The grizzly bear (*Ursus arctos*) ranged throughout Kansas prior to 1800. By 2015, the population of wild grizzlies in the lower forty-eight states was restricted to Yellowstone and Glacier National Parks, northern Washington, and a few other deep wilderness habitats in the Rocky Mountains.

James Gardiner, an early settler, wrote that a golden bear lived near the modern Turner neighborhood of Kansas City, Kansas, in the 1830s, menacing domestic animals of the Shawnee tribe. That bear survived into the 1840s, evading hunting parties of Shawnee and Wyandotte Indians (Turner High School's mascot: the Golden Bear).

Biologist Remington Kellogg interviewed James O. Pattie, an early Kansas adventurer, who chased a grizzly bear in the central part of the state:

> Here we killed a white bear, which occupied several of us at least an hour. It was constantly in chase of one or another of us, thus withholding us from shooting it, through fear of wounding each other. This was the first I had ever seen. His claws were four inches long and very sharp. He had killed a buffalo bull, eaten part of it, and buried the remainder. When we came upon him, he was watching the spot, where he had buried it, to keep off the wolves, which literally surrounded him.

In Kansas, grizzly bears declined along with the buffalo, their main food source. Settlers usually shot them on sight.

The last wild grizzly bear in Kansas had been killed by 1880.

Black bears (*Ursus americanus*), once followed forested streams into all corners of the state, although they were most common in eastern Kansas. The Kansa trapped them in great numbers along the Kaw River in the late 1700s and early 1800s. In a letter to the Kansas University Museum of Natural History, Mead reported that as late as 1864, "we killed Black Bears in Comanche County, Kansas. They had dens in the Gypsum caves, which were numerous in broken canyons, and raised their young there. We smoked them out and shot them as they ran."

A key factor in the black bear's decline was the destruction of forest habitat. The last wild Kansas black bear died no later than 1890.

Today's burgeoning deer population makes it hard to imagine that both white-tailed deer (*Odocoileus virginianus*) and black-tailed or mule deer (*Odocoileus hemionus*) were probably extirpated in the early twentieth century. Deer were an important food for both the Indians and pioneers. Unregulated hunting led to their demise. Scarce by 1875, the last wild Kansas deer might have been killed as early as 1904, but by the 1930s they were widely considered extinct in the state.

Another important food source for early Kansans, elk or wapiti (*Cervus elaphas*), were disliked by farmers because they damaged crops. The explorers Bourgmont and Pike found them plentiful, sometimes in mixed herds with buffalo. Mead wrote they were more numerous in the northern part of the state and rarely crossed east of a line running through El Dorado.

The last wild Kansas elk died sometime between 1875 and 1900.

In Kansas, the puma (*Puma concolor*), also called mountain lion or cougar, preyed mainly on deer (as it does elsewhere in its range). These large stealthy cats are rarely seen, so details of their habits and distribution in Kansas are sketchy. Zebulon Pike watched cougars stalk elk and deer in the Flint Hills when he traveled through in 1806. Mead wrote about hearing the "scream" of a cougar when he was camping with Native Americans along the Cimarron:

> In January, 1868 during extreme cold and heavy snow, I was camped, in the winter, near the mouth of Turkey creek, on the Cimarron River. About ten o'clock one night

two panthers came close to the camp, less than 100 yards, and lifting up their voices, let loose the most unearthly, blood curdling screams it was ever my good fortune to hear. Lobo, the big buffalo wolf, has a deep, profound, musical howl, which can be heard for miles over the silent, frozen plains; and their music has lulled me to sleep as I lay wrapped in blankets in the snow; but the unearthly scream of a panther close at hand will almost freeze the blood in one's veins, and for an instant paralyze almost any form of man or beast. . . . A panther's scream in the wilderness on a still night is an experience never to be forgotten. The memory of it will stay with one to the end.

The decline of deer populations coupled with the loss of suitable forest habitat contributed to their decline. The last wild Kansas cougar was shot on Monday August 15, 1904, by William Applebaugh and J. H. Spratt north of Catherine.

The black-footed ferret (*Mustela migripes*), a small weasel endemic to the Great Plains, once ranged across central and western Kansas, where it was completely dependent on the black-tailed prairie dog. Today the black-footed ferret is one of the most endangered mammals on earth.

The last wild Kansas black-footed ferret was grabbed by the gloved hand of Clifford Karnes on New Year's Eve, 1957, after he saw it running along a ditch on the side of a road near Studley. The ferret died in his captivity later that night, sometime before the ball descended on Times Square.

Little is known of pre-settlement habits of the northern river otter (*Lontra canadensis*) in Kansas. Otters were found along wooded streams in eastern Kansas and probably followed riparian habitats west across the state. Isaac McCoy saw otter sign along the Kaw in 1830 near the Vermillion River. Trappers decimated otter populations in the late 1800s.

The last wild Kansas otter was captured near Manhattan in 1904.

The Alpha

Habitat destruction, lax or unregulated hunting and trapping, and government-condoned "varmint control" were the main factors that led to the extirpation of these Kansas mammals. But with the advent of state-sanctioned harvest limits and the protection and restoration of native habitat in the mid-twentieth century, some extirpated species began to stage comebacks across the state.

Deer were the first to rebound. After a "no-harvest" policy provided some breathing room in the 1930s and 1940s, deer roamed in from neighboring states and started to repopulate their old haunts. Even when hunting seasons were reestablished in the 1960s, the lack of natural predators allowed white-tailed deer herds to boom. Since the 1990s, ten thousand cars crash into Kansas deer each year. A 2008 census at the 1,280-acre Shawnee Mission Park in Johnson County recorded some two hundred deer per square mile, possibly the highest density anywhere in North America.

The beaver (*Castor canadensis*) has undergone a similarly remarkable resurgence. Never completely extirpated, beaver fill every possible riparian niche in the state today and run afoul of landowners when they chop down trees along suburban streams for food and dam building supplies.

Elk and pronghorn antelope (*Antilocapra americana*) haven't been as successful. Today, modest reintroduced herds of wapiti range across Cimarron National Grasslands and Fort Riley. Like the beaver, antelope were never completely extirpated, but in western Kansas their numbers are thin. In eastern Kansas only a small reintroduced herd of about ninety individuals continues to hold on in the Flint Hills near the Bazaar cattle pens. Flint Hills antelope suffer nearly 90 percent mortality in their first year due to coyote predation.

Black bears wander across the state border from time to time, and a wild colony may be reestablishing itself in the Cimarron River valley, but a lack of suitable habitat has limited their return.

In December 2012, coyote hunters near Wakeeney shot what they thought was a large coyote. After inspecting it further, they notified the US Fish and Wildlife Service, which confirmed it was the first verified wild wolf in Kansas in over a century. The large male probably walked to Kansas from the Great Lakes. This was an isolated incident, and there are probably no resident wolves in the state today.

Somewhere between the great success of deer and beaver populations and the continued absence of bears, wolves, and free-roaming bison, two species that began returning to Kansas in the late twentieth century can be considered litmus tests for future reintroduction efforts. Proof that some places in Kansas are wilder than ever, these animals nevertheless face serious challenges and their futures are by no means assured. The success or failure of these animals could represent a tipping point for extirpated species in Kansas.

Between the parched valleys of the Smoky Hill and Solomon Rivers, Oakley, Kansas, has something far more valuable for survival in twenty-first-century America than a river: Interstate 70. Oakley sits near a curve on the highway about twenty miles west of the spot where passengers zooming west toward Denver first realize that western Kansas is flatter than a smashed can of Coors Light left beside a diesel pump at the Golden Ox Truck Stop in Hays the morning after *Weihnachtsfest.* Neighboring towns are lucky to still have a hundred citizens, but because of the interstate, four-bar cell reception in Oakley is the norm. Named after Eliza Oakley Gardner Hoag, mother of the town's founder, Oakley was not named after Annie Oakley, the nineteenth-century sharpshooter and showwoman born Phoebe Ann Mosey but called Watanya Cicilla or Little Sure Shot by her adoptive father, Sitting Bull. Bill Cody, their boss at the Wild West Show, won a buffalo killing contest there against Bill Comstock that once and for all decided who could rightly lay claim to the title "Buffalo Bill" (Cody killed sixty-nine bison, besting Comstock by twenty-three).

Driving southwest from Oakley on Highway 25, fields of no-till corn and wheat gradually give way to sandy dunes of yucca, prickly pear cactus, purple mallow, pronghorn antelope, and mule deer. The emptiness of the upper Smoky Hill country, where untold millions of buffalo once wandered, is a fully western emptiness that's hard to match anywhere else in the state, save perhaps the Flint Hills of Chase and Greenwood Counties. South of Russell Springs, a tiny town with a historic courthouse fifty miles east of Colorado, you start to hear prairie dog chatter augmenting the territorial ranting of meadowlarks, dickcissels, and western kingbirds.

Prairie dog habitat is endangered on both public and private lands. In 1900, a single prairie dog complex in Texas spanned one hundred by 250 miles—that's almost half the size of Kansas. Nothing comes close to that today. Like their cousins on the public lands of Cimarron National Grassland, prairie dogs on private lands inspire a confused politic. Grant money flies in all directions. In theory, a private landowner could receive funds both to eradicate and protect prairie dog colonies on the same property. Although the mallets of change keep whacking, the heads of prairie dogs keep popping up across western landscapes—at least for now.

The decline of the prairie dog was particularly bad news for the black-footed ferret. Lean, pint-sized members of the weasel family, these little vampires stalk the meandering tunnels of prairie dog towns at night, sinking their teeth into the necks of sleeping prey. Prudish for small mammals, ferrets aren't prolific and were probably never common. James Audubon penned the first scientific description in the mid-1800s. Native Americans coined at least a dozen names for black-footed ferrets in several languages, but explorers and mountain men made few mentions of the species in their journals. With a range spanning parts of twelve states, they never made it onto the radar screen of modern America. Some researchers believe Kansas had the highest density of black-footed ferrets in the world.

By the 1950s, the black-footed ferret was one of the rarest mammals on earth, and in the 1970s, when the last known colony of ferrets died off in South Dakota, most wildlife scientists presumed the worst. Then one night in 1981, a blue-heeler named Shep killed a small mammal and brought it to the front porch of a ranch house near Meeteetse, Wyoming. After a local taxidermist recognized it as a black-footed ferret, biologists swarmed tiny Meeteetse and located a colony of 120 ferrets, reviving a glimmer of hope for the species. As if an alien spacecraft had landed, researchers cordoned off the site and installed floodlights. The remaining ferrets were live-trapped, vaccinated, and fitted with radio collars. Two years later the wild population peaked at around 130.

But in 1985, dual epidemics of bubonic plague and canine distemper swept through the Meeteetse colony, and by 1987, only eighteen ferrets remained. In a risky move, the US Fish and Wildlife Service captured the entire colony and established a captive breeding program split across geographies to guard against future outbreaks. In parallel they launched an extensive search across the ferret's historic range for any remaining wild populations in a bid to boost genetic stock. Ferret mugshots were posted in truck stops and given to postal carriers. Researchers hoped that with sufficient moxie and good luck, they would locate new colonies. Ferrets are secretive, nocturnal, and subterranean; people in close proximity to black-footed ferret populations go their entire lives without seeing one. Despite the efforts, no new wild colony has ever been located.

Fortunately, unlike an earlier attempt to hand-raise black-footed ferrets in the 1970s, the Meeteetse survivors reared successive litters and the captive breeding program was successful. In 2015, worldwide population has passed two thousand, with more than one thousand individuals in the wild. The program first reintroduced ferrets in 1991 at Shirley Basin, Wyoming. Since then it has expanded to public lands and Indian reservations in Montana, South Dakota, Arizona, Colorado, Canada, Utah, and even as far south as Chihuahua, Mexico. The goal of the black-footed ferret recovery plan is to establish 1,500 breeding individuals in ten different locations. Despite the successes, prairie dog town fragmentation is still a major problem; none of the wild colonies is truly self-sustaining.

Kansas is prime black-footed ferret country, in the harmonic if not geographic center of their historic range, but largely because no suitable public land was available—bubonic plague affected prairie dogs at Cimarron National Grassland—the recovery team didn't seriously consider any Kansas sites in the early years.

Then everything changed. In 2005, Ron Klataske, executive director of Audubon Kansas, got a call from a Logan County rancher named Larry Haverfield. Along with wife, Bette, and neighboring landowners Gordon Barnhardt and Maxine Blank, Haverfield controlled 27,000 contiguous acres of shortgrass prairie—more than forty square miles—that nurtured something that forty years before would have seemed impossible: a six thousand-acre plague-free Kansas prairie dog complex, the single largest prairie dog town on the southern plains.

It wasn't there by accident. Haverfield practiced rotational grazing, the moving of cattle between pastures every few days. The net effect was like clouds of bison blowing across the landscape, creating a perfect climate not only for a bumper crop of prairie dogs, but also large numbers of swift fox, pronghorn antelope, ferruginous hawks, burrowing owls, jack rabbits, and golden eagles that came for the fine dining and hand-dug accommodations. This grassland B and B was more than just a tantalizing specter; Haverfield had set the table for one more guest, a ghost absent more than fifty years. That's why he made the phone call. Ron Klataske was an alumnus of the black-footed ferret recovery project.

Not everybody was happy about Haverfield's animal house. Some neighbors complained when his wildlife spilled over onto their properties. They felt living next to Haverfield was like living next to a fraternity that spewed out grass-loving prairie dogs instead of beer-blasted junior pledges. Prairie dogs do love grass—pretty much their entire diet consists of grasses and flowering plants—but rangeland experts believe prairie dogs make up for what they use by aerating soils as they burrow and scurry around, acting as de facto grass farmers. Regardless of the science, Haverfield wasn't trying to export his vision of high plains ranching to his neighbors. To prove it, he invited varmint hunters to shoot prairie dogs on the peripheries of the complex in an attempt to create a prairie-dog-free buffer. He even gave away lead-free ammunition.

It wasn't enough. In 2005, citing a century-old Kansas law granting township boards the authority to poison prairie dogs on private property without the landowner's permission and send them the bill, the Logan County Commission declared war on Haverfield's prairie dogs and drew a line in the sandsage: Haverfield could either exterminate his prairie dogs or the county would do it for him.

But the lid was about to tighten. The US Fish and Wildlife Service was, by now, actively searching for somewhere to reintroduce the black-footed ferret in Kansas. On the first visit, Ron Klataske knew he was looking at the equivalent of a black-footed ferret Club Med. The site was more than plausible—not only was it the finest prairie dog town on the southern plains, but Haverfield, Barnhardt, and Blank, in their initial sparring with the Logan County Commission, also showed they would fight for the right to share their lands with wildlife. In conjunction with Audubon of Kansas, the ranchers asked the black-footed ferret recovery team to officially evaluate their property as a reintroduction site.

If you think that reintroducing a native predator designed with only one purpose in life—to eat prairie dogs—might, for obvious reasons, result in fewer prairie dogs being available to search out greener pastures on adjacent properties, don't expect anybody to elect you to the Logan County Commission. When they heard about Haverfield's new plan, the commission went ballistic. The Endangered Species Act is a term that packs a four-letter punch in parts of Kansas. Fearing the Feds might show up with endangered ferrets and cut off their options, the commissioners sent exterminators who applied the rodenticide Rozol to more than 320 acres of active prairie dog towns on Haverfield's ranch. It's illegal to apply Rozol when cattle are present—the exterminators knew this—so once Haverfield found out what was going on, he quickly moved cattle onto the 320-acre field. After some Monty Python back-and-forth, the exterminators realized that regardless of which field they picked, Haverfield's team would shut them down by moving in more cattle, so they gave up and stopped applying the Rozol.

That didn't deter the Logan County Commission. In September, exterminators returned with a different chemical called Phostoxin, a broad-spectrum poison that kills everything it touches. After piping the burrows full of poison gas, they used dirt to seal the tunnels so nothing could escape. No law prohibited Phostoxin use in the presence of cattle, so playing a game of musical cows wasn't an option. Haverfield's attorney finally drove from Wichita to Topeka to get a restraining order. Once again the prairie dogs were out on bail, but it was only a matter of time before the county commission would make another attempt to destroy the colony.

During a cease-fire in the prairie dog wars, Jay Bredwell and I joined trustees of Audubon of Kansas for a tour of Haverfield's ranch organized by Ron Klataske. Klataske—a wildlife scientist with degrees from K-State and the University of

Maine—was not a passive academic. He owned a working cattle ranch and was no weekend warrior. The day I met him he nursed a bad back from hauling block salt. Klataske seemed suspicious—in a kindhearted way—of the green crowd, maybe because the green crowd has trouble getting things done in a state like Kansas where most landowners are also suspicious—and not always in a kindhearted way—of the green crowd. Of complicated veneer, Klataske was a powerful advocate of the wild, equally comfortable bidding at a cattle auction or duking it out in legislative brouhahas over the rights of endangered species. He played a pivotal and very public role in the fight to establish Tallgrass Prairie National Preserve in the Flint Hills, the only national preserve dedicated to wild lands in Kansas, and one of the most controversial battles ever fought over public and private land in state history.

The front porch of Haverfield's modest ranch house proffered a choice view of Lone Butte, a slack mesa that loomed over the north fork of the Smoky Hill River. Dickcissels, western meadowlarks, and orchard orioles called from fields of buffalo grass and poppy mallow, and down below the garden-heavy vines of buffalo gourd crisscrossed cattle trails leading out toward the rangeland. The spring had been a rainy one and the winter before it brutal. Snow covered the ground for seventy days. A once-in-a-lifetime blizzard trapped Haverfield and Bette in their house for three days and killed thirty-seven cattle and an as yet undetermined number of prairie dogs. You couldn't tell by the chattering chorus all around, though. Prairie dogs whistled and trilled from every direction. When I raised my binoculars, what seemed like hundreds scurried about and lounged in all manner of repose.

Haverfield, wearing a blaze orange pullover, blue jeans, and facial weathering from fifty years of stiff Oglalah winds, held court from his driveway and explained how swift foxes won't den near active prairie dog holes. He loved swift foxes. Save for the pullover, he looked as much a part of the landscape as the yuccas and broomweed.

As we prepared to drive up toward Cedar Canyon on the far side of Lone Butte, somebody tossed three headless prairie dogs into the back of Haverfield's impossibly derelict pickup—gifts for the swift fox family. Jay and I were going to ride in the back of that pickup, but when seats came up short for two members of the Audubon board, Klataske looked at my Pontiac Aztek and said, "You're driving." I looked at the dead prairie dogs and said, "No problem."

Crossing a cattle gate and leaving the gravel driveway for open pasture, Haverfield's ox of a truck broke trail for our yoke of SUVs. Grass swept over my grille every time we dipped down into a seep. I gunned it once, after the other cars passed

Cedar Canyon, Logan County, Kansas.

by, to splash through a wet mire at the base of the mound. Jay thought he smelled brake fluid—for all we knew those other cars had never been off road—but a half-mile double track of crushed grass in the rearview confirmed it was the faintly medicinal wake of buffalo grass and curlycup gumweed.

Everybody piled out of the vehicles at the top of an expansive ridge with a long panorama of Haverfield's ranch and the tidy neighboring farms to the north with their neat rows of grain bins. But to the south, where the ranch broke out into a wild 27,000-acre emptiness given over to prairie dogs, a completely different landscape arose, where mile-square fractals of wheat and corn were chiseled away to reveal an unhewn block of the American past. The view across that flat vista embodied the fact that "horizon" is the root of horizontal.

A few of the Audubon board members walked slowly and methodically through the field, heads down, doing something I thought was a little peculiar, but now recognize as irresistible to certain botanists and plant nerds (and one of the reasons I love hanging out with these guys): calling out the names of every plant species they knew growing on the ridge.

"Prickly poppy!" (A poisonous white flower with a yellow center also called cowboy's fried egg.)

"Globe mallow!" (Or scarlet mallow, a plant that blooms in waves.)

"Goat's beard!" (A soft giant dandelion my daughter would have loved to grab.)

Under Haverfield's tutelage, Jay and I studied a yucca plant carefully. I knew yuccas—one grew outside my front door back in Lawrence—but I never considered their culinary possibilities (at least not *in situ*—I'd eaten fried yucca root in restaurants), so when Haverfield and Klataske started munching the blooms, I stuttered to follow, but finally looked at Jay and said, "Why not?" The taste of peas came to mind. One of the trustees chortled, "Make sure they're not feeding you loco weed, man."

Haverfield pointed into the crevasse of Cedar Canyon and told us, "This is about the roughest, deepest hole I know." At this crenulated scar in the sandstone, great rock slabs were scattered haphazardly like somebody pounded his fist on a giant chessboard, a scene almost southwestern in motif, except that the constant downpour of sunlight washed the reds from the stones, leaving a uniformly stippled burnt yellow.

Haverfield liked to drive up here and reflect on the canyon's history: "We have a book back in the house; I think Bette can find it. Once, the Southern Cheyenne left their reservation in Oklahoma and the cavalry chased them to their hideout right down there in those rocks. They kept running after that, and farther north near Nebraska there was a skirmish and some of the Indians were killed."

Klataske walked up to Haverfield and pointed behind him, motioning for us to be quiet. As if on cue, a female pronghorn antelope dashed across the pasture, its baby close behind, two out of the roughly two thousand pronghorns in Kansas. Jay quietly pointed to more movement down by the rocks—jackrabbits the size of house cats munching on buffalo grass. The ranch literally pulsed with life. After we piled back into the cars and drove through the canyon toward the next stop, three burrowing owls popped out from prairie dog holes and flew off into the glare. On the boundary of the ranch, Haverfield tossed one of the dead prairie dogs toward the den of his swift fox.

After a short drive, Klataske stopped the caravan in a valley of short grass and pointed toward a flat depressed trace, with less grass and fewer yuccas, about half the width of a football field and one foot deeper than the rest of the valley floor. He called it a buffalo road. The Smoky Hill valley was once an interstate highway for bison; literally millions passed through during seasonal migrations, so the presence of a buffalo road here made sense. Frontiersmen called the Smoky Hill the best buffalo habitat on the planet. Deer traces no wider than a yucca were etched like

Burrowing owl at
prairie dog town,
Logan County, Kansas.

yellow dashes on the centerline of the ghost highway. How it managed to survive I wasn't sure, but I wondered what other fragments of the buffalo roadmap still remained more than 150 years after their extirpation. In far western Kansas every old rancher has a buffalo story or knows a place where bleached bones still wash out from hillsides during spring torrents. The absence of the buffalo defines this place.

Sometimes things just work out. Beginning in 2006, the black-footed ferret recovery team got serious about the Haverfield site and began an official feasibility study. They sent interns to make maps of the creases and crenulations of the prairie dog towns, conduct a census, and search for signs of plague or canine distemper. They held public meetings in Logan County to review the "Draft Environmental Assessment and Application for Enhancement of Survival Plan" that began circulating even before it was finished. They reassured skeptical neighbors that any federal reintroduction would not affect their livestock operations. Though the recovery team planned to roll out the red carpet for the ferrets on Haverfield's ranch, they deemed the population "nonessential" for survival of the species. Ferrets that strayed from the preserve would be on their own, Endangered Species Act or no Endangered Species Act. Meanwhile, the US Fish and Wildlife Service went border patrol on the periphery of the ranch and created better buffers to keep prairie dogs from tunneling through to colonize less friendly environs outside Haverfield's digs. They held an official period of public comment, and when it closed, counted sixteen thousand letters supporting the reintroduction of the black-footed ferret in Kansas.

The week before Christmas, 2007, fish and wildlife officials showed up with a stack of fourteen cat carriers jerry-rigged with fat spans of drainage tubing to simulate prairie dog tunnels. The slightly nervous but otherwise healthy black-footed ferrets spent their last night in captivity eating prairie dog parts and ferret chow. Shortly before sunset on Tuesday, December 18, 2007, Larry Haverfield and Ron Klataske personally released the first black-footed ferrets back into the subterranean wilds of Kansas after an absence of more than fifty years. The first ferret scrambled out of her cat cage with little fanfare, diving face first into the nearest prairie dog tunnel. In an instant, one of the last wild places of Kansas suddenly became much wilder. In addition to Haverfield's ferrets, the recovery team released ten more individuals at the Nature Conservancy's Smoky Valley Ranch farther east in Logan County. As of 2015, the black-footed ferret is the only federally endangered species ever reintroduced in the state.

Western Kansas is still majestically empty. On clear winter nights there are so many stars the sky looks like a celestial lumberjack ran the moon through a wood chipper. But all of those stars, all of that endless sky cannot hide what's missing—the gray wolf, the grizzly bear, the buffalo.

Kansas is the land of private property. If we believe the rights of private landowners trump all others, then let's go all the way and recognize the rights of private ranchers like Haverfield, Barnhardt, and Blank to create a sanctuary on their property for a two-pound underdog marvelously maladapted to twenty-first-century life, an animal literally snatched from the jaws of extinction by a farm dog in Wyoming. These ranchers are a new kind of hero, representing the best components of the Kansas character: humility, perseverance, and a tenacious thunder to do what's right.

Long term, the odds are stacked against the Smoky Hill ferrets. Ferrets that explore beyond the "safe zone" of Haverfield's property will find no friends. Bubonic plague is a constant threat—all it would take is one infected prairie dog to make its way into the colony. Perhaps more troubling, small populations like the Haverfield ferrets could eventually suffer maladaptation due to a lack of genetic diversity.

But there is reason for hope. Following the reintroduction of the ferrets, the Logan County Commission continued to push for eradication of Haverfield's prairie dogs. Finally in 2013, the Kansas Supreme Court ruled in favor of the ranch. Haverfield died in 2014 knowing that prairie dogs, swift foxes, and black-footed ferrets were safe on his property and that his family would keep fighting any new obstacles to ensure that black-footed ferrets had a place in Kansas to continue their fight against extinction.

Puma concolor—whose common names include mountain lion, panther, cougar, puma, or my favorite, *deer tiger*—was first reported from Kansas by Zebulon Pike in his field notes from a trip across the Flint Hills, probably in modern Chase County: "Passed very ruff flint hills. My feet blistered and very sore. I stood on a hill, and in one view below me saw buffalo, elk, deer, cabrie [antelope], and panthers."

An Ellis County hunter shot the last native Kansas cougar near Hays in 1904. Today, its official status remains extirpated. But is it? The presence of cougars— the ivory-billed woodpecker of Kansas mammals—is a controversial and much debated topic in Kansas. Public reports of sightings come in from all over the state, some of them making the local evening news. Everybody, it seems, has a strange Kansas mountain lion story.

Here's mine.

In graduate school, I read an article in the *Lawrence Journal-World* about a man documenting the current distribution of mountain lions in Kansas. Read carefully. Not documenting *one* solitary male jaunting through the northwest corner of the state on its way between, say, Pike National Forest and the South Dakota Badlands. He wanted to make a *distribution map*.

I'd heard cougar stories for years. They involved black panthers (which don't exist in the wild in North America), cougars "grazing alfalfa on Stranger Creek," cougars sitting on hay bales in Lawrence, cougars swimming the Kaw, spotted cougars with short stubby tails not much bigger than a housecat. Bigfoot stories. Nevertheless, the guy seemed obsessed with finding plausible accounts. I wrote him and offered to help.

I met Edwin Smith at the house near Vinland that he shared with his ninety-two-year-old mother. Edwin stood about five-foot-one, wore thick glasses that he constantly wiped with a handkerchief, and didn't comb his hair much or bother to tuck his shirts in completely. He spoke deliberately in carefully measured phrases, like he was dictating notes to his archivist. He rarely made eye contact unless you said something really stupid. He said "Bingo!" a lot.

As far as I could tell, Edwin only cared about three things: cougars, tornado chasing, and his artwork, from which he derived most of his income. He painted obsessively detailed wildlife and Christian fantasy scenes on black velvet—saber-toothed tigers locked in mortal combat, dinosaurs and bison sitting together in orange fields, macabre scenes of the lamb bleeding rivers of blood. Outsider art.

In that first meeting, he showed me his notes. He had a form for everything and an entire room filled to the ceiling with cardboard filing boxes. He made duplicates of the most important forms and kept them in separate briefcases for safety. His stock "cougar sighting form" featured a freehand drawing of the outline of a cougar, complete with identifying field marks, like a butcher's poster displaying cuts of beef, but for cougars. He preprinted cougar pads for each of the most important forms.

Edwin offered me an apprenticeship. My training would entail several in-home interviews—I was to strictly observe at first, Edwin would do all the talking—after which, presumably, I would get my own stack of cougar pads and strike out alone to gather data. Tallying my way through the stacks I calculated that Edwin had interviewed about five hundred people.

The next week, I met him at a trailer home in rural Edgerton, Kansas. He reminded me in advance that to gain trust, we had to treat people's stories with respect, whether we believed them or not.

We sat down on a floral couch, and the eyewitness, a middle-aged woman who lived with her boyfriend, served us Diet Coke with ice in small espresso mugs. Edwin took each witness through the same spiel. He definitely showed respect for their stories—a little too much respect, I would soon discover.

Edwin read from his cougar pad, checking off multiple-choice answers with the thoroughness of a detective. Things got more intense during questions about the animal's tail.

"OK, let's move on to the tail. Did you get a good look at it?"

"If you had to choose, would you describe it as three feet, five feet, or six feet long?"

"Did the tail have a noticeable dip?"

He kept firing off questions, and she did her best to answer, but the details were sketchy. "Guys, I'm sorry but I really don't remember that much about the tail," she answered. "It was really dark, past dusk. We saw it walking between the hay bales by the creek. Jasper wanted me to call the county extension officer to see if we should keep the dogs in at night. I told him, 'I'm not calling the extension office to ask that question. We're keeping them in.'"

I finished my Diet Coke. There was silence in the room as Edwin flipped pages, so I asked, "Do you remember if the tail was white?"

Edwin glared at me.

She said, "Actually, now that you mention it, once it started running away, I did notice some white. Like a hand waving good-bye."

Edwin stopped her: "That's good. That's really good. But how long was it? Do you even know if it was longer than a foot?"

She said, "A foot? Oh definitely. I wouldn't have noticed the waving otherwise. It was definitely longer than one foot."

Edwin said, "Bingo!" He scratched more notes on his cougar pad.

I met up with Edwin later on the KU campus to go over the notes. He sensed disappointment and said, "Look, these people aren't wildlife biologists. Some of them aren't even hunters or people who know the woods. But they all had an experience. Maybe they saw a cougar, maybe they didn't. I'm not there to judge them. Sometimes they just want someone to believe they aren't crazy. What would you do if you thought you were standing a hundred feet away from a two-hundred-pound cougar? Memorize the length of its tail? No, it would freak you out. You wouldn't remember things in order. It takes a while for everything to come back. I created the interview to help straighten out the facts, line them up. Sometimes it takes a couple of interviews. For example, the lady called me later that night with more details that she forgot to tell us."

"What details?" I asked.

"That when it ran away, the animal jumped over three tall wire fences like they were railroad ties."

I didn't buy it. "Edwin," I said, "the lady saw a deer. You know that, right? Not a bobcat, not a house cat, not a cougar. A white-tailed deer."

"Maybe it was a deer, maybe it wasn't. We can't be sure that the white tail wasn't the underbelly of the cougar as it jumped the fence. She said it was dark."

"Underbelly? I'm sorry, but if I see a big animal jumping fences with a white, waving tail, by the creek at night? I'm not thinking white cougar underbelly, you know what I mean?"

Edwin said, "You don't get it, Jeff." He always called me Jeff. "I have five sightings from five different people within two miles of the field where she saw her cougar, or whatever it was. What we have here are multiple sightings of the same animal."

"OK," I said impatiently, "the same white-tailed deer?"

"Nooooo," Edwin said. "If you group the sightings in eastern Douglas County and near Edgerton, this one is probably a female, since she's always close to the creek. We have another cluster of sightings south of Baldwin. Same for Lone Star,

Globe, Warden, and Tauy Creek. I have clusters of sightings north too, up past the river."

I said, "So that means . . ."

"It means we are probably looking at ten cougars in Douglas County. At least," Edwin said, cutting me off, disappointed in what he thought was my small-minded thinking. Edwin believed passionately that mountain lions were roaming the woods and prairies of Kansas; all he had to do was prove it. He called in to local radio shows, talked to grade school classes, and patiently followed up on every report sent his way. He even interviewed people at nursing homes who thought they had seen cougars years ago.

Despite his intentions, I just couldn't go along with his methodology. On the question of cougars in Kansas, I was more than skeptical, I was a nonbeliever.

I was also wrong. Fast forward to the present, and I have to tip my cap to Edwin, who has since passed away. He was right. Bingo! Cougars have returned to Kansas.

Between 1999 and 2015, the extension wildlife specialist at Kansas State University fielded more than 230 reports of cougar sightings. Wild mountain lions have been documented in the four states that border Kansas. Males maintain huge ranges, up to two hundred square miles. It made sense that a few cougars would venture across the state line eventually. It just took longer to prove than Edwin expected.

In October 2003, a van struck and killed a male mountain lion on Interstate 35 in North Kansas City. Analysis of its stomach contents and the overall healthy condition of the animal suggested it was a wild cougar, not an escaped captive. While not technically in Kansas, it was close, less than ten miles away.

The following December, geographer Mark Jakubauskis set up a motion-triggered camera on KU's West Campus after a rash of cougar sightings in the area. He captured a tantalizing photo. Some thought it was a mountain lion, although when I saw the image, I couldn't tell. Jakubauskis also collected feces near the camera, and the DNA match was positive for *Puma concolor*. Repeated cougar sightings from the area followed near the university and on a nearby golf course.

A few months later, KU biologist Chip Taylor, one of the world's foremost experts on monarch butterflies, reported a high-quality sighting near the Wakarusa River bottoms in Douglas County, Kansas.

Then in June 2004, a train killed a young male cougar near Red Rock, Oklahoma, forty miles south of Arkansas City, Kansas. This mountain lion wore a radio collar. It wandered more than seven hundred miles from the Black Hills of South

Dakota in a nine-month period. Jonathon Jenks, the researcher who tracked the cougar, reported to the *Wichita Eagle* that "judging from where it was found, compared to where it came from, it would have had a difficult time not going through Kansas."

In June 2006, Ron Klataske saw a mountain lion in the Flint Hills. He returned and made plaster casts of tracks from a sandbar in a creek. The tracks showed the retracted claws of a wild cat. They were larger than the tracks of a bobcat but not as big as a fully mature mountain lion's. A month before Klataske's sighting, two guys riding on an ATV in the same vicinity took a compelling photograph of an animal trotting up a hill. I saw the photograph, posted on the website of Audubon Kansas, and it looked like a mountain lion to me (though Matt Peek, biologist for Kansas Wildlife and Parks, told me he wasn't so sure).

Finally, in 2007 when state game warden Tracy Galvin heard rumors that a local rancher had shot a mountain lion near Medicine Lodge, in the Red Hills, he made some phone calls and soon was in possession of the pelt of a wild cougar. The landowner, who acknowledged shooting the cat and sending the body to a taxidermist in Texas, cooperated with Galvin when he realized he had illegally shot a state protected species. The first mountain lion in Kansas since 1904 probably wandered through the state in the 1980s or 1990s, but this was the first definitive proof of a wild Kansas cougar in over one hundred years.

Cougars are back, but it's less clear whether we have a breeding population in the state. Ron Klataske and other wildlife experts believe Kansas cougars are mainly sub-adult males dispersing from the Black Hills. The vagrant lions are forced out by adults who won't tolerate other males in their territory. An estimated two hundred cougars live in the Black Hills, a veritable no-vacancy situation.

Because Kansas is a deer factory, it's only a matter of time before female mountain lions recognize the great shopping and move in to take advantage. At that point, the question will be whether we choose to tolerate a breeding population of the large predators. I think we might. Many people who think they've seen a mountain lion don't call in the press or the sheriff out of concern for the cougar. Attacks against humans, while not unknown, are extremely rare; there are only about one hundred documented attacks since 1900. In South Dakota there are zero.

Cougars sometimes prey on small livestock, but usually not cattle, which are formidable animals for a predator the size of a cougar. To support a viable population, agencies like the Kansas Department of Wildlife and Parks could fund a reimbursement for producers who lose stock. Hopefully we never return to the days of poisoning and shooting large predators. Against all odds, a few of these magnificent cats seem to be moving back into the state. I hope we decide to do all we can to help them.

If mountain lions can return, what about the remaining ghosts of the prairie? Given the complex emotions and issues surrounding the return of the black-footed ferret and mountain lion, is there any hope for animals like the bison, gray wolf, or even the grizzly bear?

Maybe.

In the late 1980s, a controversial book by New Jersey researchers Frank and Deborah Popper ruffled feathers in western states (and just about everywhere else). *The Buffalo Commons* posed a vision of a postagricultural era on the Great Plains. The Poppers believed depopulation of the region was accelerating because the plains had "the nation's hottest summers and coldest winters, greatest temperature swings, worst hail and locusts and range fires, fiercest droughts and blizzards, and therefore its shortest growing season."

Agriculture, under such conditions, was a failed experiment and, so the Poppers reasoned, depopulation would continue. Rather than relying on exotic schemes for regional revival like fleecing the plains with wind-generating farms or creating Internet-enabled commerce that could thrive off the grid, they had an idea that would create a small sustainable economy and at the same time right one of the great wrongs of American history: the extermination of the buffalo. They proposed creating a 135-million-square-mile Buffalo Commons in parts of ten states. The Poppers would deprivatize the plains. It would expand upon and complete the programs of the 1930s when the government bought dust bowl–ravaged farms and ranches to stabilize soils, creating the National Grasslands. The government would pay for land it had given away for free in the days of homesteading.

Not surprisingly, the idea did not play well in Kansas. It didn't help that the two professors were from New Jersey. Some people suggested the government should buy up land in New Jersey and replace it with a million-acre pig farm because the idea was hogwash. It also didn't help that one of the key components was deprivatization.

Twenty-five years later the idea hasn't disappeared. Mike Hayden, who was Kansas governor at the time of the Popper book's publishing and one-time director of Kansas Department of Wildlife and Parks, told the *Topeka Capitol-Journal,* "When the Poppers came out with the Buffalo Commons, I was one of those who was critical of it at the time. But the truth is, I was wrong. The Poppers ended up being somewhat conservative in their estimates of the outmigration from the Plains. The losses have actually exceeded most of the Poppers' projections."

Frank Popper has said that the Buffalo Commons is inevitable; it's only a matter of when and how it will happen. I think, though, like the return of the black-footed ferret and mountain lion, there is nothing inevitable about the return of the buffalo. To some, the Poppers' vision has been an admonition, an argument that if the Great Plains can support people, then people should stay in the Great Plains. I don't disagree. But if the exodus continues, my heart is with the buffalo. A Buffalo Commons would support not only bison and other ungulates like elk and mule deer, but would also create opportunities to complete the rewilding of the plains and open the door for the great predators—the gray wolf and maybe even someday a grizzly bear or two.

The last truly wild Kansas buffalo vanished generations before I was born, and the first truly wild Kansas buffalo will likely return generations after I'm gone. But our home on the range, the homeland of the buffalo, is a vision I've carried since I was a child, since I learned the meaning of tragedy in the story of the bison. Each time moonlight illuminates a pair of green eyes on a prairie dog mound near the north fork of the Smoky Hill, each time a mountain lion leaves its five-toed signature—claws retracted—in sands along the west side of the Missouri River, we move a step closer to the whole. Someday the hooves of bison might thunder once more above the bones of men who long ago lived in cities built over the bones of the original bison. When that happens, all of our ghosts can rest in peace.

CHAPTER FIVE

Ottering

Big Cypress Seminole Indian Reservation on the way to the Florida Everglades. She hadn't said a word since Fort Myers seventy miles back. Under a billboard advertising "Swamp Safaris," I noticed a shady trail that led from the highway back into a forest of big cypress and sweet gum. It followed a slow bayou. She saw it too and said, "Pull off."

We walked. My eyes never left the refuge of the bayou as she proceeded to give me a piece of her mind that mowed down stands of saw palmetto, eviscerated epiphytes dangling from live oaks, and bled a red line east across the arc of southern Florida. That's why I saw them: two river otters wrestling on a dead log in a pool of lily pads, the first otters I'd ever seen in the wild. At that moment I would have given anything to dive into the black bayou with them. Two months later she was gone, but my love for otters was only beginning.

The northern river otter (*Lontra canadensis*) is a silky streamlined member of the weasel family—Mustelidae—a group of mammals that includes skunks, badgers, mink, wolverines, pine martens, ferrets, weasels, and sea otters. Part mermaid, part border collie, these creatures seem to infuse everything they do with joy. In winter, otters sled down ramps of snow and ice, creating a signature that looks like Morse code: hop hop slide, hop hop slide. Aquatic acrobats, they come equipped with webbed feet, a nose with a water flap, and triple-layered eyelids that work like goggles in murky water. They swim circles around schools of fish, churning up a centrifuge that funnels victims into their whiskery larder. Otters can remain submerged for up to eight minutes. They love fish, but are crazy for crawdads. Growing up to four feet long and weighing as much as thirty pounds, otters are much larger than muskrats and mink, and leaner and more elegant than beavers. They fancy a bath after meals. When they run, people confuse them for dachshunds.

In pre-settlement times the range of the river otter included the entire lower forty-eight states save for the most arid pockets of the desert southwest. This likely included all of the riparian habitats of Kansas. The eighteenth-century hunter and naturalist James Richard Mead simply wrote that "otter were common" in Kansas.

The nineteenth-century fur trade led indirectly to the extirpation of the species in Kansas. Like black-footed ferrets, they co-depend heavily on another species, the beaver, for existence. Otters are hunters, not carpenters. They sometimes den up in rocky crevices, but since these are rare in the Midwest, Kansas otters prefer the company of beavers—in particular, their abandoned tenements. In the 1800s when the fur trade nearly wiped out the beaver, otter populations plummeted. Stream pollution might have played a supporting role in their demise. Otters and other keystone predators are prone to the multiplier effect, the concentration of contaminants in ever-increasing percentages as species ascend the food chain. Whatever the cause, by the time pioneers arrived in the 1860s otters were already rare. The last wild northern river otter in Kansas was trapped near Manhattan in 1904.

They were absent for eighty years. Then, in an effort to reestablish the species in 1983, biologist Lloyd Fox and his team at the Kansas Fish and Wildlife Department (now Kansas Department of Wildlife and Parks) released twenty otters into the South Fork of the Cottonwood River. The South Fork runs through pristine prairie uplands in Chase County, the heart of the Kansas Flint Hills. It boasts a flourishing aquiculture rich with native mussels, spotted bass, channel catfish, and crayfish. The river seemed like prime otter habitat.

Not everyone, however, was happy to learn that otters were returning to Kansas. Otters are expert fish killers. In headwater streams and small ponds they can and do wreak havoc on fish populations. But the twenty new Kansas otters quietly dispersed along the Cottonwood River, some showing up later on the Neosho and at John Redmond Reservoir. By 1990 there had been few public complaints, most likely because there were few river otters. Wildlife and Parks limited the reintroduction to that single group, with no follow-up releases. One spring I spent three days searching for otters and camping along the South Fork of the Cottonwood and didn't find a trace. A 2001 fur trapper survey yielded no sightings. The future for river otters in Kansas didn't look promising.

In Missouri, a completely different story was unfolding. Like in Kansas, the fur trade decimated river otters in Missouri almost to the point of extirpation, although a relict population managed to hang on in the boot heel counties along the Mississippi. In the mid-1980s, about the same time Lloyd Fox released his twenty otters in the Flint Hills, the Missouri Department of Conservation began to reintroduce river otters—but with a vengeance. Instead of just a single river, streams throughout the state received otters and in many cases multiple stockings. Missouri has better otter habitat than Kansas, with dozens of rivers; more than three hundred thousand farm ponds stocked with bluegill, catfish, and bass; and the spring-fed streams of the Ozark plateau in southern Missouri. The success of the reintroduction exceeded everybody's expectations, and soon Missouri was swarming with otters, between sixteen and thirty thousand by the turn of the twenty-first century. These Missouri otters, bearing no Border War prejudice, began crossing the state line, dispersing west in search of new habitat. With little fanfare, the otter population of Kansas began to grow.

I was excited to hear otters had repatriated the Kaw. Ever since graduate school I had dreamed that someday I would see a wild river otter in Kansas, but just because otters were back, there was no guarantee that finding one of the secretive, mainly nocturnal mammals would be easy. My random sighting in the Everglades fifteen years back was somewhat of an anomaly; most people living in otter country never see one in the wild, full-time wildlife managers included. Marais des Cygnes National Wildlife Refuge probably has the highest density of otters in the state. Refuge manager Ryan Frohling told me that in all his years on the job he had never once seen an otter, although he sees otter sign on a daily basis.

River otters were the new wildlife success story, and almost nobody in Kansas knew it. Matt Peek, river otter expert and biologist for the Kansas Department of Wildlife and Parks, told me that by the early 2000s otter sightings in southeast Kansas began to increase. Reports came in from the Neosho Wildlife Area, Melvern Reservoir, Flint Hills National Wildlife Refuge, and most of the streams of southeast Kansas. In the summer of 2007 a park ranger at Perry Lake watched a river otter in the stilling basin below the dam. The presence of otters at Perry Lake, in the northeast part of the state, meant otters were in the Kansas River, and from there they could disperse virtually statewide. They had also repopulated the Marais des Cygnes, particularly the wildlife refuges near the Missouri border. By 2010, the northern river otter, though still rare, was definitely back, and it looked like it was back for good.

Learning to identify otter sign is the first step in locating where otters live. The best time to look is immediately after a snowfall. The Morse code trail left on frozen creeks is unmistakable evidence. Otters will always slide rather than run on slippery surfaces. After hopping for a few steps to gather steam they slide as far as twenty feet on their bellies. But year-round the best way to find otters is to look for their latrines. Unlike beavers, otters use fixed sites to do their business, often on logs near the junction of streams or at the highest point along a beaver trail between bends of a creek. In cold months, when crawfish hibernate, otter scat is composed almost exclusively of fish scales. Mink, which also use latrines, are muskrat specialists. They will eat fish, but prefer surf and turf; their scat almost always includes fur. Raccoons are expert fishers but their omnivorous habits guarantee that their scat includes seeds or corn. Since beavers eat the inner bark of trees, their scat looks like sawdust. Like it or not, I found that scouting for otters meant scouting for scat—mealy piles of green, fishy mustelid scat. When my wife figured out my new mission to find a Kansas river otter meant walking around looking for poop, she penned a little rap:

> Lookin' for an otter latrine
> On the Marais des Cygnes.

(If you ever need to teach somebody how to pronounce "Marais des Cygnes"—just remember it rhymes with "otter latrine.") Fortunately, my search for otter scat was about to get a lot more interesting. I stumbled across an article on a birding website about a biology graduate student at Pittsburg State University who live-trapped eight river otters on Bone Creek and Dry Creek in the Marmaton River valley. Marcus Jones was living the life of a French coureur de bois, at least the part that involved obsessively pursuing fur-bearing mammals through the woods and prairies of southeastern Kansas. Instead of pelts, Jones was hunting data that would illuminate the behavior of river otters in Kansas: where and how they selected den sites; what they ate; how far they ranged each night, each week, each season; and how many were victims of illegal trapping. After I talked to Jones on one of his breaks from the field, he invited Jay Bredwell and me to come down and "walk some creeks" with him. He didn't guarantee we'd see an otter ("That's a rare treat, even for me," he noted.), but we'd definitely see scat, scent markings, latrines, and tracks. Remembering my fruitless expedition to the South Fork of the Cottonwood, I couldn't wait to get out in the field with an expert who actually knew what he was looking for.

I met Jay at our rendezvous point outside Tanner's Bar in Overland Park at 5:00 a.m. sharp on President's Day. Four inches of fresh snow and beer bottles had fallen in the parking lot the night before. The digital display on the bank read fifteen degrees. In the gathering light before sunrise we drove past the frozen wetlands of Marais des Cygnes National Wildlife Area, the long yellow prairie where six hundred Confederate troops were killed at the battle of Mine Creek. We also passed the parking lot in front of Big Bear Liquors in Pleasington, located exactly halfway between Kansas City and Pittsburg, where, Jay told me, divorced parents wait for their exes to arrive on Wednesday nights for the biweekly child swap.

As we pulled into the dusty parking lot at Crawford State Lake southwest of Fort Scott, we flushed a pileated woodpecker from a red cedar. Hopefully it was a good sign. The lake is a throwback. Built during the Depression by the Civilian Conservation Corps, the dam features a road and a stone retaining wall with art deco pillars. Crawford isn't a gearhead lake; you won't see big bass boats that cost more than a bungalow. Little cottages with purple martin condos and clotheslines bunch together on the south shoreline. A strange cracker box silo house full of paper wasp nests stands at the head of Spider-Leg Trail. With playground equipment and swimming beaches, fishing docks and Coke machines, the lake seems like a summer camp waiting to happen.

Both the Dry Creek and Bone Creek drainages of Crawford County are speckled with strip pits, labyrinths of old bituminous coal mines filled with water that tends to the lime side of green. These pits provide habitat for water fowl, fish, and aquatic mammals—including otters. Farmington State Fish Hatchery, a dozen gravel-lined rectangular pits that gestate a third of the fish released annually into state lakes, lies below the Crawford County Lake dam. I'd learned from talking with Matt Peek that the fish ponds are an all-you-can-eat buffet for river otters. As Marcus Jones drove up in his state-issued purple Dodge Dakota, I said to Jay, "Assume everything that moves is an otter." I didn't want to miss anything.

For the past two years Marcus Jones had lived and breathed northern river otters. As a summer intern at Mined Lands Wildlife Area outside Columbus, Kansas, Marcus was angling for a master's thesis topic when he started hearing chatter from local fishermen about otters poaching their big fish. With the otter resurgence so fresh, formal research on their specific habits in Kansas was virtually nonexistent. Marcus started piecing together a research plan. He bought the equipment he'd need piece by piece as he could afford it. The heart of the research hinged on eight small radio transmitters that looked like yellow vibrators sealed in wax. When implanted in live Kansas otters, these beacons would allow Jones to follow the animals on their wide sojourns across the Marmaton River valley.

We drove behind Marcus to the first stop on his otter run: a Farmington fish pond one hundred feet from a beaver hole along Dry Creek that Marcus knew was inhabited by an otter. He hopped out of the truck and started assembling his listening gear. Frequency determines what size antenna you need to receive signals from radio-tagged mammals. Marcus's otter radios broadcast at 150 MHz. This calls for a handheld Yagi antenna—a horizontal bar of aluminum three feet across with three vertical bars attached in a single plane—like a housetop TV antenna from the 1970s. Marcus told us his vendor promised a two-mile effective listening radius, but the claim was bogus; to pick up a signal he had to get within *one hundred feet* of an otter.

Sometimes otters move a mile in a single night. When that happened Jones had to spend days walking creeks to pick up the trail again. Sometimes all eight of his otters moved the same day. Snapping the earplug into the Yagi, he said, "My life for the last year and a half would have been a lot easier if they'd worked like they were supposed to."

Marcus, who had no previous trapping experience, used Number 11 leg-hold traps to capture the otters. It didn't take long—about two weeks. Besides eight mature river otters, he caught two coyotes, two raccoons, and two beavers. One of the beavers, as he was freeing it, bit a chunk out of his rubber boot next to his big toe. He wiggled his toe through the gash to prove it. Each time Marcus bagged a new otter he transported it to a Pittsburg veterinarian's office in a specially designed three-gallon plastic drum fashioned after a sketch he found in the *Journal of Mammalogy*. He had to dance up and down waving his arms to scare the otters into the barrel. The vet not only performed the surgeries to implant the radios for free, Marcus said, but "put up with me slopping nasty wet otters through his office; he'd even meet me on Saturday nights." The entire procedure was both effective and safe; they didn't injure a single otter during the captures. Officials at the Kansas Department of Wildlife and Parks were so impressed with Marcus's pluck they hired him to collect river otter data for the department.

We hiked out onto a well-worn single-track trail that led from the fish pond, up over the levee, and down into the ravine of Dry Creek. Marcus raised and lowered the Yagi, slowly pivoting a quarter step and then repeating, like he was blessing the fish pond. As he listened in his earphone for the faint ping—like a submarine's sonar radar—I asked if we would see any otter latrines near the den. He looked down at my boots and said, "You're standing in one."

Below my feet, piles of pale green gruel littered the levee, like oatmeal made from fish scales. I was standing in, or rather on, an otter's bathroom. A squeamish sense of victory swept over me. At last, fresh otter scat. I hoped it would lead to an actual otter sighting.

We bushwhacked through buck brush and rose briars down to the banks of Dry Creek to check two Moultrie digital field cameras Marcus had tied with bungee cords to the trunks of sycamore trees to monitor otter crossings at night when the animals are most active. The flash memory was empty—no pictures from the night before—but back at the truck Marcus grabbed his laptop and pulled up some spooky night shots of wide-eyed coyotes and huge surly beavers, their eyes blown up like moons from the unnatural light of the flash. There were other pics of muskrats, mink, raccoons, and rabbits. Best of all, though, were the photos of his river otters. In one shot, he captured four otters on a midnight raid of the fish farm. There were dozens of rare daytime shots of his favorite otter frolicking in the snow during a two-day cold snap. The otter, Marcus said, was clearly intelligent and playful, curious about Marcus and his camera. He'd take a few steps toward Marcus and bark, then make trilling sounds like a purring cat, and then go back to frolicking in the snow.

His research had already produced one interesting data point about the diet of otters. In Kansas, at least, otters prefer lobster but will settle for *poisson* if they must. Their diets consist completely of fish in the winter, but as temperatures warm they switch over to a diet of pure crayfish.

He told us, "Crayfish are shredders. There's more organic material in these little creeks than in the main lake—leaves falling into the creek mainly—so the otters follow them up here." Marcus walked us along a series of beaver dams on Dry Creek. We checked a bank lodge on the edge of the lake. After that we drove to a series of connected strip pits—canals formed in the ruins of old bituminous coal mines—near Garland. There we climbed down a steep bank—slippery with frozen springs—to get a look at an otter den in the deep indention of a sycamore root wad. Marcus picked up the radio signal; an otter was in the den.

I said, "So now you reach up in there and grab him, right?"

"Noodling?" Marcus asked. "Haven't tried it."

Scat marked the front of the den, some of it fresh. Marcus explained that since otters are mustelids, they produce an anal gland secretion for scent marking.

"It's a unique smell," he said. "When I'm walking creeks I can smell where the otters are before I see the dens."

He picked up a wad of scat, ungloved, and shoved it toward my face, saying, "Smell it."

With Marcus standing there so fresh-faced and earnest, I couldn't say no. Besides, if scat smelling turned out to be a litmus test for prospective otterists, I wanted to pass.

"Ahem," I said after taking a small but believable whiff. "Smells like a fishy pawpaw."

"Pawpaw? That's a new one," he said. "You've got to be careful when making identifications solely based on scat. Other animals eat fish—raccoons for example. When there's any doubt it's better to get a second sense, like smell, involved. I don't recommend tasting."

I asked Marcus what other cool things he's seen while chasing otters. "Bobcats, for one. I've seen six of them this winter. I found an eagle nest that the district biologist didn't know about. That's kind of still a big deal down here. Tundra swans."

Then he paused and added, "Otters are cool in themselves."

Indeed.

We made a few more stops, but unfortunately didn't see an actual otter. Nonetheless, I was happy enough that Marcus took us to mustelid school. Now with field skills, we could look for otters on our own.

Before we drove home, Marcus wanted to make it clear that Wildlife and Parks wasn't interested in his research solely to arm, with numbers, any future (and almost inevitable) decision to reinstitute a trapping season on otters. He told us, "Kansas will have a trapping season, and maybe soon. But if you ask me, we have otters on the Neosho, down near the border on the Verdigris; they're at John Redmond and Marais des Cygnes, now they're on the Kansas and from there they can spread out across the state. We've got the seeds in place. I think we should give them ten more years so those seeds can take hold and grow."

Marcus knew that, although things looked good now, there was no guarantee river otter populations would continue to grow. A few months back, he lost track of his favorite otter—the one he jousted with in the snow. The signal went dead. He walked miles of creeks with no pings from the Yagi. Eventually he found its skinned carcass dumped along the creek, the victim of an illegal poacher.

After Marcus said goodbye to us and hopped back into his truck for the drive back to Pittsburg, he jumped back out to show us a note somebody had left on his seat when we were down by the otter den. It read, "Call me, I'm interested in your otter research," and beside it was a name and phone number.

Jay mentioned later that the guy who left the note could easily have grabbed Marcus's camera equipment or laptop from the truck since the windows were open. Hopefully it was a good sign, not just that southeast Kansans are friendly and hospitable, but that some people in the state want to see river otters survive.

Marcus's hard work had paid off. In his brief career as a salaried field biologist, he was starting to make a name for himself as the Kansas otter guy.

Back home in Lawrence, otter fever hit hard. I figured my best chance would either be at Perry Lake thirteen miles away in Jefferson County or Marais des Cygnes National Wildlife Refuge sixty miles south of Lawrence. I was curious, however, about two forms submitted by Douglas County fur trappers that Matt Peek told me about. In response to a voluntary survey, two licensed Douglas County trappers reported finding otter sign in the last year. These were not confirmed sightings; they didn't hand over a carcass to wildlife officials and no otter was trapped incidentally. There was no photograph. But I considered it potential. Nobody had documented a river otter in Douglas County since the 1800s, but because of the Perry Lake data, I knew they were in the Kansas River, which crosses the northern part of the county. I reasoned that my daughter Chloe and I might have a real chance to document the presence of river otters in the county if indeed they were here. This would be more exciting than, say, finding the first occurrence of a woodland bird expanding its range westward because trees had encroached on what once was prairie. It would be proof that a part of Kansas's wild past had returned. Heavy with a sense of history, I started wondering where to look.

A riparian woodland and sloughgrass wetlands once covered the extensive bottomlands that straddle the Wakarusa River south of Lawrence. Geomorphologists call rivers like the Wakarusa "misfit" streams. During the Pleistocene, a catastrophic flood scoured the Wakarusa's floodplain after a massive ice dam on the Kaw River collapsed. Before the flood, the ice dam had diverted water from the Kaw into the Wakarusa, creating an enormous flood plain. Today the small stream enjoys a wide berth—an empty nester in a valley much too big for itself.

After the completion of Clinton Lake in the early 1980s, the natural patterns of spring flooding in the Wakarusa changed. Today, a once expansive complex of wetlands has been reduced to a single square mile on the south side of Lawrence, a jewel called the Haskell-Baker Wetlands. Bounded by the Wakarusa River on the south, a channelized stream—Mink Creek—connects the river to the numerous pools and sluices of the wetlands. These pools teem with Canada geese, marsh wrens, red-winged blackbirds, cormorants, great blue herons, and dozens of other bird species. On cold, rainy spring nights, hundreds of small-mouth salamanders cross the roads that surround the wetlands. Some years volunteers stand guard, directing traffic around wads of amphibians, saving salamanders by the bucketful, at least until the next time they try to cross the road. Monarch butterfly congregations in the thousands have been reported in trees along the Wakarusa during peak migration in the fall.

The wetlands are significantly wilder than in the early twentieth century when it was drained to create farmland for Haskell Institute (now Haskell Indian Nations University). At the time, Haskell was a government boarding school where Native American children were sent to be "civilized." This meant, among other things, learning how to farm, so for a time the wetlands were under cultivation. When the days of Haskell farming ended, the waters of the Wakarusa gradually began to reclaim the property. After the land was deeded to Baker University in nearby Baldwin, the new curators built canals to stabilize water levels, helping to transform the preserve into today's thriving wetland complex. According to the studies conducted by Baker University students and staff, thirty-five species of amphibians and reptiles, thirteen species of fish, 333 species of plants, and twenty-two species of mammals are known from the wetlands. When we started our search, northern river otter was not among them.

The next Saturday morning I decked Chloe out in her winter gear so she and I could take on the frozen wetlands. February was almost over, but winter still held a firm grip on eastern Kansas, as it had for the past hundred days. The current of the Wakarusa kept it from freezing, but Mink Creek and most of the pools at Haskell-Baker Wetlands were solid enough to skate on. We hiked the half-mile to Mink Creek and began combing the banks, checking each beaver trail for scat, just like Marcus had taught us.

It didn't take long. We saw it on a high saddle between the creek and a frozen pool, on a trail littered with cattails and partially chewed twigs. Scat. The telltale sign Marcus taught us to look for. Light green, consistency of gruel, 100 percent fish scales. No way was it *this* easy, I thought. Had we really found sign of a Douglas County otter, or just pyrite—fool's scat? I took some photos of the droppings along with some tracks we found in the snow and emailed them to Marcus. Although the tracks, he said, were probably canid, he thought the scat looked good; the consistency and prominence of fish scales was promising. He told me to make sure there was no fur (mink) or seeds (raccoon) mixed in with the scales. I thought about taking a sample and mailing it to him, but wasn't sure if even Marcus would be cool receiving a UPS parcel filled with mustelid scat.

Back at the wetlands over lunch the next day, I noticed an intermittent trail on Mink Creek. It looked like someone had shoveled snow for about twenty feet, walked a few steps, and started shoveling again. Using my binoculars I could see this trail started at the end of Mink Creek by the Wakarusa and continued for a mile through the heart of the wetlands. The tracks had frozen and thawed too many times for identification. Otters have five webbed toes. The fifth toe is sometimes difficult to see in the track. The webbing and fur are sometimes visible in tracks left in mud. The toe has a classic candle flame shape. You usually find otter tracks in bunches; like other members of the weasel family they bound down the trail, leaving several footprints in proximity. I snapped some good pictures of the Morse code signatures and went home to ponder the evidence.

That evening I emailed Roger Boyd, senior professor of biology and director of natural areas at Baker University, and manager of the wetlands. He told me that as far as he knew there were no records of the northern river otter anywhere in Douglas County and that I had probably found signs of a mink. I agreed, in theory. I had watched mink play in the wetland sloughs a number of times. Both species are mustelids, but river otters are dog-sized, much larger than mink. But mink are more common in wetlands than otters, even where both species thrive. Otters prefer to ply the open waters of rivers and lakes in search of fish, their winter fare. Mink eat muskrat to the exclusion of almost everything else; otters only eat muskrat in a pinch. Boyd told me the muskrat population at the wetlands was in an upswing.

However, he was very supportive of my search and told me to let him know if I still thought I'd seen otter sign. I uploaded the evidence from my camera and emailed him a link to the pictures. Late that night he emailed back, "Well, you may be onto something!" He said he couldn't tell much from the scat, but the tracks appeared to be much too big for mink and with the dragging line in the middle it looked quite convincing. He said that if we had one otter, there were probably others and to keep him posted if we found more tracks.

I was determined now to get convincing evidence that the northern river otter had returned to Douglas County after more than a century. One option was a field camera like the ones Marcus used. Before that, however, I wanted more definitive evidence such as a track. It still seemed possible the animal leaving the Morse code messages was a mink. As if on cue, the following day it began to snow just before sunset—big wet sticky flakes that would make the wetland a blank journal ready to record the night's activity. Chloe and I got to the wetlands the next morning before dawn; we wanted to get there first, before walkers with their dogs obscured any potential evidence. A half-inch of snow covered the trail. We entered the wetlands at the north entrance one hundred feet or so from a busy road. A single beaver trail,

Otter tracks along Mink Creek in the Baker Wetlands, Douglas County, Kansas.

strewn with cattails and flakes of young cottonwood, crossed the walking path. A half-eaten sucker fish sat on top of ice that was covered in blood. Tracks were everywhere. Chloe and I cased the scene like a mustelid CSI unit.

Fresh scat covered the ground and new slides at multiple locations led from the trail down onto the ice. At the base of one of the slides that ended in a cattail pond, I placed Chloe's ruler up against a five-toed track in the snow: it measured three inches long, more than two inches larger than a mink print. The tail print was clearly visible in the slide. I took pictures of more tracks as we followed the fresh Morse code trail all the way to the Wakarusa. Back home I was able to crank down the contrast on the photos and build an outline of the imprints. Not only were these tracks much larger than a mink's, but the toes also had the candle flame shape. Chloe and I were past the point of no return now. We had to either see this river otter or capture a photograph.

That night I ordered a field camera on eBay and emailed the latest evidence to Marcus and Dr. Boyd, who replied, "There is little question in my mind that this is an otter, especially from the size of the tracks." He also gave me permission to put up the camera. Marcus told me the slides were "100% otter, in Canada they use helicopters to look for this kind of pattern when doing population surveys."

Now all we had to do was get the money shot. I wasn't at all confident we would be successful. The camera wouldn't arrive for a week. Meanwhile, a warm front was heading our way. Spring can land overnight in Kansas, and the first day of March was almost upon us. What if otters only ventured into the wetlands on carpets of ice?

The next week, at a Jayhawk Audubon Society presentation on the status of the ivory-billed woodpecker in northeastern Arkansas, I looked around at the birders in the auditorium and realized nobody "mammal-watched," at least not in the same way people bird-watched. I told Jay I'd spent the last week birding for otters and that Christina was confiding to friends that all I wanted to talk about was scat. He said, "Pretty soon people will just call it ottering."

While I waited for the field camera to arrive, I kept making trips to the wetlands. Every day it got warmer and I didn't see any new sign of scat or tracks. Finally, on a balmy afternoon, the UPS guy brought my camera. The only ice that remained was in the deep shade of the northern part of the wetlands. At sundown, Chloe and I strapped the camera to a black walnut tree near Mink Creek and aimed the laser pointer at the otter slide where I had taken the best pictures of tracks. Chloe crawled across the trail like an otter so I could train the infrared temperature sensor. When she crossed its field of view, the camera took three shots spaced one second apart.

That night I could hardly sleep. Every time my cat rolled over at the foot of the bed I dreamed an otter rustled under the covers. I finally got up and left for the wetlands with the first hint of light on the eastern horizon. I found no new otter sign, but the camera had recorded seven "events." I popped out the memory card and raced home to see what we had.

Two events were pictures of Chloe bellying across the trail the night before. The last picture was a close crop of my nose as I took the camera down. In between I had good shots of a mink chewing its hind leg, a beaver marching morosely ahead on the trail, the hind-end of a raccoon, and a rabbit. But no otter. Every day for the next week we followed the same routine. Chloe and I placed the camera near the latrine site at dusk and I hightailed it back to look for evidence the next morning. We got photographs of stately beavers crossing between waters with shiny coats and stern demeanor. Mink were more common than I expected; we shot half a dozen. I worried that, like the purported 2005 rediscovery of the ivory-billed woodpecker in Arkansas, *my* ivory-billed—the northern river otter—would turn out to be the much more common American mink, in this case a mammalian equivalent of the pileated woodpecker, which is often confused for the ivory-billed. I was no tracker or trapper. I hadn't even trapped a mole in my backyard. Even though they looked rock hard to me, maybe the three-inch tracks I had photographed had melted out before I got to them, blowing up ordinary mink tracks into otter proportions. Mink are the common aquatic predator of the wetlands. My photographs proved that whatever made the tracks visited a latrine, but mink are also latrine builders. Maybe this was a mink latrine.

I worried about the veracity of my sighting at least in part because of a generations-old controversy about the construction of a road south of Lawrence. In the 1980s, the Kansas Department of Transportation unveiled plans for a new highway, originally called the South Lawrence Trafficway, designed to relieve traffic congestion in rapidly growing south Lawrence. Because the proposed road would run through the Haskell-Baker Wetlands, it became a polarizing issue. There was little room for compromise between people who wanted to reduce traffic congestion and people who wanted to preserve the last large piece of wetlands in the Wakarusa bottoms. The original environmental impact statement concluded the road could be built with minimal impact to the wetlands, but environmentalists didn't believe it. In 1985 trafficway opponents cast nearly 30 percent of the vote for county commissioner to Agnes T. Frog, a fictitious write-in candidate created to draw attention to the locally threatened northern crawfish frog (which is probably extirpated in the wetlands today). Talk of the trafficway made normally congenial Lawrencians, united among other things by Jayhawk Nation, act like Border War Jayhawkers turned loose in a room of Missourians.

After a quarter century of lawsuits, the future of the trafficway was still in limbo. Many wetlands supporters wanted the road built south of the Wakarusa River, missing the wetlands altogether. KDOT was pushing for an alignment between Haskell Indian Nations University and the northern edge of the wetlands. This would result in the destruction of about one hundred acres of the preserve, including one of the otter latrines I'd found.

Northern river otters were a protected species in Kansas at the time of my search, but not a federally threatened or endangered species, so their habitat, the wild places where they lived, were not protected. Nevertheless, the discovery of otters in the wetlands—the return of a species missing in Douglas County since the 1800s—would possibly help galvanize public opinion in favor of preserving the northern section of the wetlands. Chloe and I wanted to find an otter, but if we could help save this beautiful wetlands preserve while we were at it, so much the better.

The morning after Leap Day, February 29, 2008. A skim of ice covered the trail as I marched out to get the camera. Even before sunrise a strong south wind brought spring north from Texas in indiscriminate gusts. The sound of red-winged blackbirds calling from their cattail perches was like pagers buzzing on a Wall Street trading floor in the eighties. I found no new otter sign at the crossover point, but the camera logged seventeen events, most likely of a single industrious muskrat making trips to get mud for a new den along Mink Creek.

I took the camera home and hooked it up to the computer for a quick peek at the night's activity. The first couple of shots were false events caused by sunset and the temperature differential it briefly creates, which confused the camera. The industrious muskrat was there, making its yeoman trip in search of mud.

Then I opened the computer file that contained shot number three. The time stamp read 9:43 p.m. A long, sleek mammal headed toward Mink Creek, fresh off a steep climb up the creek bank just a few hundred feet from the Wakarusa River. The first picture clearly showed the wet pointy otter tail, the webbed feet, the long neck. There were two more pictures, taken just before 11:30 p.m., the same otter headed back from the wetlands toward the river. The last picture was the best, a clear shot of the face, mouth open, reaching back to groom, a face nobody had photographed in Douglas County in over a century—probably ever—captured on a day that only comes once every four years. Chloe and I stared at the image together for a moment and finally I shouted, "We've got it!"

I was ecstatic. These pictures were the culmination of fifteen years spent dreaming that Kansas waterways would once again host the agile gymnastics of river otters. Just a month before I'd never seen otter sign *anywhere*, and now we'd found one in our own backyard. I emailed the pictures to Roger Boyd. Our shots proved that the trappers' reports from Douglas County were right. Otters were back, and probably had been for several years. As Marcus told us, the seeds for a full otter recovery were firmly planted and beginning to germinate, and our grainy four-megabyte image proved it. We had to drive to Kansas City later that morning, and during the ride Chloe studied the photograph in the back seat. As we crossed the Wakarusa on K-10 she said, "We just crossed the Wakarusa River, home of the river otter."

The river otters of Kansas are still rare, a well-kept secret in our rivers and wetlands, but signs indicate they will rapidly fill every available niche in the eastern part of the state. The return of the otter is a wildlife success story. It proves that work to clean up the nation's waterways is paying off. It shows how the resurgence of a species like the beaver can have a rippling effect; without a large beaver population the return of river otters would have been impossible. It also shows that preserving wild places like the Haskell-Baker Wetlands is paramount if we want to share our lives with wildlife.

Matt Peek hopes that Kansans and otters can coexist, that we won't have the same "otter problem" that exists in Missouri where some consider them a nuisance because of their supposed impact on commercial fish farms and Ozark bass fishing. Peek said, "The problems in the Ozark headwater streams are completely different than what we have here with our farm country streams. If they get into a commercial fishery they can do some damage, but there are ways to mitigate it. We have them in our hatchery at Farmington and have even relocated a few. But it's a manageable problem."

I hope so. Otters belong in the streams of Kansas, their rightful homes. Those waters are *wilder* for having otters, and we, in turn, are privileged to live in a time when a species like the river otter can be restored. I think Kansans will embrace the return of the river otter. The *Lawrence Journal-World* covered news of our otter rediscovery on the front page. The story received an unusually high number of comments on the paper's website. The Saturday after the story ran a man I didn't know called me around 10:00 p.m. to say he and his family were driving by the Haskell-Baker Wetlands and noticed an unusual road kill. They had followed the news of the otter rediscovery. He pulled off the road to examine the animal. It was the otter. Out of respect, he moved the body to the shoulder of the road on the banks of Mink Creek where it, no doubt, had climbed out of the water to cross the highway. Over the cell phone I could hear his children in the back seat, crying about the death of the Haskell-Baker Wetlands river otter.

I drove to the wetlands around midnight. When I pulled off by the slough I saw the remains of the unlucky little guy—a mink—carefully arranged next to the north canal. I stood there with him for a few minutes before I got back in the car to drive home. The night air was steeped in a faint sweetness, more stirrings of spring. Overhead, waves of snow geese flowed north like silent V-shaped army divisions. Somewhere out in the pitch expanse of the wetlands the otter prepped for another night hunting in the murky waters of Kansas.

Postscript 1

In the years since we grabbed our night shot of the Haskell-Baker Wetlands otter, all evidence continues to indicate accelerated growth of northern river otter populations across the state. Otters *are* back! Kansas Wildlife and Parks opened a carefully monitored, limited season on otter trapping several years ago. Trappers are limited to two otters per season against a maximum statewide limit (in 2013 it was 100), and trappers must send the lower canine teeth to the Kansas Department of Wildlife and Parks upon capture.

Postscript 2

The eastern leg of Kansas Highway 10—formerly called the South Lawrence Trafficway—is slated to open sometime in 2016. Opponents of an alignment south of the Wakarusa River failed to block construction of the road through the portion of the wetlands where we tracked our otter. In exchange for land lost to the new road, Baker University has built extensive new wetlands southwest of K-10, greatly expanding the overall size of the preserve. Wetland managers have reported river otter sightings in the newly created flood pools.

At least three otters—probably many more—have been killed by cars on K-10 southwest of Lawrence.

CHAPTER SIX

The Renegade Streams
of Eastern Kansas

Decriminalize canoeing in Kansas.
Bumper sticker

The Ninnescah, Mill Creek, the Marais des Cygnes, the Chikaskia, the Black Vermillion, Shoal Creek, Fall River, Grouse Creek, the Marmaton, the South Fork of
the Cottonwood, the Neosho, the Verdigris, Wakarusa, Bloody Run, Illinois Creek,
the Little Osage, Spring River. These are the renegade streams of eastern Kansas.

Pristine they are not. Booby trapped with low-head dams and a century of
farm country refuse, most look more like Willy Wonka's Chocolate River than
clear western streams. But they harbor unexpected surprises. One hundred-pound
flathead catfish haunt murky bends no angler's hook has probed in decades. High
in the folds of prairie buttes, emerald gardens of watercress and red glacial boulders
encrusted with pink papershell mussels cleanse spring-fed headwater tributaries.
American mink stalk muskrats in still backwaters. Pecans, persimmon, and pawpaw chill arboretums of hushed darkness. Southern redbelly dace, creek chubs, Topeka shiners, central stonerollers, and other tiny jeweled fish inject a kaleidoscope
into the muddy currents. Thinking about these rivers makes people like me want
to strap a canoe on the roof rack and hightail it out to the waterways of the prairie.

So it is with forbidden fruit.

In a turn of the screw, Kansas, with less public land than any other state, also
has the most draconian regulations in America governing access to state waters,
which are public resources. For putting paddle to puddle—any puddle, that is,
except the big federal flood control reservoirs, state and municipal fishing lakes,
a few small stream segments on public land above the public reservoirs, and the
Kansas, Missouri, and Arkansas Rivers—canoeists have been hauled off to jail for
trespassing.

I once floated a serene section of the Marais des Cygnes—the River of Swans—with my brother-in-law. Floating this river was a family tradition for Steve. His father spent the first week of every August there setting trotlines. Our route hugged the Chippewa Hills, a limestone upheaval west of Ottawa covered with mature oak-hickory forests. We followed bends coiled tight as a rattlesnake, played tag with a pair of pileated woodpeckers, and spooked a half-dozen beavers. The river felt like a muddier version of an Ozark headwater stream sans the Milwaukee's Best crowd. We were in no hurry. The fourteen-mile trip took the better part of a day.

During the float, Steve and I likely passed close to the lost grave of Mokohoko, the Sac and Fox leader. His people buried him secretly at night in the Chippewa Hills. In the 1870s and 1880s, he led his small band in stubborn resistance to just about everybody—the main Sac and Fox tribe, Indian agents, the US government, and a flood of Kansas settlers. Twice Mokohoko's people were "removed" to Oklahoma and forced to march south 150 miles under guard. Both times they snuck back to Kansas, finding their way home to the Marais des Cygnes valley where they eked out a hard and humiliating existence, squatting near lands taken from them, making their gardens along a river they had sacrificed everything for.

Now, more than one hundred years later, floating Mokohoko's river—Steve's river—we had no way of knowing that a feud one hundred miles to our south would soon spill out of Cherokee County and go all the way to the Kansas Supreme Court, dramatically affecting our rights to be on the Marais des Cygnes and most Kansas streams. The feud would lead to a precedent that sooner or later affects anyone seeking the last wild places of Kansas.

Shoal Creek rises up in the hills of southwestern Missouri, flowing west toward the Spring River in extreme southeastern Cherokee County, Kansas. Cherokee County, tucked in the lower right corner of the state, contains the entirety of the Kansas Ozarks, fifty square miles of bitternut hickory, white oak, cold springs, and shallow caves that are home to several species of amphibian found nowhere else in the state.

In the late 1980s, rare salamanders weren't the only wildlife spilling west across the state line. Shoal Creek was a party stream—sort of. It didn't have the gunwale-to-gunwale traffic of eastern Ozark rivers like the Current or the White, but in spring and summer, dozens of boats—many of them glorified floating breweries—embarked from Joplin, Missouri, and cruised west, crossing the state line near

Galena, before taking out at Lowell, Kansas, on the Spring River. Most people respected the rights of property owners along the way, but some didn't.

Jasper Hayes was a lifelong Cherokee County farmer who owned land on both sides of Shoal Creek. In the spring of 1988 he got fed up with boaters "littering, sunbathing in the nude, and having sex" on his land. Taking matters into his own hands, Hayes ran a strand of baling wire across the narrowest section of the creek on his property. By the next afternoon someone had taken it down. The following day he replaced it with reinforced steel wire. That didn't last either.

Finally, Hayes put up an electric cattle fence that completely spanned the fast-moving Ozark stream. An electric fence is the last thing any canoeist wants to face on a stream with tight turns like Shoal Creek. You'd have three ways to react *if* you saw the fence in time: drown; grab it, get shocked, and flip the boat; or portage and trespass on private property. When a float guide from Holly Haven Outfitters encountered the fence, he complained to the county, arguing that it was an imminent danger to his customers.

Chris Meek agreed. As Cherokee County attorney, Meek believed paddlers had a right to float the public waters of the state. On June 11, he filed a declaratory judgment on behalf of Holly Haven, seeking to confirm that the public had a right to use Shoal Creek for recreational purposes. He ordered Hayes to remove his fence.

On September 22, Cherokee district court judge David Brewster issued a ruling that surprised almost everyone. The court sided with Jasper Hayes on grounds that Shoal Creek was not in fact navigable, since, because of a federal law, nobody was likely to use it under ordinary conditions as a highway for commerce. This was because the major products of the region—wheat, corn, soybeans, cattle, and hogs—could not be transported by boat on Shoal Creek. Because Hayes owned land on both sides of the stream and riparian landowners adjacent to non-navigable waters owned the soil *ad medium filum aquae*—to the middle thread of the creek—it was his right to put up a fence and keep paddlers, including the clients of Holly Haven Outfitters, from floating it. They lifted the restraining order.

Chris Meek, however, was certain the district court got it wrong. He believed Brewster misinterpreted the federal definition of navigability and ignored a long tradition of access to similar streams throughout the state for the purpose of recreational paddling. Spurred on by the Kansas Canoe Association, the Geary County Fish and Game Association, and the Kansas Wildlife Federation, Meek appealed to the Kansas Supreme Court. He would soon discover that paddlers and fishermen weren't the only groups carefully following the case.

Under US federal law, water, like air, is a natural resource shared in common by the public. Virtually all legal jurisdictions allow canoeing and kayaking on *navigable* streams. In some states, the right does not extend to non-navigable streams because, the reasoning goes, if a stream isn't navigable, traversing it is as much hiking as floating, and hiking on private property without permission is trespassing.

Navigability is an issue of federal law. A stream navigable by boat will likely be used in some fashion to conduct commerce. States cannot tighten the federal definition, but they can loosen it and allow access to streams not strictly navigable in the federal sense. Many do just that.

States with robust recreational floating industries usually have promiscuous definitions of navigability. Alaska, Minnesota, Virginia, California, Connecticut, Idaho, Iowa, Wyoming, Montana, New Mexico, the Carolinas, South Dakota, Tennessee, Utah, Ohio, and Oklahoma allow the public to float any stream that can sustain a canoe, kayak, inner tube, washtub, or boogie board (although a few stipulate that the stream must be navigable for at least half the year under normal conditions). Those states consider recreation itself commerce.

Other states take a more arcane approach. In Washington a river is navigable if it can support a bolt of shingles. A stream is navigable in Alabama, Michigan, Missouri, Vermont, West Virginia, Nevada, and New Hampshire if it can transport logs or railroad ties. Maryland and New Jersey allow public navigation only on tidal streams while New York allows it only on nontidal streams. Mississippi defines any stream navigable that flows better than one hundred cubic feet per second. Texas defines any stream navigable that is wider than thirty feet for its entire length.

Because Kansas never adopted a state definition of navigability, paddlers' rights were a murky topic. T. J. Hittle, founding member and past president of the Kansas Canoe Association, has arguably logged more miles on Kansas streams than anybody since the French coureurs de bois. According to Hittle, the debate over legal access began in the late 1960s when recreational canoeing first started to become popular. Opinions flowed from many sources—Attorney General Vern Miller, Lt. Governor David Owen, the Kansas Water Office, and various legislators—without converging. There was no clear standard or law that spelled out whether paddlers could float Kansas streams without first gaining permission from landowners.

Short of the Kansas Legislature enacting a special law, Hittle and others believed that the courts would eventually decide the matter. Hittle told me, "What I thought as president of Kansas Canoe Association was that if we could ever take this thing to the Supreme Court, because you were floating on public water, there was no way they could keep canoeists or kayakers off the streams. Because we weren't actually touching the land, we were floating on public water and there shouldn't have been any problem."

When the Kansas Supreme Court agreed to hear *Meek v. Hayes* in the fall of 1989, it appeared that Hittle would soon find out whether or not he was right.

Chris Meek is tall and wiry; he could pass for singer Neil Young's kid brother. We met in Lawrence at a former Internet café turned hippie breakfast spot on a sparkling fall morning.

Meek told me that even before the case he sympathized with paddlers. He and a law partner floated Shoal Creek many times in their own canoe, and Holly Haven Outfitters shuttled vehicles for them. He knew the owners. But Meek completely agreed that Hayes had every right to keep people off his property. "This was a law enforcement issue," he said. "Statutes were already there protecting his property rights. If someone drags their canoe up onto his land, they're trespassing. If they throw something on his land, they're littering. These were crimes anywhere in the state of Kansas. It didn't matter whether they got to the property by creek or county road. Hayes was protected by the law. I was concerned about the paddlers. That electric fence was a public nuisance. Somebody was going to get killed."

Meek said that, at the time, every prosecutor in Kansas would have made Hayes take his fence down. "Eight or nine counties in western Kansas had followed our argument," he said. "Only Colorado had ruled that landowners could control access to the water up to the middle point of the stream. We had evidence that Shoal Creek was navigable based on the federal definition. Even though we lost in district court, I was confident we'd go into the Supreme Court and win. I didn't think it would be that big of a case."

That's where he was wrong. It *was* a big case. Not yet thirty years old, Meek didn't realize that legal wrangling on a stage as big as the Kansas Supreme Court was certain to attract the interest of big players in backroom Kansas politics if it involved the rights of farmers and private landowners—or if it smacked of environmentalism. Those big players were the Kansas Farm Bureau and the Kansas Livestock Association. Without meaning to, Meek had rolled out a powder keg and lit the fuse. He soon found out it was a short one.

In 1986, four years before the Supreme Court ruled on *Meek v. Hayes*, a bill was introduced into the Kansas House of Representatives to amend the following line in the constitution: "All water within the state of Kansas is hereby dedicated to the use of the people of the state, subject to the control and regulation of the state in the manner herein prescribed."

House Bill 2835 would have added, "All water of the state which can serve a beneficial purpose is hereby declared to be public waters, and the public shall have a right to make a nonconsumptive use of such water obtaining an appropriation. The public character of the water shall not be determined exclusively by the proprietorship of the underlying, overlying or surrounding land or on whether it is a body or stream of water which was navigable in fact or susceptible of being used as a highway for commerce at the time this state was admitted to the union."

This amendment was for paddlers. It would have put Kansas in league with states like Missouri that allow open access to virtually all rivers and streams. But the Kansas Farm Bureau flexed its muscle in the statehouse. The Farm Bureau had a long adversarial history with environmental groups. They fought proposals to create a Tallgrass Prairie National Park in the Flint Hills. They litigated against western Kansas ranchers who wanted to manage their rangelands to protect native species like the black-tailed prairie dog (a Farm Bureau lawyer told a newspaper he was always for landowners' rights, at least the rights to rid the land of prairie dogs, otherwise he supported the "government's right to do the job" for them). With pressure from the Farm Bureau, House Bill 2835 died in the House Energy and Natural Resources Committee.

Later the same year, the Kansas Canoe Association, in conjunction with the Kansas Department of Wildlife and Parks, tried to establish the Kansas Recreational River Act. The act would have been similar to the National Scenic Rivers Act, creating a way for the state to designate select rivers with "outstanding fish and wildlife, recreational, geologic, or scenic values," open for the public "to enjoy and use through non-contact river recreation." Hittle, who worked on the project, said that "after it got to the floor of the senate, the Farm Bureau jumped on really hard. They got together and said, 'We want to kill this bill so badly that no other environmental group will ever bring this before us again.' So when they passed it out of committee it went to the general senate and lost thirty-nine votes to one. Only the bill's sponsor voted for it."

The Kansas Farm Bureau has successfully bullied state agencies that tried to improve river recreation opportunities. According to Hittle, the defeat of the Kansas

Recreational River Act rattled the Department of Wildlife and Parks. Shortly afterward, they shredded their inventory of state-produced brochures on Kansas rivers. Things have changed in recent years; the climate is less hostile. The department has helped private groups like Friends of the Kaw establish access points on the Kansas River, but they still don't offer classes or information on paddling safety.

Despite the pressure, Meek wouldn't budge, even after voters ousted him as county prosecutor—partly because of negative publicity associated with the case. He prepared for the Supreme Court battle on his own dime, adamant that federal law was on his side and that Kansans had a right to access their rivers.

Arguments in the case got under way in the late fall of 1989. From the outset both sides agreed on one thing: Water was a public resource. The Supreme Court's job was to decide where a landowner's rights ended and the public's rights began. To win, Meek had to convince the court that the dividing line was the stream's normal high-water mark. Because of federal law, if Shoal Creek was navigable, Hayes couldn't fence paddlers out if his ownership didn't dip below the high-water mark. The goal was simple—Meek had to prove that Shoal Creek met the federal definition of navigability.

But the federal definition was complicated. In a previous court case, *United States v. Holt Bank*, the court ruled that beyond mere functional navigability (navigability "in fact" in legal lingo), title to a navigable stream's riverbed must have passed to the state at the time it was admitted to the union. So between existing legal precedent and current statutes, a stream was federally navigable if and only if, under natural conditions and normal stream flow, it could support commerce on the day the state joined the union.

Questions of navigability had come before the Kansas Supreme Court before. In 1927 a landowner on the Neosho River sought reparations because the county dredged gravel for public roads on his property. The court decided the Neosho was not navigable, largely because of Holt Bank. At the time of statehood there was evidence that ferries and sawmills used the river for commerce. Under normal conditions a small boat could make the fifty-mile trip from Oswego to Humboldt. But in a number of places, shallow riffles required portage. The court believed that these shallows made it impossible to use the river to transport typical farm country products like grain and livestock. Because of this, the court ruled that the Neosho was non-navigable.

In total, courts had ruled on six rivers, with the score tied at three. The Kansas, Missouri, and Arkansas Rivers were navigable. The Neosho, Delaware, and

Smoky Hill Rivers were non-navigable. To break the tie in favor of paddlers, Shoal Creek needed to have met federal navigability requirements on January 29, 1861, the day Kansas became a state. Like the Neosho, Shoal Creek had shallow riffles that required portage, and in dry years even a canoe required more draw than the stream could provide. There was no reason to believe it had ever transported grain or livestock. However, Meek presented evidence that John Link, the owner of Ozark Quality Products, made several canoe trips each year to collect plants to sell at his business. He also showed that Holly Haven Outfitters had run group floats on the creek between Joplin and Lowell for years. The Kansas Wildlife Federation presented evidence that the creek's natural condition was largely the same as it was when Kansas became a state, so if it could support commerce today, it could have supported commerce in 1861.

But Meek took the argument beyond "navigability in fact." He argued that states were free to make it easier for people to access public resources. He showed evidence that Wyoming, Idaho, Arkansas, and California had reinterpreted navigability as a stream's capability to provide recreation for the public. Hayes's attorneys countered that such a reinterpretation would radically depart from the direction Kansas had always taken in such matters. In a similar case, the Colorado Supreme Court upheld trespassing convictions against two canoeists claiming that "a long established judicial precedent is desirable, it is a legislative and not a judicial function" to make these sorts of legal changes.

On the last day of testimony, a representative from the Kansas Wildlife Federation tried an appeal to common sense. The people own the water of a state. Courts should tread lightly when considering whether to let state governments restrict the people's access to it. The right of citizens to float their streams and rivers was self-evident. This public trust doctrine had been applied to river rights in Mississippi and Montana. The Montana constitution explicitly states that "all surface, underground, flood and atmospheric waters within the boundaries of the state are the property of the state for the use of its people and subject to appropriation for the beneficial uses as provided by law."

After closing arguments, Meek thought he had a decent chance of winning. He told me, "Many of the Farm Bureau's claims were just ridiculous. A guy from western Kansas asked a question in oral arguments. He had creeks that were dried up 99 percent of the time, but he knew that after four days of rain there was enough water to run a raft. If these dry creek beds come up suddenly and people want to canoe, do I have to cut my fences to give them access? I thought to myself, who in the world is going to say to themselves after four days of rain, 'Let's head out to western Kansas to canoe?' But he was really worried about it. They were obsessed with what-ifs."

In its decision, the Supreme Court agreed with one of Meek's critical arguments: Shoal Creek met part of the federal definition of navigability. Because of John Link and Holly Haven's commercial use of the stream, it qualified as a highway of commerce. But on the issue of title, the court disagreed with Meek. They ruled that, at the time of Kansas's statehood, the title to Shoal Creek's riverbed did not pass to the state, in fact Shoal Creek was less navigable than the Neosho River, which by the Webb case was officially non-navigable. The court drew heavily on a 1979 Colorado Supreme Court ruling that showed there was no legal reason for courts to adopt a "modern" standard of navigability. If a state's constitution restricted the public's rights to access streams, it was the job of the legislature to change the constitution, not the court. Not only did Shoal Creek fail to satisfy all federal conditions of navigability, but the court also disagreed with the Kansas Wildlife Federation's argument that the right to access public resources should overrule the Kansas constitution.

Therefore, on January 19, 1990, The Kansas Supreme Court upheld the Cherokee District Court's original decision. Shoal Creek was not navigable. Hayes had the right to fence any part of the creek on his land. Kansas paddlers—without prior permission from landowners—were renegades in the eyes of the law. In adopting Colorado's position, the court also squashed any further possibility of litigation, ruling that the *legislature alone* would be responsible for any deviance from the Holt Bank standard in future situations involving paddlers and Kansas streams.

So the rules are clear. Canoeing is only legal on the Kansas, Missouri, and Arkansas Rivers (though crossing private property to gain access requires permission). Paddlers are restricted to sandbars and banks below the normal high-water mark.

But *Meek v. Hayes* didn't prevent somebody from asking adjoining landowners for permission to go canoeing on their property. Though each landowner along the route would have to consent, it was still theoretically possible to legally float streams other than the Kansas, Missouri, and Arkansas. How hard would it be, I wondered, to take a street-legal float on a typical small Kansas stream? Would I need a wilderness permit or a law degree?

I decided to find out. I chose the same section of the Marais des Cygnes that Steve and I had floated years back. I would have to locate every landowner along the route and hope they were sympathetic toward a canoeist trying to follow the letter of the law and have some fun on the waterways of Kansas at the same time. I knew canoeists still floated this section of the river. I hoped the renegades who paddled with impunity hadn't soured landowners toward all Kansas paddlers.

Compiling a list of riparian landowners along the upper Marais des Cygnes in Osage and Franklin Counties was a multijurisdictional exercise made easier by a modern innovation—GIS. Geographic Information Systems are georeferenced electronic databases that county governments use to store property information. Shari Perry and Roy Baker, from Franklin County, and Becky Bartley, from Osage County, helped me create parcel maps along the course of my proposed route. After examining data linked to each parcel, I came up with a list of thirteen landowners. The list seemed manageable, but I hoped thirteen didn't foreshadow any bad luck. Lucky thirteen, lucky thirteen, I thought to myself.

Selecting the hopefully more propitious date of July 14 for the float, I had three weeks to gain permission. It seemed like plenty of time. I made a postcard with two checkboxes so recipients could give me a thumbs up or thumbs down on the trip. I used registered mail to ensure receipt.

Meanwhile, it began raining in the Marais des Cygnes valley. In Ottawa, twenty miles below my put-in point, the city closed the protective floodgates for the first time in a decade. Farther down at Lane, farmers heard stranded raccoons chattering in the trees above Pottawatomie Creek at night. John Brown's Osawatomie almost washed away to Missouri.

With the waters still rising on the Marais des Cygnes, our postal carrier knocked on the door one early Saturday morning and handed my wife some slips of withered cardstock. She yelled downstairs, wanting to know why somebody mailed me a Puffins cereal proof-of-purchase tab that we owed seventeen cents on. Apparently my homemade postcards weren't up to code—they required additional postage. I'd used free Wildlife Federation return address stickers, the ones with lemurs on them. Christina raised an eyebrow and handed me the cards. "If anyone gives you permission to float that river it'll be because they think you're a Cub Scout."

Apparently the Cub Scout strategy worked. The first six postcards were checked "YES." I had permission from nearly half of my landowners and almost two weeks remained before the float. Two of the postcards included friendly messages: "Yes, but only if we can come along." "Sure, but be careful of Miller's dam if you go farther." On another of the slips, somebody wrote in "Hell" before the "Yes" and finished it off with an exclamation point.

By the time the Ottawa floodgates reopened and the Marais des Cygnes began to subside, I had twelve postcards checked in the affirmative. One found its way to an absentee landowner in Germany who signed off, "Auf Wiedersehen." Only one more postcard remained missing, but by the Fourth of July it still hadn't come in the mail. I looked up the landowner's name on whitepages.com and called, leaving voicemail. It took three days to finally get him on the phone.

I explained who I was and what I was trying to do, but I think he had trouble hearing me at first. After a few moments, though, it clicked. He said, "You're the one who wants to run a boat down the river. I got your card. I'll be watching for you next Saturday."

Watching for me?

"I'll be down there watching in the woods and I'd better not see any canoes floating by." That was it. Before I could try to convince him otherwise, he hung up. I called back—several times—but he didn't answer.

So much for lucky thirteen.

Discouraged, I thought of one more tactic to salvage my legal float. The next Monday I drove to Franklin County to research portages around landowner thirteen's soybean field. It didn't take long, driving around with my maps, to realize several miles of walking would be required to circumvent his property. I'd need to contact new landowners and ask them if I could haul my canoe across their fields so the guy in the woods wouldn't have to chase me off his land. This was getting ridiculous (or *more* ridiculous); I wanted to float the Marais des Cygnes, not hike around it with a canoe yoked to my forehead. I'd made a reasonable effort, but enough was enough. The trip was off.

It was the most complicated permit procedure I'd ever gone through for a two-hour float that I didn't make. My wife called it performance art—a canoe trip without the canoe or the trip.

I agree with the Kansas Supreme Court. Shoal Creek and the other renegade streams of eastern Kansas are not highways of commerce. They are highways of history, highways of wildlife, highways of adventure, highways of the imagination, highways to the last wild places of Kansas. They are also, like it or not, highways clearly marked "no trespassing."

The story of Kansas canoeing is not all *Grapes of Wrath*. We have three excellent navigable rivers: the Missouri, Arkansas, and Kansas. In 1995, T. J. Hittle put up the first Kansas Canoe Association website, with an interactive map of the Kansas River and a series of links to river gauges that helped paddlers plan safe trips on the Kaw. (In response Hittle received anonymous threatening emails that he "just decided not to worry about it. I wasn't going to let them keep me from encouraging people to use their own rivers.") Friends of the Kaw launched kansasriver.org a few years later. New access ramps are opening on the average of one every nine months. The first book on Kansas streams, *Paddling Kansas*, by Dave Murphy, was published in 2007. It covers every legally floatable stretch of river and stream in the state. Canoe races—the Kawnivore 100 and Gritty 50—attract hundreds of boats each summer.

But there's still a void. Slipping at dawn onto a quiet stream a stone's skip wide, gliding past stands of pecan and maple with barred owls peeking down from the branches, is a small stream experience. There's no better way to discover the essence of a place than to explore it from the seat of a canoe or kayak at river's pace. In a great irony, *Meek v. Hayes* had little effect on Shoal Creek. By the time the Supreme Court ruled, the electric fence was gone and nobody ever put it back up. Hayes died in the early nineties. Shoal Creek is still a party stream.

Years after the Supreme Court decision, I wondered if the hardline positions held by political foes of river access had softened. To find out, I spoke with Terry Arthur, general counsel to the Kansas Farm Bureau. Their stance was pretty much the same as before. He said, "If you have a navigable stream, you've got people coming across your property all the time trying to get to it. People aren't very good about respecting private property rights if they know they can boat, or fish, or hunt ducks, or whatever. To get to the river, people will have to cross private property, which is our biggest concern, or they would have to use some sort of authorized entrance that the government might have. Besides the possibility of vandalism, if you've got people floating down a navigable stream people won't respect your property rights. They feel perfectly entitled to stop the boat, get off, run around on your land, start fires, leave litter, let your cattle out, and whatever else."

Despite Meek's argument that property owners are already protected by existing laws, I know that Arthur is right. Some people are idiots. In Kansas, trespassers have been busted breaking their necks on ATVs, poaching alpacas, cooking meth, and cultivating pot on other people's land. Is it any wonder that farmers and ranchers don't text state representatives and ask them to pass new legislation making it easier for yahoos to access their property? Despite vandals and yahoos, however, I believe three sound reasons exist that should make private landowners take another look at river access.

The first concerns liability. Missouri's 1983 recreational use statute provides riparian landowners virtually complete immunity from litigation by paddlers. You can leave unattended chainsaws running twenty-four hours a day or let your pit bulls sunbathe on the sandbar. It doesn't matter; paddlers can't sue you if they get hurt. If the legislature ever decides to loosen its chokehold, Kansas law should include similar protections.

The second reason is economic. Arthur said the Farm Bureau believes people should profit from the use of their land. The Kansas Department of Wildlife and Parks operates a walk-in hunting and fishing program that pays good money in exchange for public hunting and fishing access in open seasons. Users don't have to contact anybody for permission. Participating properties are clearly marked. This can be an easy source of income for absentee landowners who aren't worried about people tromping through their front yard. A Scenic Rivers Act could provide a similar payment. With the economics of family farming and ranching getting tougher each decade, such recompense could be a new source of farm country income.

The last reason is less tangible. Today, most Kansans live in cities and suburbs and have little exposure to traditional rural lifeways. An enhanced connection to place, especially to the land, is a great way to educate people about life on the other side of the Interstate. Floating prairie streams would give people a reason to visit rural Kansas. It could foster an investment, not just of money, but also of passion to preserve these places.

When the majority of the Sac and Fox tribe agreed to leave Kansas for a reservation in Oklahoma, Mokohoko and his people refused to surrender their lands along the Marais des Cygnes, saying it "would be like putting our heads in the mouth of the great Bear's to be eaten off." The lack of access to Kansas streams pales in comparison to the tragedy of Mokohoko, but the story of his people is the story of a love of place, a love of a river valley. Perhaps there will be a day when paddlers can once again legally float the beautiful River of Swans. If that day comes, I hope they will think of Mokohoko resting in his unmarked grave somewhere in the shaded valley of the Chippewa Hills.

The Ninnescah, Mill Creek, the Marais des Cygnes, the Chikaskia, the Black Vermillion, Shoal Creek, Fall River, Grouse Creek, the Marmaton, the South Fork of the Cottonwood, the Neosho, the Verdigris, Wakarusa, Bloody Run, Illinois Creek, the Little Osage, Spring River. These are the renegade streams of eastern Kansas.

CHAPTER SEVEN

Badlands

In Kansas, waves of bluestem once sailed prairie schooners and montane cumulonimbus still blow across the plains like clouds of buffalo, but ours is not a land of oceans or mountains. We can, however, claim one landscape that in other places is also a tourist draw: badlands. Not *bad lands* in the pejorative, despite our rap sheet as Great American Desert, Dustbowl, Tornado Alley, and flyover country, but badlands in the geologic sense—those rugged western landforms starved for water and sculpted by erosion. From the Lakota *mako* (land) *sica* (bad), the term "badlands" was first used to describe the whimsically eroded mixed-grass hill country of the Lakota homeland in South Dakota. Although the landscape of the Dakota Badlands is unforgiving (in an Old Testament way), nearly a million Aquafina-clutching vacationers exit I-90 every year to visit Badlands National Park and its maze of buttes, pinnacles, and spires. It's a place of little comfort, but many comfort stations.

The Kansas badlands don't attract tourists and you'll be hard pressed to find a public restroom. We have no badlands parks—national or otherwise—and signs are few. Spectacularly under the radar, hidden on ranches and private property, sequestered from the imagination, the Kansas badlands are a reminder of the incredible diversity of landforms in the state. Sky islands—bastions of topographic relief that harbor unique flora not found on the tablelands below—top their friable mesas and buttes. These landforms are wild and harsh at the core, eroded by minerals that seep into groundwater and streams, some too alkaline to drink from. The soils that manage to cleave to eroded hillsides are seldom arable. These hills might not have a silver lining for agriculture, but as a setting for wild places, they're like Black Hills gold.

A great rainy day read, the physiographic map of Kansas segments the state by its common landforms and geologic history. The great Kansas landscapes occupy most of the real estate: the High Plains, the Flint Hills, the Smoky Hills, the Glaciated Region, the Osage Cuestas. If the physiographic regions were musicians, the Osage Cuestas would be Green Day—popular, brutally honest, but somehow mainstream nonetheless; the High Plains would be BR549—Grammy-nominated, Kansas-born and influenced a little by the high lonesome sound; the Flint Hills would be Wilco—unplowed, rough around the edges, and beholden to no record label; the Glaciated Region would be Natalie Merchant—smooth, nurturing, and a little past their prime; and the Smoky Hills would be Fiona Apple—rarefied, artistically pure, and prone to overgrowths of loco weed. But if you start in extreme western Kansas and trace your finger east along the Oklahoma border, you'll run into a small peninsula surrounded by the High Plains on both the north and west. This is the Red Hills region, which, if it were a musical act, would be the Velvet Underground—not many people ever listened to them, but everybody who did started a band. Most Kansans will never visit this mysterious plateau, also called the Gypsum or Gyp Hills, and relatively little has been written about the area. Otherwise rare in Kansas, caves are common in the Red Hills—Barber County alone has more than one hundred—inhabited by swarming colonies of bat species found nowhere else in the state. J. R. Meade wrote that these gypsum caverns were once home to a large population of black bears.

The wildness that Meade experienced echoes to this day. In the fall of 2007 a rancher shot a mountain lion in the heart of the Gyp Hills, the first wild puma confirmed in the state since 1904. More buffalo wander these gypsum cleavages and soap weed canyons than anywhere else in the state. Southern Comanche County contains some of the most pristine, biologically diverse wild places remaining in Kansas today.

The Red Hills were considered sacred ground to the five principal tribes of the region—the Comanche, Kiowa, Plains Apache, Southern Arapaho, and Southern Cheyenne. The map of places held sacred to the native Kansas tribes is mostly lost today, but an ample literature documents a spiritual connection among the Gyp Hills, the Medicine River, and original peoples of the state. Badlands are contemplative landscapes. The power and sanctity of the Red Hills has managed to survive into the twenty-first century.

Driving west away from the Kansas Turnpike on US Highway 160, a road almost exactly as long as the Missouri River, rolling hills soon give way to the flat valley of the Chikaskia River. As the Great Plains near, wind becomes the primary element. Farmhouses hunker down against pine shelter belts slumped north in mute surrender. The prairie-burning season was almost over, but chimneys of smoke still smudged the horizon, carbon giving back to carbon. I saw a roadkill porcupine just outside tiny Argonia, which in 1887 elected Susanna Salter as the nation's first woman mayor (when Susan B. Anthony introduced her to a convention of suffragettes, she slapped her on the shoulder and said, "Why, you look just like any other woman, don't you?").

Beyond Wellington, Highway 160 slides into a run of counties that have been losing population for decades. Grain elevators stand like gravestones in towns that can no longer support even a funeral home. Billboard space is so cheap that advertisers compete for your conscience:

"Take a stand for our life and land: Stop the landfill!"

"Smile. Your mom chose life."

The Red Hills straddle the ninety-ninth meridian in parts of Barber, Clark, and Comanche Counties, constituting a total of 550 square miles. Stereotypes of Kansas fall flat here. The soil is martian red. Canyonlands, sandstone buttes, and mesas create a skyline that looks more like Arizona than Kansas. Tables of gypsum, a mineral that occurs as flat, diamond-shaped crystals of selenite and as a silky pink crust called satin spar, cap the tallest hills. Gypsum is used to make cement, plaster, and drywall, also called gypsum board. The National Gypsum Company's mine near Sun City is one of the ten largest gypsum mines in America.

Gypsum is soft, scoring two out of ten on Mohs' scale of hardness (the value one is assigned to talc and the value ten to diamond). You can make a scratch in gypsum with your fingernail. Shallow caves form easily when water erodes through the porous rock. The caves eventually dissolve and break up into natural land bridges. A partially collapsed section of a thirty-five-foot by fifty-five-foot bridge that once arched over a creek still stands near Sun City.

The first line of buttes and mesas rose up on the horizon behind a billboard that featured a larger-than-life image of Martina McBride, the country singer born in tiny Sharon, Kansas. By then, sand-choked streams had replaced muddy creeks, and fresh green wheat looked like a patina of lichen on the clay pot burnish of red soil. By the time I reached Medicine Lodge I was in the heart of the Red Hills. Driving into town, I saw a man sitting with a cat and two little boys, deftly casting flies into a sandy pool of Elm Creek.

The name Medicine Lodge has a sadness to it—a lost western kind of sadness—like a line of cattle slowly walking through the forgotten remains of a buffalo wallow. On October 21, 1867, the Kiowa and Comanche tribes signed a treaty with the United States government near the confluence of Elm Creek and the Medicine River. It was the last of a series of treaties signed that year by the tribes of the southern plains. William Tecumseh Sherman was present, as were Kit Carson, Jesse Chisholm, and a grandson of Daniel Boone. Black Kettle; San-tan-ta, the Kiowa leader known as the "orator of the plains"; and Little Raven, leader of the Arapaho who bore a striking resemblance to Andrew Jackson, were among the better-known Indian signers. In all, sixteen thousand Native Americans and six hundred government representatives assembled for the proceedings.

Perhaps because the Kiowa in particular viewed the Red Hills and the Medicine River as sacred, the meetings, after convening at Fort Larned, were moved south to the Medicine River valley. For many years Plains tribes had traveled to a lodge at the confluence of Elm Creek. The waters were restorative, softened with naturally occurring epsom, a mineral used in spas. Streams in the Red Hills advertise salinity in their names: Salt Fork of the Arkansas, Bitter Creek, Salty Creek, Pucker Creek. But the healing waters and peaceful history of the setting didn't do the Indians much good; the treaties resulted in each tribe ceding vast amounts of land in exchange for diminished reserves in the Oklahoma Indian Territory.

If the community of Medicine Lodge had relegated the history of the treaties and the Kiowa to a corner in the county history museum, it wouldn't be the first. Few memorials commemorate the key events of Kansas Native American history. Moreover, the town of Medicine Lodge wasn't incorporated until thirteen years *after* the treaties were signed. But Medicine Lodge remembers its role in Indian history. The Stockade Museum displays replicas of the original lodges along the Medicine River. Signs pinpoint where the treaty events occurred. Starting in 1927, the community has commemorated the Treaty of Medicine Lodge with a triennial pageant in a natural amphitheater south of town. Windows of shops and gas stations are stenciled with welcoming slogans ("Indian Treaty, fill up here"). If you didn't know about the pageant you might think the treaty had happened last week. With the exception of Council Grove, no other Kansas community stewards its Native American history like Medicine Lodge.

The town was also once home to prohibitionist Carrie Nation, who began her temperance work in Medicine Lodge, but teetotaling as a movement had a short lifespan here. Nearby Sun City is home to Buster's Saloon, one of the most cantankerous western-style bars in Kansas and the last business left in the mostly deserted town of eighty (although against all hope I found a Sun City website that celebrates the town's history and promotes local adventure travel and hunting). The bar has closed more than once in the last twenty years, but I stop there and drink a red beer whenever I'm in the area.

Past Medicine Lodge, the wide panorama of the Red Hills emerges. Some first-time visitors who expect an arid western landscape are surprised by the soft appearance of the range, mostly because of the wealth of western red cedars (*Juniperus scopulorum*), the quintessential plant of the Gypsum Hills. The dark evergreens literally choke the steep draws between mesas and dot hilly slopes like loose herds of cattle. Some of the cedars were old when the treaty of Medicine Lodge was signed. The plants are well suited for life in this semiarid landscape. If one season is too dry, the trees save their fruit for the next year, reaching maturity on either a one- or two-year cycle. The crops of light blue berries lure winter flocks of mountain bluebirds hundreds of miles east of their normal ranges in the pinyon-juniper foothills of the Rockies.

Lost in scenery, I suddenly remembered to look for my turn onto a dirt road nine miles west of Medicine Lodge—I hadn't zeroed the odometer—but after another mile I saw my landmark, a white cross, stuck like a toothpick in a hill topped with gypsum meringue. I turned, crossed a cattle grate, and drove down a twisting dirt road toward a group of horse trailers parked beside a campfire ring and a full-sized lodgepole tepee. It was only two o'clock; I was an hour early for check-in at Gant-Larson Ranch.

A line of five riders, one on a mule, came down the trail that led through the cedars to camp. I waved and drove past the trailers and up another hill to a kitchen trailer with a sign that read "Cowboy Cafe." I knocked on the door and someone inside yelled, "Use the east entrance!"

It was hot for this early in spring, probably about seventy degrees. I took off my lime green pullover and let myself in through the screen door. Four men were sitting at a table using paring knives to peel what I thought were frozen chicken livers soaking in stainless steel bowls. Nobody looked over at me. Three of the guys still had their riding chaps and neckerchiefs on. Four hats hung on hooks below a portrait of a boy roping a steer in the shadow of a gypsum-capped mound. After a few seconds of uncomfortable silence I pulled up a chair next to a man in his mid-sixties wearing a Farmland cap with the logo worn off. Continuing to slice the slippery pieces of meat, he said, "You must be the hiker from Lawrence."

Bob Larson's ranch is hands down the best place for trail riding in Kansas. Since 1972, when he and his wife, Charlene, hosted their first trail ride as a joint project with the Medicine Lodge Chamber of Commerce, thousands of riders have ambled across the ten thousand acres they own or have access to. Some of the ranch's annual events include Carrie's Cavalry Ride (no men allowed), two all-comers rides in May, and an all-mule ride. Near the campsite there's a bathroom with a shower, but no electrical hookups.

I didn't have a horse, but when I spoke with Charlene Larson on the phone she told me bikers and hikers were more than welcome to strike out on the horse trails with or without an animal companion. Sitting there in the Cowboy Café, though, I got the feeling I was supposed to have a horse with me.

Bob grabbed another handful of the slippery globs and continued paring. He said, "We're working on dinner, which starts at exactly seven o'clock. You're invited."

I asked what was in the buckets.

"Rocky Mountain oysters."

I've spent a share of time in western places, a good share compared to most eastern Kansans of my generation, but I'd never watched anyone prep Rocky Mountain oysters, or calf testicles. Some consider them a delicacy—the same people who eat pickled quail eggs from a jar or beef brain and scrambled egg sandwiches. Delicate, yes, but delicacy?

Bob's son walked into the room and introduced himself. I asked if the oysters were from the ranch. Bob said, "My partner and I run 350 cows. We take them from calf to slaughter. We use a small slaughterhouse near Dodge. You're looking at about a year's worth of oysters. We remove the outer sheath when we castrate the calves, but there's still a membrane that needs to come off. If you don't freeze them first they're too slippery to run the knife along."

Ouch.

One of the other guys said, "Make sure you come back for dinner. Bob lays out quite a spread. We coat the oysters in flour and deep-fry them in fat over a propane fire. Not the healthiest for you, I guess."

The guy sitting next to me chuckled, "We don't look like the healthiest fellows do we?"

Before I left to hike, Bob gave me a map of the ranch and suggested the best places to get up into the hills and how to reach the river without crossing onto his neighbor's property. As I was leaving he reminded me, "Dinner at seven."

Medicine Lodge River is the official name the US Geological Survey gave the stream in 1968, when it revised the quad maps for Kansas, but the Kiowa called

it *A-ya-dalda-pa*. Most locals just call it the Medicine. A spate of spring thunderstorms had spread the waters across the width of the sandy gulch, which I could
easily wade near the Forrest Road bridge on the edge of the Larsons' property.
Swallows swooped low to scoop insects off the surface. Jeep tracks beckoned toward a path downstream, but I wasn't sure who owned the sandbar—a broken
strand of barbed wire stretched across the stream. I brought a wet fingertip to my
lips to sample the salinity of the water but then stopped when I noticed a beaver
lodge a hundred feet upriver. Rocky Mountain oysters were one thing, amoebic
giardiasis another.

I looked south toward Oklahoma. Red dirt mingled with the sand beyond willow breaks. In the bluffs above the far valley, earthy sandstone cliffs looked dry
and foreboding. This thirsty place reminded me that, even here at the eastern edge
of the Great Plains, water is scarce, a rare commodity that is both sculptor and
sculpted, wielding the power to give life and take it away; a definition of divine.
Maybe this was one of the reasons the Kiowa held this river sacred.

After a half-hour along the Medicine I backtracked to a trail that ascended into
the high ridge of mounds near US 160. I started hiking up toward a canyon. *Any*
ascent in Kansas is notable, especially one that involves a structure that can pass
for a canyon. There was little evidence of recent rains on this trail; sage, soap weed,
and fringed puccoon grew between slag heaps of broken gypsum. Above me, more
broken gypsum had tumbled down in great piles. I picked up a piece the size of a
sand dollar. Milky white webs punctuated with emerald and garnet hues looked
almost like mother of pearl. It was like standing in a field of rock candy.

I walked through the canyon until I found a little trail that led to the top of the
mound. My heart pumped harder as the trail steepened. Swallows dive-bombed
me to protect their nests thirty feet up in the cliffs. I stopped to catch my breath
and turned to look at the valley of the Medicine. Vultures circled near the Cowboy
Café. I hoped they were stealing the main course. Lush cedars grew in crags. I
continued climbing straight up, making footholds in the gypsum sludge. Finally, a
short scramble around a steep needle brought me to the flat summit.

A few feet of elevation brought a new world of vegetation. Lush bluestem car-
peted the top of the mound. Blue flowers, which I hadn't noticed on the climb
up, bloomed by the dozen. Some plant species in the Red Hills prefer the tops of
buttes, possibly because they receive little or no grazing pressure. Three molded
anthills looked like southwestern furniture—ottomans from hell. A few pocket
caves along the sides of buttes were visible in the distance. The cover of cedars in

these remote canyons and a ready supply of white-tailed and mule deer made it easy to see why mountain lions—or at least one mountain lion—had returned to this part of the state.

After savoring the view for a few minutes, I felt my stomach start rumbling. It was a bittersweet churning because I wanted to spend more time in the hills and I knew what awaited back at the mess hall. Nonetheless, I picked up my backpack and started down. Squeamish or not, I was starved.

Outside the Cowboy Café, the Larsons and a group of about twenty riders gathered around four deep fat fryers that sizzled away in the fading light. The first fryer was filled with onions, the others with shrimp, potatoes, and, of course, a pot full of oysters manned by Bob himself.

I worked through the buffet of homemade broccoli salad, German potato salad, green bean and fried onion casserole, smoked ham, cowboy beans, and custard pie. As the sun set over Bison Butte, I pulled up a lawn chair next to Crystal, who was visiting with her mule and a sway-backed palomino named Bucket Seat. They were training for the next weekend's women's ride. She explained that a horse will love you if you spend enough time with it, but a mule is like a cat. "If a mule doesn't take to you after awhile, there's no hope," she said. "You'd be better to trade it for a horse."

The people at the table across from us were talking about a recent cattle rustling. Crystal shook her head and said, "It's a big problem. People can make a lot of money pinching steers."

Crystal was almost completely blind. She told me that if I came down to the bonfire later I should tell her who I was; she wasn't good with voices when she was drinking. Since she couldn't drive anymore, she rode her mule almost everywhere. The Mennonite grocery near her home in Newton had a hitching post out front.

After Bob passed through and checked on Crystal's drink, she confided to me, "What the Larsons do is priceless. They open up this incredible land for us; none of the folks you see here could find trails like this if it weren't for the Larsons. Some of the guys helping cook have been coming for twenty years. It's like a big extended family."

Bob came back and took a seat on an overturned washbasin. He told me how he and Charlene had met when they were in college at Kansas State University. Bob had never heard of the Red Hills, but Charlene's roots were firmly entrenched. Her grandfather homesteaded and slowly built up his rangeland, but after he died the children divvied up the original ranch and sold some of it. When Bob married Charlene, he married the Red Hills too. They settled near her family's ancestral land and eventually repurchased her grandfather's original ranch. In the years since, they used money from the trail rides to bolster their holdings and by 2012 owned almost three thousand acres. They open all of this up to trail riders.

The Larsons' trail ride business is a successful example of how ranchers and farmers can use supplemental income, in this case from tourism, to sustain a traditional operation. I heard some of the riders talk about how much they'd love to "retire" like Bob, but looking around I could tell it was a lot of work. Bob said, "No matter how much you love trail riding, this becomes a job really fast. You're going to do the regular work of your ranch and then work all weekend on tourism. You have to have realistic expectations."

I asked if any of his visitors were surprised to find a landscape with buttes and mesas in Kansas. He said, "The trail riders are one group. They appreciate the land. But some of the people most surprised by what we have here are new professors from KU."

When new tenure track professors are hired, the University of Kansas sends them on a five-day Wheat State Whirlwind Tour to expose them to Kansas culture. The Gant-Larson Ranch is sometimes on the itinerary. Bob said, "In the past, I've ridden the bus around the county and played tour guide. Everyone is always surprised to see the Gyp Hills. At the end of the day we bring them back to the Cowboy Café and lay out our usual spread. The first time, we cooked KC strips and rib eyes grown right here on the ranch. Some of the professors weren't much interested in the meat, and I don't blame them; we could all do to live healthier. But we had a few who've never had real corn."

"Real corn? Do you mean corn on the cob?" I asked.

"Yes. Real cob corn. We hold out one of the fryers and boil the corn, husks and all. It takes exactly eleven minutes. Those professors who wouldn't touch our finest steaks started peeling into that corn. Before long we had to bring out another bushel." He smiled and, in a quieter voice, said, "They were like a yard full of hogs."

Tension between the rights of landowners and the public have a long history in the Red Hills. In the 1890s, dissention between Barber County ranchers—who favored communal access open range—and settlers—who were claim stakers and fence builders—almost broke into warfare. Cowboys and farmers exchanged gunfire on a number of occasions. Owners' rights prevailed in the end, of course, but the bankruptcy and consolidation of farms and ranches a century later shows that going it alone has a price. In some ways, the Gant-Larson Ranch is a throwback to the days of the communal range. By developing a tourism component, the ranch can remain private and on the tax rolls. By opening up the land to a limited number of people who want to experience one of the last wild places of Kansas, traditional family ownership can continue in a time of increasingly corporate operations. The state promotes the ranch and other similar operations through the state agritourism campaign. Not every outfit can expect to be as successful as the Gant-Larson trail rides, but the program is one of few where Kansas government has promoted public access to private lands in a mutually beneficial way.

Before I said goodnight to everybody, one lone Rocky Mountain oyster—golden brown and shimmering with grease—still sat in the middle of my red plastic plate. Nothing I learned in "man school" excuses my behavior, but I just couldn't do it. With a flip of the wrist I tossed my plate, Great Plains sushi and all, into the trash can as I shuffled off toward camp. Not one bite did I take. What kind of man was I?

Life doesn't hand out many second chances, but through sheer coincidence, the specialty of the house at the roadside restaurant on the way back to Lawrence was *real* Rocky Mountain oysters. I ordered chicken salad and iced tea and mulled over my options as I took my time eating the food. When the waitress asked if I wanted dessert I cleared my throat and told her I'd take an order of Rocky Mountain oysters.

She looked at me like I'd just asked her out on a date. "Honey," she said, "we only do those on the weekends."

I had crossed an invisible line. Around wildlife geeks or geographers or maybe even programmers I could have gotten away with it, but say the word "myotis" one too many times around artistic women and its meaning will forever morph into the comic.

Christina: "Oh to hear the gentle mewing of the cave myotis."

Chloe: "Indeed, I yearn for its gay and cheerful song."

We were somewhere between Elm Mills and Sun City—or was it Minonga?—headed toward Schwarz Canyon in the wilds of the southern Red Hills ranch country. I'd explored gypsum caves before, but the caves of Schwarz Canyon stand out in the annals of Kansas speleology: Hubbard, 1934; Dunnigan and Fitch, 1967; Kuntz, 1973; Stan Roth and his students, 1959 through the early 2000s. The bats of Schwarz Canyon had fascinated Kansas researchers for decades. It's one of the most biologically diverse wild places left in the state. Phyllis and Dee Scherich had generously offered to lead us up through the canyon to the caves. Christina and

I were excited, but I oversold the trip to our daughter; she was bored sick of my yammering on about pallid-ear bats, big-eared bats, Brazilian free-tails, and the cave myotis, or cave bat.

In this part of the state, people direct you to GPS coordinates rather than postal addresses, but I brought the wrong GPS device—my smartphone—and couldn't get a signal. After about an hour driving in circles on jeep trails (the only signage chides you to yield the right-of-way to cattle) I pulled over to consult *Kansas Atlas and Gazetteer.*

Chloe, realizing we were lost, put down her Japanese manga book and started rapping:

> He was leading us around like Moses,
> In search of the cave myotis,
> He was really starting to feel his 'oatses,'
> Then he realized he couldn't work his GPS.
> Daddy couldn't work his GPS!
> Daddy couldn't work his GPS!

"Do something useful," I said and gave her the atlas to see if she noticed something I missed. Oatses? Christina and I walked up the path to check out a road-killed slender glass lizard, the elegant legless lizard that seems abundant in the Gyp Hills. We picked a few buffalo gourds, a member of the cucumber family that is endlessly fascinating to people from eastern Kansas, taking care not to uproot the plants because Native Americans, who prepared the root for medicine, believed killing a buffalo gourd vine might bring injury to your family. After a few minutes Chloe yelled to us from the car, "I think I figured it out!"

It's hard to pick a wildest place in Kansas, but if biodiversity and sheer visual grandeur are your measure, Schwarz Canyon—Schwarz is often spelled Swartz in the literature—wouldn't be a bad choice. Phyllis greeted us outside their ranch house near the canyon. Most people throughout the state know the Scherichs from sold-out trail rides they used to host to raise money for a local medical clinic and their incredible knowledge of plants native to gypsum soils (Phyllis was past president of the Kansas Native Plant Society). We played with two vibrant green and pink collared lizards in their rock garden until Dee brought the pickup around to take us up toward the canyon. We had a lot of driving ahead of us, none of it on proper roads.

Badlands topography in the Red Hills near Schwarz Canyon, Comanche County, Kansas.

After repeatedly fording the Salt Fork of the Arkansas as it grooved back and forth through sandsage and small stands of elm and plum brush, we left the open range for a series of switchbacks up into a grassy plateau beyond a badlands that hugged the river. A monsoonal June and July had made up for months of drought. I couldn't believe how lush the grasses were. Near Lawrence, there would be a section road every mile in a prairie like this, but we followed two undulating ruts through a sheer biomass of grass. Finally, after about fifteen minutes, Dee stopped the truck next to a three-foot-deep green nutsedge sump as perfectly circular as a contact lens.

I took out my binoculars and scanned the horizon. Buffalo wallows. Dozens pocked the high shelf for miles out toward the canyon. I started to whisper to Chloe that we were standing in the middle of a time machine but stopped myself; she was old enough to feel the strange mojo of this buffalo ghost town without my commentary. In a time long past, bison had rooted in the damp seeps of this plateau. They literally carried the soil away with them in their coats, an all-natural insect repellant for megafauna.

We weren't yet in Schwarz Canyon proper, but a great view north across the broad sweep of the Salt Fork valley with its gypsum-capped buttes and mesas stood before us. Dee pointed out cedars growing not only in steep draws, but also along the river bottom and ridge slopes. Without strategic fires set by Native Americans to improve buffalo habitat, red cedars behaved like nonnative intruders, changing the prairie. Dee battled constantly to suppress the onslaught, but the dry years limited his ability to prune back the overgrowth with fire.

Driving south again between small valleys and ravines, we discovered the prairie was literally alive with animals: toads, a Texas horned lizard that Dee grabbed and tossed to the girls in the backseat, collared lizards, jackrabbits, cottontails, wingless zebra-striped locusts, box turtles, and above us turkey vultures and Mississippi kites riding the thermals. Earlier that morning in Elm Mills, the "Gyp Ozarks" south of Pratt built up around the mill race of an eighteenth-century flour mill, Chloe and I saw a Mississippi kite circling high above the water. As we watched, the bird extended her talons, dialed us into her radar, and damned if she didn't make a three-hundred-foot death-plunge right at our faces! We ducked back toward the cabin. She called off her sortie, but I'd never felt so like prey in my life.

After another twenty minutes cutting parabolic swaths across the buffalo tableland, we descended slowly into the southern canyon, where the valley floor rose almost to the height of the surrounding prairie. A slurry of gypsum gravel and mushy slate-like slabs that broke easily littered the ground—you wouldn't want to build a countertop with this stuff. Dee led us into a dark cedar-choked hollow. The temperature dropped ten degrees as we walked without ducking into the biggest gypsum cave I'd ever seen. Lichens, mosses, and tiny ferns grew on rocks lining the passage, and fifty feet back a wire rigging screwed in to hold lanterns surrounded a well-used circle of rocks under a ceiling caked with the soot of hundreds of fires.

In the late 1950s, Lawrence high school biology teacher Stan Roth started bringing students to this cave to conduct an annual bat census and camp in the murky dank of the hollow—cave camping in Kansas, complete with all the guano and cave mold you could slither through. This speleodormitory was roomy enough for at least a dozen high school sophomores and assorted cave myotis. When I spoke to Roth about those trips he told me, "We surveyed in the winter, mainly because that's when school was in session, but also because that's when bats are less active and easier to approach. Several Red Hills species occur nowhere else in Kansas in any number and, in fact, are at the northeast extent of their range in North America. This includes the cave bat, or cave myotis, the pallid bat, the big-eared bat, and the Brazilian free-tail bat."

He admitted, "One thing I found meaningful was to show kids that the reputation Kansas has as being flat and boring is not deserved." I'll bet it wasn't boring. I could just imagine the pranks those kids dreamed up sleeping in a cavern full of Brazilian free-tail bats.

The cave tunneled down through the gypsum toward another entrance, but none of us were up for spelunking so we climbed back out to the gypsum flat, then crawled on our hands and knees under red cedars to the second entrance. Dee suddenly stopped and shushed us: "I thought I heard something roar."

"Something roared?" Christina asked as she grabbed my arm. It sounded like a nighthawk to me, but I knew if a Red Hills mountain lion snoozed in there with the bats I might have to stop her from trying to get close enough to pet it.

We slowly approached, but whatever roared either made its escape or climbed farther back into the cavern (though I wondered if Dee had the prankster spirit of those high school campers—if so, he also had a poker face to match). This side of the cave housed a maternity colony—a neonatal ward for bats—so we didn't walk all the way in. Roth's bat counters took a separate change of clothes and carried everything out in trash sacks so they wouldn't infect the colony with white-nose syndrome, which can wipe out entire bat colonies.

In the gypsum soil of the cave's periphery Phyllis took us to plant school. I'd never heard the term "gypsiferous" before—it refers to plants that thrive in gypsum soils—but they grew all around: paper flower, gypsum blue-eyes or stout scorpion weed, Stevens' nama, sand lily (the original Velcro; Dee threw a handful at me—it stuck). Eventually we climbed back out, doing a final limbo under those spiky cedar branches. Christina and I looked at each other—we were soaked in sweat and covered with gyp dust and Red Hills Velcro. When we got back into the truck, Chloe whispered, "No cave myotis."

Heading out, we retraced the sweeping loops through the prairie pasture but this time angled east, past epic sandstone pinnacles and rounded buttes that resembled hand-built pots, through another series of sandsage washes, and up a final steep set of jeep tracks. As we climbed out of the truck, the light suddenly and dramatically changed; sunset was near. It was like somebody applied a "land of milk and honey" Photoshop filter so the golden light of a Hudson River School masterpiece would bathe our first glimpses of Schwarz Canyon—a real estate agent's dream scenario. We stood on a chalky gypsum ledge that dropped 150 vertical feet, which strangely you didn't notice until you stood right next to the plunge. The canyon was well hidden; you had to ascend into the bluffs to see it. The walls were about an eighth of a mile across. Dead cedars, living cedars, an aspen-like grove of mulberries, gnarled cottonwoods, and smaller stands of salt cedar filled the draw, and even more cedars climbed canyon walls. Golden eagles wintered here; I could see why—vultures soared on the thermals below us. We didn't hike down—that would be a trip in itself—but I wondered how long it would take to reach the mulberry trees at the bottom.

After basking in the light for a while we drove back toward the house. Along the way we ate fruit from plum brush that grew everywhere, searched the ruins of a mostly vanished general store from the 1800s, looked at one of the most potent natural springs I'd ever seen in Kansas, and toured a field where Dee had put red flags next to individual prairie gentian plants, some showing soft blue bell–shaped blooms. I wondered if they were threatened, but Dee said he marked them "just because they're beautiful."

Finally, we drove through the Salt Fork of the Arkansas one last time. We were filthy and tired and the river was crystal clear as it ran across a pure sand bottom. Dee asked if we wanted to stop and wade. Chloe almost lost her kid passport when she looked at me with "no" in her eyes, but five minutes later she was splashing through the foot-deep current chasing toads and minnows. All my life I've been mildly ashamed of Kansas streams—by standards of the American West they're a muddy, polluted lot—but not the Salt Fork of the Arkansas after a rainy June and July amid tens of thousands of acres of unplowed prairie, cared for by two of the most learned stewards of Kansas land I'd ever met. The experience completely renewed my belief in the last wild places of Kansas.

Driving home around 10:30 p.m., we stopped to gaze at an almost unbelievable show of stars, the kind of scene that makes you want to say, "Behold!" Light pollution has ruined the dark sky in eastern Kansas, but not in the southern Red Hills, even with a slight haze from fires in Canada. The horizon was cavern black; the structure of the Milky Way unrolled like a map illuminated by eerie yellowish zodiacal light.

That's when Chloe saw it: "Daddy look!" We switched on our flashlights and about one hundred feet away a huge awkward bat flopped down on the road next to a small elm tree grasping at a moth and then flew off again in the direction of Schwarz Canyon. Chloe said, "God, it really is a cave myotis."

Once we got back into the car I turned toward her in the backseat, but she cut me off: "I know, I know, Daddy. You don't have to say it."

It's almost impossible to knock Schwarz Canyon, with its delicate gypsiferous plants and bat caves and buffalo wallows, but I couldn't shake the feeling that something was missing there. The prairies were in terrific shape—not showy, but more diverse than anything in the Flint Hills. Big predators were long gone like everywhere else in Kansas. But two species in particular—the prairie dog and the buffalo—seemed to haunt the canyon with their absence. Prairie dogs were at the eastern edge of their historic range in the Gyp Hills but once thrived on native sandsage prairies before poisoning campaigns decimated their numbers in the 1940s and 1950s. Bison had been extirpated since the 1870s.

Here's a quiz. How many head of cattle does the largest contiguous ranch in Kansas run at peak capacity?

Give up? Zero.

In 1999, two years after Strong City's Z-Bar Ranch became America's first Tallgrass Prairie National Preserve, Turner Enterprises, owned by media tycoon Ted Turner, bought the remaining Z-Bar property in Barber County. After tacking on the Double-H Ranch in 2000, it's now the largest contiguous ranch in Kansas, with more than forty-two thousand acres of prairie and a pristine section of the Salt Fork of the Arkansas.

But the Z-Bar is no ordinary Kansas cow farm. They've enrolled more than thirty thousand acres in the lesser prairie chicken recovery program. They've petitioned for water rights to rehabilitate a wetland for migratory birds. They fight red cedar and tamarisk encroachment like an alien war using a custom-made tree-killing machine that you maneuver from a cockpit like a fighter pilot, deftly swinging a wicked beam-mounted circular blade that deli-slices red cedars at their base. But most remarkably, the Z-Bar is completely dedicated to production of Kansas's original cash crop—the buffalo.

The best thing they ever did was to hire Keith Yearout in 2000. At the time, he and his wife, Eva, lived in South Haven with their four children and 140 head of bison. Bringing Yearout on board was like hiring Willy Wonka to run the Chocolate Factory; when it came to bison he had the golden ticket. President of the Kansas Buffalo Association, he lived and breathed bison. Almost overnight Z-Bar became one of the most progressive livestock operations in Kansas. Today the ranch has more than sixteen hundred bison. One in ten buffalo on earth live on a Turner ranch.

With his long braided mustache, Yearout resembles a buff David Crosby. His Kansas street cred is unassailable—he served as a Sumner County commissioner—

but he does things his own way. He prefers to pronounce the "Arkansas" of "Arkansas River" like the name of the state, not the more vernacular "Our-Kansas." His deep knowledge and enthusiasm for buffalo is contagious.

Yearout and I rattled around the prairie in his pickup truck on a blazing July afternoon. We covered so much ground I left with the impression that the ranch was about the size of a small New England state. Yearout is a personable guy and really knows his stuff. As we drove, he gave me a crash course in Z-Bar buffalo husbandry, much of it deeply technical. The basic philosophy, though, is simple. Kansas used to be one big wildly successful buffalo ranch. Restore the buffalo wilderness, prairie dogs and all, and buffalo will prosper.

Ranchers too often think like farmers who own cows, Yearout explained. But the key to success lies in the soil and grass management, so Yearout focuses most of his resources on maintaining native range, fighting invasive cedars, and stabilizing farmed-out soils.

Segue to prairie dogs. Yearout's team mows for them when it rains too much and clears brush on the outskirts of their villages to dissuade predators. Since 2000, prairie dog suburbs on the ranch have sprawled from thirty to five hundred acres, and if Yearout has his way, Z-Bar will become the third Kansas black-footed ferret reintroduction site once they reach the minimum one thousand acres required by conservation guidelines. If given the choice, Yearout told me, cattle and buffalo will spend most of their time on prairie dog towns because burrowing cultivates palatable species like buffalo grass and various gramas.

Hundreds of prairie dogs scattered as we drove through one of the main towns on the way up to the ranch's central plateau above the Salt Fork valley. The serpentine upland escarps steeply on mesa edges, and we stopped frequently to scan for buffalo. They weren't cooperating. The Z-Bar practices rotational grazing, and all sixteen hundred bison were out on a rugged section mostly sequestered from the freshly graded trails we drove on.

Sixteen hundred bison is a big chunk of buffalo meat, and I kept thinking we'd round the bend and suddenly be all *Dances with Wolves*, but Yearout told me it doesn't work that way. Buffalo travel in groups of no more than thirty or so. "Nobody, including buffalo, wants to breathe the dust that a thousand bison would kick up," he said. If a neighbor's cow accidentally gets in with the buffalo, they'll walk it to death. They're constantly on the move. I saw a few shaggy heads perk up above the rise from time to time, but the main herd stonewalled. It was 107 degrees; if I were a buffalo, I knew exactly where I'd be.

Yearout stopped the truck. We walked down to a deep green buffalo wallow filled with nutsedge, exactly like the ones at Schwarz Canyon. An adjacent sump was full of actual mud and hoof prints. Two wallows separated by twenty feet and 160 years. The buffalo didn't reuse the old ones. Maybe the nutsedge confused them or the soil was too compact, but I wondered if they felt the mojo of the ancient bison and avoided the old wallows out of a deference or homage or some buffalo Spidey sense.

Many Red Hills ranches can trace their roots all the way back to the Comanche Pool, the 1.2-million-acre grazing commons that spanned Barber and Comanche Counties in the 1870s and 1880s. Nobody properly owned the land then; members grazed their herds on the open range before fall roundups. The Comanche Pool is gone, but ranchers throughout the region find a wistful solace in its memory.

Heritage precedes endurance, and endurance aplenty is necessary to weather the austerities that Kansas ranchers face. But the geography of nostalgia is useless for mapmaking. I've met ranchers who are wonderful stewards of their histories but seem less able to rise up to more immediate challenges. To sustain the old ways and fragile native ecosystems sometimes you need to throw a crazy tree slicer into the mix and hit back hard against invaders. Operations like the Z-Bar and some of the ranches near Schwarz Canyon are fighting a battle that harkens back to something much older than the Comanche Pool—the lost prairie wilderness itself—but the link between ecosystem and bottom line necessitates a pragmatic approach that favors science and technology over nostalgia. Sometimes I think wild lands management needs more of that in Kansas.

But technology and science are not enough. The Z-Bar is going strong after fifteen years. That wildlife and native ecosystems can be synergistic with commerce is, in fact, prairie justice incarnate—how fitting that the biggest contiguous ranch in Kansas is being given over to the buffalo, never mind they're bound for the table; keystone species like bison have always been fair game for the smorgasbord. But thirty million buffalo once vanished overnight. I hope that fifty years from now the Z-Bar and ranches like it are still around, that they find a way to tap into the heritage that has sustained their neighbors since the days of the Comanche Pool.

Behind ranch headquarters, the Salt Fork of the Arkansas loops north across a cottonwood bottomland where the enormous broken hulks of dead trees are scattered across the flats. Before I left, Yearout drove me to the river's junction with Mule Creek. It was here that the Comanche people, fierce Lords of the Southern

Plains, spent their last winter in Kansas before the treaty of Medicine Lodge forced their exile to the Oklahoma Indian country. We both stood there in the swelter for a few moments. Bobwhites, dickcissels, and cicadas broke the drone of my tinnitus, otherwise it was stone silence. I knew that somewhere nearby, sixteen hundred bison were going through their timeworn rituals. Perhaps their return is as fitting a tribute to Native American heritage in the Red Hills as we can hope for, the last winter of the Comanche reborn as a new spring for the buffalo.

Like the Red Hills, the High Plains also surround the Cheyenne/Arikaree Breaks, although because the region is so small—only thirty miles long and a couple of miles wide—they really don't constitute their own physiographic province. Flanking the Arikaree River and its tributaries in the extreme northwest corner of Cheyenne County, Kansas's other badlands are every bit as stunning and unexpected as the Red Hills.

One big difference is their erosional substrate, the material from which they were sculpted: red sandstone in the Gyp Hills and loess in the Arikaree Breaks. Loess is a fine glacial soil that covers rock gorges, canyons, gravel ridges, and even small mountains lying far beneath the surface of the Great Plains. Loess and other high plains depositional materials are a result of erosion that wore down the Rocky Mountains. Runoff over the course of millions of years deposited this fine slurry across a vast swatch of the Great Plains.

Perhaps even more than in the Red Hills, Native American history echoes across the Arikaree Breaks. Nowhere else in Kansas is the drama of the Indian Wars more evident. A great Cheyenne warrior was killed along the Arikaree, and thousands of Native American survivors of one of the seminal events leading up to the Indian Wars came here to regroup and plan their next move.

Like the Red Hills, the Arikaree Breaks have virtually no public access—only a state-sponsored scenic drive on Kansas Highway 27 north of Saint Francis. Brochures lure would-be travelers with dramatic photographs but then warn them to stick to public roads and stay in the car. Anywhere you set foot is trespassing.

My kind of place.

I was glad to be well provisioned when I pulled into the High Plains town of Saint Francis tucked up against Colorado and Nebraska in the corner of Kansas. It was late Sunday afternoon and everything was closed. I wondered if the blue laws were still in effect. A bored, rowdy group of young guys wearing cowboy getups wandered the parking lot at Cook's Empire Motel. Three of them, propped in lawn chairs on the bed of a Ford pickup filthy with dried mud (bumper sticker: "My other car eats oats"), sang off-kilter harmonies to the strumming of a drugstore guitar. Their buddies made weak attempts to lasso a carpet-upholstered trash can painted like a bull (I thought it looked like a Muppet). I watched them miss thirty consecutive throws from point-blank range. Finally, after first checking to make sure the motel's manager wasn't looking, one of the guys grabbed an armful of warm Coors cans from a trash bag and passed them around. I wished they could have passed me some of the idle time on their hands.

The badlands northwest of Saint Francis—the Arikaree Breaks and Cheyenne Breaks, usually just called the Arikaree Breaks—follow the rugged, treeless draws of the Arikaree and tributaries of the South Fork of the Republican River like a wild border along an otherwise flat landscape engineered for maximal production of row crops. The plains north of Saint Francis are a tableland of tame wheat fields, evenly spaced hay bales, and listing cotton clouds. The sky seems to stretch into the next life. The Arikaree Breaks tear a gash into this vision of tame paradise, a linear crack where the wild past creeps in, a reminder that bison and Indians and the lonesome emptiness of soap weed and antelope once dominated this land.

Unfortunately, nowhere is access more of an issue; public land just doesn't exist here. I planned to drive the Arikaree Breaks Wildlife Trail until a network of county roads took me to the literal northwest corner point of Kansas, a singularity that overlooks the valley of the Arikaree. The geographic datum marking the convergence of states is a public landmark surrounded by private property. A landowner had graciously provided access via his cattle roads to reach the remote location. The guy lassoing the trash can gave me a goofy look as I drove away from the motel. "Thanks for being you," I thought to myself.

The Western State Bank clock read eighty-seven degrees; the sun had robbed this cold spring of its vigor as I approached the river a mile outside of town. The South Fork of the Republican continues into Nebraska, where it meets the North Fork. From there it snakes back south across the state line before angling toward its rendezvous with the Smoky Hill River in Junction City—the birth of the Kansas River. The river wasn't named after the party of Lincoln, but after the Kitkehahki, or Republican, band of the Pawnee. I slowed to read a hand-lettered red metal sign on the edge of the cottonwood thicket: "Cheyenne Indian Prayer Site on north side of republican river here. Dog soldiers and warrior societies perform certain prayers and dances related to the buffalo hunt."

This was the first Native American spiritual site I'd ever seen commemorated on a sign in Kansas, as much lamentation of the fact that our old unwritten history is forever lost as it is a monument to the site. Another reminder is the road north from Saint Francis. This was once harsh buffalo country. At just over thirty-six-hundred feet in elevation, Saint Francis recorded the all-time low temperature in Kansas for August: thirty-three degrees. Today the uplands are devoted to row crops. Except for hapless pheasants always ready to take a suicide plunge across the highway, wildlife in the uplands is minimal. Plum Creek's crystal blue spring-fed waters flowed across waving grass flush from recent rains and snowmelt. Wooden barns and outbuildings of ghost farmsteads weather on in the Cherry Creek valley, where the last bull bison was killed in 1887. Near the breaks the road begins to cut through solid cliffs of loess—some taller than thirty feet—pocked like Swiss cheese with the nests of bank swallows.

Finally, after one last rise of unsustainably lush CRP grass, the Cheyenne Breaks struck like a frontal assault. The ground literally broke out from under me, a deeply crenulated valley plunging three miles across, dissected, dissonant, and western. Unlike the Red Hills, where gypsum and sandstone resist the erosive forces, nothing guards the loess cleavages from the chisel of water and wind that carve the landscape into a devil's garden of yucca, cholla, and prickly pear cactus; prairie rattlesnakes slumbering in deep crevices, dreaming of summer; air redolent with sage. I got out of the car and took in a deep breath of emptiness.

I continued west via county roads toward the breaks on the Arikaree River itself. Incredibly, snowbanks remained in the bottoms of loess crenulations, giving the finger to the eighty-plus degrees of mercury. Little bluestem grew in roadside swales. It doesn't matter whether you're in eastern or western Kansas; wherever bluestem rises, the wild places of Kansas can't be far. Prairie dogs gossiped in the hills lining the descent into the valley of the Arikaree two miles from the tri-state corner. The Arikaree Breaks proper are not as dramatic as the Cheyenne Breaks, but they seem wilder because of the river, which percolates through the sands and makes fleeting appearances in stagnant pools and short jogs of current. In normal flow, the river has no substantive channel and certainly nothing that looks like an island, but nevertheless, a few miles to the west of the Kansas border, an "island" was the site of a battle that is remembered as the last significant act of Indian resistance on the Kansas frontier: the battle of Beecher Island, where the Cheyenne warrior Roman Nose was killed.

At Devil's Gap, a few miles east of Beecher Island, I carefully drove down a jarring jeep trail that crossed the Arikaree and led up into the yucca breaks where Colorado, Kansas, and Nebraska meet. Ghost buildings of failed ranches and telephone lines strung low between glass insulators enhance the abandonment of this place, where time could decide to flow backward and cattle lazing beside the river might shape-shift into bison with the failing light. The sand shores of the river are a spooky ghost yard of dead cottonwoods. Three calves blocked the road with legs folded. I stopped at a respectable distance and waited for the mother to gather them up. Finally, after driving very slowly for three miles, I arrived at a small fenced enclosure in a valley of winds. A golden eagle soared high above.

Someone had painstakingly preserved the history of attempts to pinpoint the exact location where the three states meet. Each of the previous locations is commemorated with its own datum; a historical plaque sits next to a mailbox with a guest book inside. I grabbed a can of Bud Light from my cooler and opened a packet of tuna. It was hard to believe this remote treeless plain was part of Colorado. A rectangular abstraction itself, Colorado boasts three "three corners" and one "four corners," a veritable playground for cartographers. Nothing here evoked ski slopes, or shot glasses adorned with bighorn sheep in mountaintop gift shops, or legalized marijuana. They should give eastern Colorado back to Kansas; we'd know what to do with it.

On my way back to Saint Francis, I went to see an unusual monument to the survivors of the Sand Creek Massacre, one of the most infamous events of the Indian Wars. Following the attack on November 29, 1864, the survivors retreated east toward the sacred buffalo waters of the Smoky Hill. As word spread across the plains, a group of three thousand Indians, which consisted of Sioux bands led by Pawnee Killer and Spotted Tail, the Cheyenne Dog Soldiers, a band of the Northern Arapaho, and the surviving members of Black Kettle's people, joined forces at Cherry Creek close to present-day Saint Francis. They used this base to stage attacks against white outposts. These early skirmishes evolved into the Indian Wars, which would culminate at Wounded Knee in the shadows of the Dakota Badlands a quarter-century later.

Tobe Zweygardt, a Cheyenne County metal sculptor of Volga German descent, created a series of pieces from discarded metal and barbed wire to honor the survivors of Sand Creek. Dedicated to the spirit of survival that held the Cheyenne together in the dark days following the massacre, *Cherry Creek Encampment* is part historical monument, part installation art. I stayed long enough to watch the sunset behind the wrought iron buffalo. Back at the motel later, I fell asleep listening through cardboard walls as my neighbor spent hours talking on the phone to his wife about poisonous snakes.

Native American history and spirituality still resonate in the Kansas badlands. The badlands themselves are microcosmic landscapes reduced to the elemental: earth, wind, water, the memory of fire. Naked and exposed, the wild outweighs the civilized. I think it would be hard to spend much time in the Red Hills or the Cheyenne/Arikaree Breaks and not believe that rivers are sacred. The Medicine, the Salt Fork of the Arkansas, and the Arikaree are old western buffalo rivers. Their importance to life in the badlands is self-evident.

Visit the Kansas badlands if you can. Property lines will stand sentry at every turn, but walk the county roads into the heart of these seldom-traveled dreamscapes. Introduce yourself to the locals. Over many years, the people I have met here are eager to share their stories. I hope more people will open their ranches and farms, sustaining local economies and allowing people to experience these lands that seem close to God, or Manitou, or the big bawdy coyote howl that sounds the welcome to the Big Empty.

CHAPTER EIGHT

Big Springs Go-Go

Lester Bishop had seen American goldfinches mob a feeder before, but after hanging the new Droll Yankee from the gutter and going back inside to his window seat with its unobstructed view of the broad Verdigris River valley, nearly two dozen of the radiant yellow birds were already busy peeling thistles with their stout pink beaks. Weeks can pass before the first finch discovers a new feeder, but on rare occasions they seem to appear immediately, like when you drop a bar magnet into a plate of iron filings—the polarity evoking an instant molecular expression from the fragments, swirling them into the pattern of the field, briefly exposing a page from the blueprint of creation. All morning a steady stream of goldfinches came to the feeder, swarming out of the prairie and the wooded draw of a creek near the house where Lester was born sixty-five years earlier.

Located on the eastern edge of the Flint Hills, the farm had been in Lester's family since the Depression. Don't try to find it. It's swaddled in a deep buffer of private land that spans counties. The uppermost reaches of the Verdigris form an aimless drainage; backwaters and creeks meander along an ecotone where the tame cornfields of the Osage Cuestas yield to the wild magnificence of the Flint Hills. This land plays coyote with outsiders. Once I watched a Ford Explorer disappear around the bend of a prairie mound so symmetrical it could have rolled off the line at a Dolly Madison bakery; thirty seconds later, three cowboys rode around the other side on ponies. We've been turned around in that backcountry for hours— with plenty of gas and not a care in the world, mind you—but dumbstruck by the fractal maze of cottonwood draws and limestone-capped knobs. At dusk, fog lifts from creek bottoms like the smoke of ancient cooking fires kindled in deerskin wikiups. I've smelled bison musk mingled with lilac on a soft May wind. It's a place where you can still lose yourself.

In Kansas there is no cow more sacred than the family farm. Agriculture defines middle America, but it's fickle, prone to the rough edges of the world economy and the depredations of locusts, red spider mites, fungal eruptions, droughts, blizzards, tornadoes, dust storms, and scourges that seem nothing if not biblical, despite the fact that Joseph Smith, founder of the Mormon religion, apparently believed the site of the Garden of Eden was in Missouri just east of the Kansas state line. Small farms, like small businesses, have fewer resources to ride out such vagaries. Even as frontier Americans were funneling west in the nineteenth century, staking claims on what had been disparaged as the Great American Desert, powerful socioeconomic forces gathered that would doom a way of life that was over, for most families, almost before it began.

Make no mistake, if the plowing of the tallgrass prairie and the slaughter of the North American bison herd—the unforgivable American sin—were perpetrated to quilt the prairie states in a fabric of family-owned farms, it was an abject failure. The era of the family farm sputtered out in less than three generations as market forces shuttled the majority of farmers on toward the information age, an age that would take place in suburbs that were heaped over the graves of the old farms, which themselves were planted on the grimacing memory of the prairie, the buffalo, and Native Americans.

Farming brought my own family to the Midwest after the Civil War, but by 1930—only seventy-five years after the Kansas territory opened to pioneer settlement—my grandparents had abandoned their farms for the growing Kansas City metropolis. Today Americans plant roughly the same acreage as a half-century ago, but farms are bigger (the average family farm was 733 acres in 2015) and a growing percentage is corporate owned. The Future Farmers of America, 4-H, and the Grange (the once radical farm "fraternity" otherwise known as the Order of the Patrons of Husbandry) have long been declining. The Jim Brothers sculpture *American Farmer* in downtown El Dorado is subtitled *An Endangered Species*. Even certain native species have been affected. The eastern spotted skunk once ranged widely in the state. It was abundant as late as the 1940s, but is probably extirpated today; there hasn't been a verified sighting in over a decade. Spotted skunks favored chickens, corn, mice, and eggs, all easy to find on diversified farms. DDT might have played a role in its demise, but biologists point to the decline of the family farm as the main trigger.

The Great Plains continues to leak young people. Manning the harvest, once a major community event, is getting tougher on small farms. Sometimes the youngest person in the field is past retirement age. Great-grandparents in their eighties or upwards commonly pitch in. Farming has become an expensive hobby for many who have to rely on nonfarming income to stay solvent. In 2014 there were about two million family farms left in America, down from about seven million in 1935.

It's hard to overstate how this flight from the countryside has influenced the psychology of wild places in farm country. On farms, the land itself was focal, the connections between nature and people obvious. The cultural memory of wild places in the Midwest developed against a backdrop of farm life rather than just through the eyes of explorers or frontiersmen. But today there is more than just physical distance between farm country and the rest of the state. As Kansas band Danger Bob sang, "I wasn't born in a barn. I don't have to live on a farm." I was raised at the edge of the cornfields and walked past cows and horses on a daily basis, but farm life was as familiar as Mongolian reindeer herding or Cambodian rice paddy cultivation.

But this wouldn't last. My search for wild places took me into the heart of farm country. As much as I disdained the barbed wire and no trespassing signs that kept me from exploring my beloved Kansas creeks, rivers, and prairie fragments, the farmers and ranchers who let me search for arrowheads and morels in their spring fields were also usually more than eager to share their enthusiasm about the Kansas outdoors or talk about plans to disc their brome and plant big bluestem. I found I had common ground with people from small towns: We all gave a damn about geography. I lived in a rented farmhouse for a year while I wrote my doctoral dissertation. The smokehouse still smelled of burnt alder and apple wood, and every week during the summer a man came by to look after the soybeans. But the way I viewed family farms and their relationship to the last wild places of Kansas really changed after I started making an annual journey with one of my best friends to the Flint Hills.

Alan Ziegler grew up in Greenwood County, on the Verdigris River, but by the twenty-first century he was splitting time between Singapore and the rainforests of northern Thailand. His job as a tenured geography professor involved fieldwork on tropical hydrology and erosion in rainforest-covered soilscapes. Research took him to Burma, Laos, Vietnam, southern China, Java, Kyoto, Tokyo, and Ethiopia, but Alan didn't brag about his wanderings, preferring to discuss KU basketball, Kansas City restaurants, or nest predation of bobwhites in northeast Kansas. After he finished his PhD at the University of Hawaii, he began to make an annual December pilgrimage back home to Kansas to spend time with his mother, Margaret, and her husband, Robert, and to hunt deer with an old friend of his mother's, Lester Bishop. Lester and Alan had a lot in common, most notably a faint but constant force pulling them back to the Verdigris country.

Lester too had an established life far from his agrarian roots. A well-respected character in Topeka, he required no more than a couple of beers to grab the Dobro and unleash a hoedown on the room. A baron of local bluegrass royalty, he included some of Kansas's most notable musicians, artists, and intellectuals in his circle of friends. His memory was wikipedic and he was one of the best listeners I ever met.

One time he taught us how to roast a deer haunch over hickory coals in an oil drum his brother salvaged at a ranch auction. Lester could tell a Harlan's hawk from an immature red-tailed and distinguish chickadees—black-capped from Carolina—by their call notes (one-two vs. one-two-three-four). He kept the laws of the hunt—as imparted by the Kansas Department of Wildlife and Parks—like the Sabbath. Lester might grit his teeth and smile politely if someone told a story about evading the game warden, but he and Alan followed hunting regulations to the letter. They would debate the fine points of how to use the angle of light to determine exactly when the last shot of the day could be taken. I had never shot a gun in my life, but by the way they talked about deer I imagined them outfitted in wapiti hides, stalking through the reeds with atlatls and bois d'arc quivers.

I don't think Lester ever planned to live in the Flint Hills. After his mother moved to Topeka, the farmhouse fell into a state of willful disrepair—more from respect than neglect. For a time, it served as their hunting lodge. Brown deer blood smeared on the wood floor in the kitchen thinned to a trail of bloody boot prints like a crime scene, drawers and shelves empty save for a collection of stone-sharpened cleavers, three kinds of hot pepper sauce, a refrigerator packed with meat wrapped in clean white butcher paper, boxes of shotgun shells, and a dog that wheezed when it curled up on the rug by the door.

After Lester's mother died, he started taking long weekends at the farm and began to resettle the first floor, bringing down antiques and decorations from upstairs bedrooms that had been sealed off. From the wall above a bed, he took a mounted bobcat that had been sewn onto a backing of delicate green and orange floral chintz and edged with pinking sheers. Taxidermy had frozen its face in a lifeless snarl and robbed luster from the fur, which had faded to the color of soggy graham crackers. This was neither bobcat nor toy—only the claws seemed fully real; one was cracked off, but the others looked ready to tear loose of their froufrou bondage and crawl back outside. Perhaps it sought some prairie set aside for similar unfortunate creatures—stuffed pets, talking bass, reanimated herds of bodiless antlers, families of squirrels sewn into doll clothes and rigged with wires enabling them to enact unnatural scenes like squirrels playing badminton, squirrels sitting on benches waving, squirrels playing poker and smoking cigars. From his kitchen table, Lester could point to the exact spot where his brother shot the cat.

He expanded a bathroom off the kitchen and put a copy of *Trees, Shrubs, and Woody Vines of Kansas* on the toilet tank. He rolled linoleum over the bloodstains in the kitchen, and at night the hearty aroma of hickory smoke funneled up the chimney again. His cousin found a poster from 1980 advertising "Night of the Living Bluegrass." He started cutting spindly cedars for Christmas trees, partly for conservation, since cedars are choking out prairie remnants on the edge of the Flint Hills, and partly because they came with their own ornaments: bagworms. Every shelf was loaded with books.

Outside the house, a small grain silo, barn, and several sheds constituted the homestead. The house itself was a cozy enough box, long ago accreted by the land, formed from sunlight that fed the bur oak groves above the Verdigris from which its timber came. Ancient cedars, with bark that looked like old people, stood like sentinels, blocking the view from the road—instead the house and yard opened up toward the broad valley of the Verdigris River, which ran through the property along a series of north-facing bluffs covered in the same grasses that had been there since the last Ice Age.

The bird feeders at the farm brought in a fantastic array of native birds, like a reanimated James Audubon watercolor. Familiar city birds like starlings and Eurasian sparrows were absent, but brown creepers, Carolina chickadees, nuthatches, hairy woodpeckers, red-headed woodpeckers, grosbeaks, siskins, waxwings, and orchard orioles were regulars. Harriers and Cooper's hawks preyed on the smaller birds.

Between the river and the house, a creek curved through a series of fields before feeding into the river at the edge of the property. Some years the fields lay fallow; other years they hosted winter wheat, soybeans, or grain sorghum. Aging oil wells labored night and day, slowed by rust or arthritis.

But the farm was defined in every way by its one abiding distinction: the river. The name Verdigris comes from the old French, *verte grez*, the "green of Greece," also the common name for copper acetate, which is released when seawater laps against copper or bronze from shipwrecks. Near its confluence with the Arkansas

River in Arkansas (a grand junction of Kansas rivers, the Neosho feeds in a mile to the east), a series of locks and dams allows barge traffic to ply the river all the way down to the Mississippi. After the Cherokee treaty of 1834, the Verdigris was the dividing line between lands of the Osage and Cherokee. It flows over 250 miles from its headwaters near two feeder branches, the South Fork, which rises up in Chase County, and the North Fork, which begins near Big Springs.

Christina and I began to measure time by our annual trips with Alan to visit Lester, sometimes with his parents and other friends. One year we showed up early and nobody was around. Walking alone in the soybean fields and looking up at the soft pastel of grasses slumbering on the river bluffs, I realized why I was beginning to love the place so much: It was still wild. Yes, it had been farmed over, but the bluffs south of the river and the draws that fed the Verdigris concealed the daybeds of deer. Prairie chickens, upland sandpipers, wild turkeys, owls, and coyotes were frequent visitors. The Bishop place was a farm, but the farm hadn't completely uprooted the natural history of the landscape. The Jeffersonian grid was warped.

During that walk, an eerie sensation came over me. I had a conspicuous feeling we weren't alone; there was a presence with us in the fields. At first I thought it was only my imagination, but the feeling stayed with me all day. Subtle but hard to dismiss, it was like meditating with someone in a dark room, aware only of their awareness, or lying down to sleep in a forest where a bear lived.

Goldfinches are masters of minutiae. The males buzz through the air, pursuing their mates and scanning the ground with crackerjack vision. I once watched four goldfinches forage a jeep path next to a wetland slough, sweeping down from tree-top heights to pluck individual seeds no bigger than the head of a pin from the ground. They gather the down from dandelions and milkweed to pad their nests and collect spider silk to adhere them to stems.

A two-inch layer of ice covered the Verdigris, but a hidden pocket of Indian summer warmed the air following two frigid weeks that took care of the mosquitoes. Hung over from his thirty-five-hour commute, Alan had been lying in a patch of brome grass with our daughter, Chloe; they were using their fingers to trace the lines of cirrus clouds that brushed across the deep blue solstice sky like coarse strokes of a horsehair brush. Earlier we had wrestled three turnips almost as big as pumpkins out of the winter garden. They were bigger than Chloe's head. "Has Lester entered one of these things in the fair?" I asked.

"That's what everyone asks," Alan said.

We grabbed four Busch Lites from the kitchen—supplies for our two-mile hike to the river bluffs. It would be my first chance to see the other side of the river. We stopped to change clothes in the barn. Old horse tack was stowed in a corner, tossed together with rusting lengths of barbed wire. Broken barstools and the ruins of a makeshift saloon were the real working equipment of the barn. They had rigged it more for bluegrass music than making hay.

The girls were outside. Christina climbed the creaky ladder of the grain silo that was completely encircled by creeper vines shorn bald by the cold. Lester had told her a barn owl lived in the silo and she hoped to sneak a peek. It wasn't home, but a pile of owl pellets—nuggets of fur and bone regurgitated by the birds after they eat—were scattered at the base. Christina extracted three mouse skulls from the mess. With flesh extruded and little bits of fur still clinging to the cheeks, the horror of the final journey was frozen on their faces. She plopped them in her pocket and looked at Chloe, in pink boots and coveralls, trying to wipe mouse fur and owl sign from her hands. I said, "I'm glad there's a creek on the way."

Dressed in olive hunting pants and a black turtleneck sweater ("The problem with Kansans is they wear too much brown."), Alan led the way. Our route was a horseshoe trail taking us across the creek via a pioneer's ford (near the spot where Alan and Lester once cooked us venison borscht in a black cauldron while we sipped Dewar's from a flask). It wound through a field of green winter wheat, across the Verdigris, up the steep crag of a limestone mound, on up and up, switching back before following a ridge to the crescendo atop the high bluffs south of the river where the Flint Hills meander along the western sky. Finally, the trail recrossed the Verdigris along a stone shelf where herons come to crack mussels (the gravel bar looked like the shambles of a Mardi Gras party).

The closest meander of the creek girdled the roots of an elephantine sycamore, its crenulated core wrinkled, the bark peeling away. Chloe gathered up the spiky balls, telling me they were sweet gum. We crossed on a dry limestone bed studded with crinoids. Hoisting Chloe between us, we shuttled her over a tangle of thorny primrose on the high bank and climbed out into a wheat field.

Suddenly Alan pointed to something moving in the green winter wheat. "Check it out!"

"Opossum?" I squinted to see an animal waddling toward the next bend of the creek as Christina took off running in pursuit. Alan raised his binoculars, still pointing, and yelled, "Armadillo!"

Some people who haven't seen one are very skeptical that armadillos exist in Kansas, so I will clearly and calmly restate my claim here for what it's worth. I stood next to a living armadillo in eastern Kansas, studied all nine of its leathery rings and its two tiny ears that in a stretch might be mistaken for cute. I admired its iguanadine claws and fine armor hairs. Christina, born for the moment, ran as fast as she could across the wheat field and wedged herself strategically between the creek and the animal. I cut off its passage to the north and we converged, closing to within five feet. Just as Alan caught up, it shot between Christina and me and crashed into the forest. Alan continued the chase into the buck brush; the armadillo briefly climbed into the buried cab of a postwar pickup truck before scurrying off toward the Verdigris, the truck apparently not in any shape for a getaway.

Nine-banded Armadillos are expanding their range northward, maybe to escape a rash of bad nicknames down south: possum in a halfshell, poverty pig, Texas turkey. The first armadillo sighting in Kansas was from Osage County in 1909. A second sighting came from Chase County in the 1930s. These were probably escapees, stowed north on freight trucks. But by 1950 specimens were being collected intermittently. Along with fish crows, pileated woodpeckers, ringtails, and painted buntings, armadillos are moving north with warmer winters into what once was probably only an occasional part of their range. Over the past decade I'd counted four or five road-killed armadillos on the highways near Lawrence, but I'd never seen a live one in the state before.

After the armadillo made its getaway, we crossed the last field and picked our way through tall reeds and volunteer ryegrass until we stood on the banks of the frozen river. We held onto Chloe while she slipped around on ice as cloudy as a cataract, frozen and thawed so many times that her ghostly reflection was a warning to us as parents. After eating some wasabi peas and finishing the Busch Lites, we followed Alan along a mountain goat trail up into the bluffs that loomed three hundred feet above. Rose vines suckered my shoelaces loose every few steps. Chloe scrambled like a marmot. As the trees thinned and we approached the top, the trail crossed a spindle of ground with steep drops on either side; a fire-charred blackjack oak kept watch atop the first false summit. The next bluff was an easier hike. It opened into a glade with uniformly spaced oaks growing in the native prairie that rolled out like carpet across the last hill and a long flat plateau punctuated by a dimple knob of rock and grass at the very top.

Amid the wild prairie was a graveyard of deer bones and gut-shot oaks, gnarled, broken, and partially burned. The bones themselves were weathered like driftwood. Alan identified some: scapulas, astragalus, metapodials, mandibles, and others that I can't remember.

Christina was busy checking out the burns on the trees. Some of the oaks were half-dead, the brown leaves of last summer clinging only to certain limbs. "What on earth happened here?" she asked, as if God smote the ridge.

As the girls examined the dried bones and splintered trees, I kept walking toward the final thirty-foot rise, the highest point along this stretch of the Verdigris. I knew there would be a clear unobstructed view of the meandering river, the adjoining fields, the farmhouse, and the deep prairies of the Flint Hills not far beyond. I didn't wait to hear Alan describe how Lester sometimes hauled up the butchered remains of deer, or how an ice storm wounded the old grove, leaving it vulnerable to a prairie fire that got out of hand the next spring.

Instead I was in my own world: I felt the strange presence again. Christina was looking around nervously, and I wondered if she sensed it too or if she was just trying to keep Chloe from falling to a certain death over the side of the steep cliff. Whatever this presence was, it felt old, like an Ozark hill worn down from mountain. I kept walking because I wanted to see the farm in its unity, in one single sweeping view, as if comprehending the wholeness of the place would explain the feeling I'd been having, or else lay it to rest.

I crested the last hill. The farm stretched out before me. In the field west of the creek between the river and the farmhouse, several decades of plowing had started to erase the work of the river's old meanders, but a swath of land perched above the high-water mark of recent floods caught my attention. The stubble of last year's crop—soybeans—was like an ever-changing garment that covered an underlying anatomy of forgotten walls and pathways pressed into the sandy soil. I was no archeologist, but the crescent-shaped disturbance looked like the ruins of a small settlement, like the farm's house and outbuildings had been gently lifted and used as a stamp to brand a mark by the river. An old Indian encampment?

I looked back behind me, and Christina had hoisted Chloe up on her back. She was exhausted. I took one last look at the disturbed spot by the river. In the far distance beyond the farmhouse, the Flint Hills began in earnest, stretching to the western horizon. It would be a magnificent place to live.

Chloe was so tired she had almost fallen asleep standing up, but she refused to put down the two deer femurs. I wanted to tell Alan about what I had seen and what I thought it might mean, but this wasn't the time; it would be better to wait until we could return to the spot alone. We took turns carrying Chloe down the bluff and across the river, making it back to the kitchen in time for a meal of turnip greens in Vietnamese pepper sauce, sweet potatoes, venison, and a sample of roasted black bear one of Lester's friends shot in New Mexico. As we ate, I wanted to confess my theory that the farm was built on an old Indian village, but the most reasonable explanation was that the imprints in the field and spooky vibe were nothing—at least nothing worth mentioning.

Many people believe that Kansas has no culture, no worthwhile history, and that the proof is our lack of architectural monuments. We certainly have nothing like the Parthenon or the Great Pyramid of Giza. But even in Egypt and Rome, the "culture" is buried in trash heaps behind these architectural marvels or, more commonly, in regular neighborhoods and farm fields. For every museum piece plucked from the tomb of a pharaoh, a hundred others were dug from nameless trenches and unheralded sandbars. By this standard Kansas history scores well; our troves of cultural debris have been combed to good extent, exposing a long, intriguing history of habitation that goes back beyond the last Ice Age.

A great place to study it is the Kansas State Historical Museum in Topeka. A few months after we returned from our hike to the high bluffs above the Verdigris, Chloe and I spent a rainy Saturday afternoon checking out the museum with Tim Hindman and his son Sam. The exhibits proceeded chronologically. You could literally walk along a timeline of Kansas history, beginning with the earliest archaic peoples who speared wooly mammoths, progressing through the Woodland Period and the Kansas City Hopewell, before continuing to European immigration, Bleeding Kansas, the dust bowl, and finally to the era of punk rock on the prairie. Yeah!

We were going to quickly run through, but while Tim took a cell phone call and Sammy plunked himself down in the middle of the floor, declaring the whole place a bore, a small collection of finely fluted arrowheads caught my attention. Each was no more than an inch long, seemingly better suited for hunting mice than deer. Beside the arrowheads, a full-sized replica of a grass lodge built by the Wichitas filled an entire room. It could easily sleep a dozen. The Wichitas lived to the south and west of the Osage when Francisco De Coronado encountered them in the 1500s. Like other tribes in the area, they gardened and relied on buffalo and deer. The Wichitas also built hunting shelters stretched from buffalo, deer, and elk hides, but in their permanent villages, slough grass and big bluestem were the primary construction materials for massive lodges. When Chloe and Sammy made a break for the 1950s and Tim dashed off to chase them, cell phone fumbling, I got that funny feeling again that I'd felt back on the Verdigris.

Moving from the lodge back to the tiny arrowheads, I carefully examined the site map describing where they were found. I wasn't sure I was reading the map right, but it looked like the majority were from sites along the upper Verdigris. Thinking back to my perch atop the river, on that highest mound, I retraced my memory of the faint impression above the river bank, this time imagining a giant hand taking three or four of the large grass mounds and stamping the earth with them. This would certainly describe something similar to what I remembered.

Then squinting carefully at the fine print on the map, I read the name of the archeology site that produced the points: Bishop.

Was this the same Bishop? It had to be—the spot on the map was exactly where the Bishop farm was located. Was the disturbed rise I saw literally the remains of an old village site? Had there been other families besides the Bishops who had called that spot by the river home, each choosing a site slightly farther out from the bank, like planets with concentric orbits? Was the farm one of the many powerful wild places in Kansas that drew people back generation after generation or was the presence not human at all, but a part of the draw of the place itself?

I wasn't sure, but I knew I was starting to rethink my ideas about why people built such strong connections to family farms. Alan was out of contact doing field-work in Thailand, but I left him an email asking if he knew anything about the exhibit at the museum and what, if anything, Lester knew about the people who apparently had also called his farmstead home.

A month later Alan returned my email. As I suspected, the artifacts at the Kansas State Historical Museum were from the farm, from the same fields near where I'd noticed the disturbance along the river. Several different sites had been excavated by professional archeologists, and in the 1970s Lester's farm was elected to the National Register of Historic Places because of the cultural significance of the finds there. Alan said he had told me some of this when we were in college, but at the time I didn't know or care enough about archeology or Native American history to pay attention. Alan said most of the sites were from the Woodland Period. This was a long time before the Wichitas were building grass lodges in the vicinity, but since the Woodland cultures of the Verdigris valley quite possibly were ancestors of the more modern Kansas tribes, it was possible their lodges would have been similar.

I was impatient to get back to the Flint Hills. Fortunately, Alan planned to visit in November, several weeks earlier than usual, and for our annual visit Lester planned to take us to see two unusual landmarks that were virtually unknown outside the area. Archeological evidence tied these sites to the same cultures that had used the Bishop property a thousand years earlier.

Foraging patterns might best describe how goldfinches find new feeders almost before they are installed. During the breeding season the birds whistle through the air like fighter pilots. I've mistaken them for hummingbirds. But when the bright males shed the last of their regal breeding plumage in autumn, they loosen up, put down their territorial spats, and join together in small flocks to make a short winter migration. These birds generally don't fly across the Gulf of Mexico to Cancun like many small songbirds. Goldfinches that winter in Kansas tough out the cold by ranging widely in search of the dried seeds of sunflowers, compass plants, purple coneflowers, and ragweed, or better yet, plastic tube feeders. Maybe they recognize farms for what they are: thistle feedlots. Goldfinch feeders abound in farm country. Each flock has a few warriors; when they find a new feeder, the other birds follow their cue and descend in force, appearing to come out of nowhere.

The jumping-off point to the Big Open lies just beyond the first cattle grate west of the Bishop farm. A thin road that follows the Verdigris to its headwaters before fording the spine that divides its drainage from the Neosho's takes travelers into a realm of unfenced aboriginal prairie that stops time in its tracks. More animal trace than road, it should be one of the seven wonders of the prairie, winding along bluffs and knobs through Greenwood and Chase Counties, crossing under the Kansas Turnpike by the Bazaar cattle pens (where caged cattle can still watch wild antelope wandering freely). The surrounding pastures are thick with prairie chicken leks. On hot summer days whippoorwills and nighthawks sleep right in the middle of the road. Once we found a snapping turtle almost as big as a manhole cover walking beside the gravel, looking back over its shell like a hitchhiker.

Indian summer was in full blossom. A south wind brought parcels of warm air up from the Texas hill country. Our destinations were a remote hill that figured prominently in the technological history of the upper Verdigris, and Big Springs, a large spring at the head of the river. Both spots were buried deep back in private lands, but we didn't stop to get permission. Everyone here knew Lester.

A mile after we forded the first stream (the water lapped the tops of the wheel wells) Lester ditched the gravel for a faint jeep track in the prairie. Terra firma in the rearview, we jarred our bones over every hillock toward a high point of land accented by a windmill spinning so fast it overfilled its cattle trough. The vista afforded us a glimpse into a world of hills that all looked the same to me, but Alan and Lester both pointed out one particular barbed hill at least three miles away. A deep ravine with no clear passage blocked our way. Lester schemed about how to coax the Explorer down and over; I prayed our plan would be to get out and walk. Lester asked Alan, "Down along the fence over there, to the right?"

The fence was 250 feet below us. The most reasonable way for the Explorer to descend was end over end.

Alan said, "You did this last time. We got up to the pumping station and had to retrace our steps."

Christina nudged me. I looked out her window straight down into the ravine. An old pickup was crushed like a beer can at the bottom.

Somehow Lester and the truck bushwhacked through the grass—upright for the duration—with Chloe bucking in her car seat like she was in the rodeo. According to plan we turned right at the fence, wiped out a gigantic ant hill, turned right again, and then came to another fence. Dead end.

Alan whispered diplomatically, "Told you."

Lester backtracked up the hill, gunning the engine to the summit. I looked out across the valley toward the knob we aimed at; it didn't look any closer. Back on the main road we crossed the ravine (second bath for the wheel wells) and found another set of ruts leading to a windmill. I figured we were back where we started, but Lester said, "This is it."

As we drove up to this windmill the hill was noticeably closer and I saw a trail heading in the right direction. This *was* it. The wind was so strong it shredded Lester's Jayhawk antenna flag. He put the Explorer in gear and we slowly approached the volcano-shaped mound (there are no volcanoes in the Flint Hills). Parking at its base, Lester said, "In the sixties and seventies archeologists worked their way across most of the sites along the Verdigris, cataloging what the old farmers had in their attics, rediscovering the old sites and doing fieldwork."

This was one of the important ones, a quarry for stone that was used to make tools like arrowheads and scrapers—a "Flint Hill" in the proper sense. The top was a barren pile of rocks. Lester explained that chert deposits were weathered and exposed on the mound. The tensile qualities of the rock were apparently amenable to creating fine tools. This natural landmark had been a destination for Native American tribes as far back as the early Christian era. The quarry stones were worked on site into blanks that could be carried home for further refinement.

Alan asked in a voice so quiet I had to lean toward him to hear, "Lester, what made them think that some of the Indians came from hundreds of miles away?"

"Shells and coral."

The wind, now a force, almost ripped the Explorer's rear passenger door off when Christina opened it and Chloe tumbled out of her car seat and began sailing like an orange and white kite down the hill toward a little creek. The hill had a great view of the river in three directions. Lester and Alan and I spread out along the mound to pick up rocks. Alan tossed me a finger edge of shiny white chert, lightly fluted on one side. I picked up a salmon flake of flint, fluted on both sides with a flat base where a larger striking stone had cleaved it from the mother rock.

I'd heard of Pipestone National Monument, a Minnesota quarry site that was a source for pipestones dating back a thousand years or more. Like Pipestone, this hill was a source of raw materials for the technologies of the time. It's big too, almost half the size of Pipestone. But almost nobody had ever heard of it and fewer visited.

The wind blanketed all sound—I could see Lester and Alan talking and Christina yelling at Chloe to put up her hood, but I only heard wind, a lonely west Texas wail, cutting everyone off from me even though they were in plain view. The presence, however, was all around. Every rock I picked up, every tiny translucent flake, every scraper-sized half-tool, even the bigger fist-sized chunks of flint, showed human handiwork. Generations of people had left their mark here; grasping a fist of flint was like shaking hands with one of the ancients.

Chloe had always been a good hiker, but the wind and tall grass had taken their toll; she filibustered at the creek, and Alan and I had to walk down and haul her back to the Explorer. We looped around the quarry hill and negotiated the pasture trail back up to the main road. Lester drove just a short distance until turning onto another unlikely trace on a ridge that led farther out into the emptiness. It widened into a dirt road that descended into the Verdigris valley. We drove past alternating fields of soybean stubble and black willow until we reached the river—really a creek at this point, and not very wide at that.

One of the first things I learned about Alan was that his father's family once owned the headwaters of the North Fork of the Verdigris. Alan pointed it out as we drove, but Lester was taking us to the spot often considered the river's actual source: Big Springs. Clear and cold, Flint Hills springs are legendary for their purity, and since most of the region was never plowed, the original hydrology of the landscape has been preserved, so that many ancient springs still run much as they did in centuries past.

We left the car where a foot trail joined the road and hiked in toward the site. It was getting colder, but the valley protected us from wind in the river bottom, and for the first time we could hear the sounds of the land around us. Great horned owls called in the distance. Females would be searching for nesting sites as males gerrymandered their districts after a long summer and fall spent hunting and building up strength for the winter mating season. This was the last hike in of the day, and though I'm sure Chloe still had plenty of energy, she conned Alan into hoisting her up onto his shoulders for a ride.

Entering the river on the arc of a tight curve, the spring was prolific enough to scour a deep hole in the creek bottom; discarded Styrofoam worm cups floated in a watercress garden below the biggest hole, broken folding chairs and Stroh's beer cans evidence of summer nights spent fishing for flatheads. Everyone but Chloe was exhausted by the time we made it—as much from fighting the wind at the quarry as from walking to the spring. Alan suggested we sample the spring water— he'd survived several bouts of giardiasis—and took a small taste.

I said to Lester, "If the quarry or this spring were anywhere else, there would be weekend crowds for sure."

Alan added, "If they were on public property."

"Well, right," I said. "But almost nobody even knows about this spring besides a few fishermen. How many people do you think have been here in the last half-century. A dozen?"

When the few farms in the area dug their wells or joined rural water districts, I wondered if the old spring had been forgotten. Lester chuckled at the question, though, and said, "This spring isn't known for water, but it used to be one hell of a party spot. They called it Big Springs Go-Go."

"You used to party here?" I asked.

"Not me. People drove down from the city to light bonfires and drink beer. Every once in a while someone would get their car stuck and the ranchers would come haul it back to the road."

A coyote howled in the distance and soon another answered in kind. Nothing in the vocabulary of this landscape suggested a Go-Go. Maybe a no go. Beyond the borders of Emporia, Manhattan, and Wichita, the Flint Hills have never been heavily populated, but for centuries people have gathered at wild places, many of which not only still exist, but also, to some extent, are still wild. Even when you're alone out here, you're never really by yourself.

For some time Alan and I had been planning to canoe the entire Kansas River, and on the drive back from the spring we discussed moving the schedule up, shooting for the next year when his current NSF grant ended and he could take some time off. Lester carefully steered along the prairie ruts in the fading light; they had driven these paths a thousand times but still, at just the right angle, they were unfamiliar, new.

I was satisfied. In a small way I could read the rhythms of this place, the seasons of habitation, the comings and goings of the people, of the different civilizations. The enduring wild places and natural landmarks here, like all over Kansas, still subtly called out to people who knew how to listen, who could weave themselves into the story of the landscape. I hoped I had left a little of my own presence here, to join the others whose bodies are scattered and forgotten in the prairie, but whose dreams are still stacked like cordwood between Lester's house and the Verdigris.

The North American bird migration was finished for another year; bald eagles and juncos had replaced turkey vultures and orioles at John Redmond Reservoir twenty-five miles away. Soon winter would descend on the prairie and late-blooming asters would recede into hibernation along with the many living things that made their home among the grasses—everything except the wind and the river. Of course the river is alive, but its life unfolds slowly, over centuries. The life of the Verdigris River has interconnected with the life of Alan and his parents and Lester Bishop. I fancy that at some time in the past, the river—part of the Great Mystery—started calling to Lester's ancestors in Ireland. It was only an itch at first—perhaps generations ignored it, staying put among the Gaelic hills of County Westmeath and the barony of Kerricurrehy. But the river persisted, and eventually his great-grandparents sailed for America. Their descendants arrived in Kansas in time for Lester to be born here sixty-five years ago, to take part in a role designed for him back before the grasses came to these hills, before the bedrock heaved up from beneath the ancient sea.

South of Emporia, a cedar break hides the remains of a small cemetery. Most of the people buried there were born in the area, but some left for places like Petaluma, California; Evergreen, Washington; Edinburgh, Scotland; and the suburbs of Kansas City and Wichita. Brought home to rest, their bodies physically are like exotics, weeds, no longer native, like Russian thistle or salt cedar. I'm not saying this is a bad thing. Lester took the same path, as did Alan. But Lester was called back and he established a rhythm so close to the land that his very body is built from the energy of deer, prairie chickens, giant turnips, and sandhill plums that grow on the good water of the Verdigris. Death will bring no alchemy. When he merges back into the earth nothing will change, his body already being the land itself.

The loss of the family farm is a multifaceted cultural phenomenon that means different things to different people, but what I never understood (and as an outsider, will never truly penetrate) is the loss of a deep belonging, a personal connection to a single place. Some private property is private like a Native American religion: esoteric, given by the Great Mystery for a time to a group, a family, even to a single person. I could honor a sign that read, "Posted: No trespassing on this land for four generations or until we have completely digested its secrets and wonders, died in its hills, given back our bodies and the ways we have learned for the next four generations to discover." Such farmers don't own the land, it owns them, and being forced to walk away from such strong connections must bring an unquenchable grief.

At least one birder, not in the mainstream of ornithology, believes there is another theory about how goldfinches find feeders: they don't. The feeders call them in, or the act of placing the feeders triggers a ripple in some morphogenetic field that goldfinches understand. Do the birds find the feeders, or do the feeders find the birds, and who would be qualified to tell the difference except the birds themselves? And they're not talking.

CHAPTER NINE

Bardo on the Kaw

If the human race has one common denominator, it is hatred of head winds.
John McPhee

Between the western and eastern city limits of Topeka, first light and sunrise, river miles 0 and 171, and two stream banks veiled in a thick shroud of ice fog, Alan Ziegler and I mindfully ferried my seventeen-foot green Old Town canoe around logjams that rose up like ghosts in the swirling brown water. For years we'd planned to float the entire Kansas River, especially the wildest section that crossed the Flint Hills. It was supposed to be my chance to slow down for a change—to three miles per hour—but now even that seemed fast.

The story of the Kansas or Kaw River is inseparable from the story of the Kansa or Kaw People. The 732-mile stream originates in the foothills near Limon, Colorado, and spills into the Missouri at Kansas City, but is named Kansas only for its final 172 miles, from the point near Junction City where the Republican River anoints the currents of the Smoky Hill. Those first 560 miles, the miles of the Smoky Hill River, belonged to the buffalo; the last 172 miles belonged to the Kansa and ran through the heart of their nation. Their villages vanished more than 160 years ago but the river keeps their stories.

In its first miles, the river crosses the Flint Hills, the last great dominion of the tallgrass prairie. At a humble pace of three miles per hour it rolls past Junction City, Fort Riley, Ogden, Konza Prairie, and Manhattan. Emboldened by a stiff drink from the Big Blue River it then dilates and winds through the small prairie hamlets of Saint George, Wamego, Belvue, and Maple Hill. By the time it skiffs Buffalo Mound on the north, the Kaw starts to resemble its mother, the Missouri. Entering the "Breadbasket of the Nation," in the language of 1950s newsreels, the lower Kansas flows through Topeka, Tecumseh, Lecompton, Lawrence, Eudora, DeSoto, Bonner Springs, Edwardsville, and finally Kansas City, which was named not after the state, but the river. Along the way it gathers its tributaries to present to the great Missouri: the Smoky Hill, the Republican, Wildcat Creek, the Big Blue, the Vermillion, Mill Creek, Shunganunga Creek, the Delaware, the Wakarusa, Soldier Creek, Turkey Creek, and many others.

Once much abused, this river—which couldn't be gunned into oblivion like the buffalo or plowed up like the prairie—became the sewer of a rising agricultural empire and the towns that served it. In the late 1800s and early 1900s the offal of slaughterhouses; raw sewage from towns and cities; every agricultural compound that could be sprayed, spread, or splattered from the hind end of a John Deere; and enough fecal matter to smell clear from the moon were all dumped into the river. Riparian borders—wild groves of cottonwood, sycamore, pecan, willow, pawpaw—were cleared so that the riverbanks, no longer buttressed by the forest's web of subterranean roots and fibers, threw themselves into the roil during high water, making the river turbid, shallow, and wide.

After the flood of 1951, which inundated Kansas City's West Bottoms, the federal government built eight flood control reservoirs that radically changed the fluvial dynamics of the river. Seasonal floods no longer recharged sloughgrass wetlands in the alluvial floodplain. Dams blocked blue catfish, flatheads, pallid sturgeon, and American eels from reaching their traditional spawning grounds. By the 1960s, after a century of pollution, the Kansas River was a toxic dump. Catfish weren't safe to eat. State and local agencies issued fish consumption advisories. Grandmothers who as children swam the shallows and skated frozen backwaters began to warn their grandchildren: "Stay away from that river!"

The horrors of change weren't all ecological. In the early 1800s, the Kansa, a culture entwined with the history of the river for centuries, suffered an encroaching wave of tragedy and chaos that would reach a climax in the villages of three traditionalist leaders along Mission Creek, at the mouth of their river, the Kaw. Every day thousands of people drive by the scene of this drama without realizing that an epic struggle once unfolded there. The Kansa built dozens of villages in the Kaw Valley. Ruins of their earth lodges persisted well into the twentieth century. Faint rings in unbroken prairies near the river still bear witness to where earth lodges once stood. Occasionally new ones are discovered—an amazing connection to a lost time.

The Kansa weren't the only people whose history haunted the Kaw. An eccentric French wannabe aristocrat and rake, infamous for deserting his post and taking up with other men's wives, might have laid eyes on the river before 1700. In 1724 he led a remarkable expedition deep into the homeland of the Kansa and witnessed firsthand the Kaw Valley when it was yet a Garden of Eden.

These stories, and until only very recently the river itself, were largely forgotten. But for years they compelled me to undertake a complete float of the river. In my lifetime the wild essence of the Kaw had rebounded. People are usually surprised to learn that the river is much cleaner today than at any time in the last 125 years. A through-float of the Kaw was number one on my list of trips into the heart of wild Kansas.

Alan Ziegler was one of only two or three people with whom I could conceive of doing a trip like this, but there was a problem—location. Alan lived in Thailand. Once a year he made a three-week trip back home in early December when ice usually covered the river. It would take a rejection letter from half a world away to begin a sequence of events that eventually made it possible for us to push our canoe into the cold water of the Republican River one hundred feet away from Kaw River mile 0.

The Kansa (pronounced by going light on the "n" of "Kon-za"), or Kaw people, were living near the confluence of the Kansas and Missouri Rivers in 1601 when Juan de Onate, a Spanish conquistador known for chopping off the left feet of his Native American captives, encountered them (but probably not the river) during one of Spain's several futile attempts to find a city paved with gold in the grasslands of Kansas. The tribe's shape-shifting name, which has suffered more than 120 different Spanish, French, and English spellings, probably means South Wind People. The prevailing southerlies that blow across the prairies near the Kaw are a defining feature of the landscape, as much a part of the region's circulatory system as the river itself—the name is truly hyper-local.

By 1600 they had split from their fellow Dhegiha-Siouans, the Quapaws, Omahas, Osages, and Poncas, all of whom eventually migrated west, probably from the Ohio River country. When French explorers started trading with the Kansa for furs, they were concentrated at the "Grand Village des Canzes," in present-day Doniphan County, Kansas, on the Missouri River. The Kansa were the most powerful tribe of northeastern Kansas by then. They had intricate customs and their own language, even though the entire tribe numbered around fifteen hundred people, less than the population of my high school. The French were astonished to see little girls younger than ten carrying one-hundred-pound loads for great distances. Work roles were gender specific. Women planted, cooked, and butchered the kill. Men hunted and defended the tribe from their traditional enemies, the Osage and Pawnee. The men went naked (except for a small breech-cloth) year round, even in the middle of winter, and bathed in the waters of the Kaw no matter how cold it was.

After brief encounters with the Spanish, the Kansa established close trading relationships with French coureurs de bois, freewheeling forest runners who lived in close proximity with the tribes and often took Indian wives. One of them, Éti-enne de Veniard, Sieur de Bourgmont, was one of the strangest characters ever to set foot in the Kansas prairie wilderness. Think Keith Richards without the guitar or the heroin. Or maybe with the heroin. No one could have been more different from the sturdy and prudent American pioneers who followed him to the Kaw River valley 150 years later. He fancied himself an aristocrat and took on major airs with everybody he met. He slept with other men's wives. He despised authority. In the late 1600s he was effectively exiled to North America after being accused of poaching on the royal hunting grounds of the Monastery of Belle-Etoile in Normandy, a serious offence. He deserted his command at Detroit after an In-dian attack (fellow deserter Betellemy Pichon got lost in the wilderness, shot and ate a member of the starving party, and was later captured and sentenced to have his head broken with a rock until he died).

Deserting might have been an easy choice for Bourgmont because the husband of his lover, Madame Tichenet, had just discovered their affair. Bourgmont lived on the lam for a while, relying on his charm to form a close relationship with the Mis-souri tribe. He took a Missouri wife and explored the river named after the tribe as high up as the Niobrara. He named the Platte River, and was probably the first European to see the Kaw River. By the time he published his field notes—"Exact Description of Louisiana, of Its Harbors, Lands and Rivers, and Names of the Indian Tribes That Occupy It, and the Commerce and Advantages to Be Derived Therefrom for the Establishment of a Colony," a name that sounds like a patent to me—Bourgmont was back in good graces with the French government.

In 1720, France decided that a more formal relationship with the plains tribes would be necessary to keep Spain away from its fur trade on the prairies. They also wanted to build a fort near the mouth of the Kaw River to help establish a peace treaty with the Padoucahs, a badass plains tribe that made life miserable for the Kansa. With his knowledge of the Missouri River, Bourgmont was the perfect man for the job, but by 1720 he was back in France, living a soft and opulent life with a new wife and family, and scheming ways to elevate his title. But his time in America wasn't finished. Soon he would find himself at the "Grand Village des

Canzes," preparing for a crazy road trip across the prairie before there were roads
or road trips.

Alan Ziegler had procured an impressive series of grants in his years as adjunct
professor of geography at the University of Hawaii, but anticipating a three-month
lull in his schedule, he emailed me to ask if late October or early November was a
good time to be on the river.

For years we'd kicked around the idea of floating the Kaw and the navigable
portions of the Arkansas and Missouri along the Kansas border. But my problem was time. I had a young daughter and a rewarding but demanding job that I
loved—at best I could only cobble together enough time to float the Kansas River.
October usually was the perfect month for the Kaw: warm days and nippy nights,
bald eagles migrating south to replace the vultures, nobody on the river.

About a month before the trip I started working on our equipment. Instead
of taking separate boats—a solo canoe and a kayak—Ziegler and I could make
good time paddling tandem. My longest day trip had been only about twenty miles.
Ziegler and I would need to cover that much and more every day to make it to
Kansas City in the week I planned to take off work.

Unfortunately, we soon had a big problem. The day Alan stepped off his plane
from Thailand it began to rain in the upper Kansas basin. Squalls swept back and
forth like an automatic carwash. The upper tributaries of the Big Blue River went
crazy out of their banks. Tuttle Creek Lake, the long flood control aneurism on the
Big Blue, steadily rose.

The Big Blue River is the Kaw's largest tributary; after it joins the main river
the Kansas instantly doubles in volume. Sometime in the 1790s the Kansa abandoned their Grand Village des Canzes and built a new capital, the Blue Earth Village, near the mouth of the Big Blue River. Not far away from the Smoky Hill
buffalo country, the nearby prairies and rich alluvial forest had enough game to
easily support the 130 lodges of Blue Earth Village that were strung out along a thin
peninsula of land between the Big Blue and the Kansas.

The village was like a commune of earthen geodesic domes. The lodges were
circular, with a pole frame and rafters that supported an exterior covering of skins,
bark, mats, or grass. A caulking of heaped soil provided a weatherized seal around
the base. A hole in the roof allowed smoke from cooking fires to escape. Wooden
platforms lined interior walls for storage. Two or three families lived in each lodge.

Privacy was nonexistent. Sometimes at night, with no warning, warriors would burst in and start beating on the lodge pole, announcing the start of a Dog Dance. Fires would be kindled. Alcohol wasn't involved, but it was nonetheless a serious party that could go on for days. It completely freaked out the white people.

After May planting, the tribe abandoned the village for a summer bison hunt along the Smoky Hill that lasted until late August. Nature took care of the gardens in their absence—sometimes they completely died, sometimes they didn't. The Kansa didn't sweat it either way. When food ran low in winter they sucked it in and fanned out over the Kaw Valley and east to the Missouri to hunt beaver, deer, elk, turkey, and bears and let their horses eat the bark of tender young cottonwoods.

The day before our planned departure the Big Blue was releasing sixteen thousand cubic feet of water per second, eight times the normal volume. The entire Kansas River basin was soaked, and more rain was in the forecast. I had to make a tough call. We couldn't push the start date out any longer and still float all the way to Kansas City, but paddling out into the flood would be insane. The toughest waters on the river are usually Class 0—no rapids—but now, in addition to standing waves that approached Class 3 below the Bowersock Dam in Lawrence, the river was booby-trapped with cottonwood and sycamore missiles that could easily take out a canoe. We would have to wait three days and forfeit our dream of making it all the way to Kansas City in a single float. Instead we'd salvage what we could and turn our trip into a through-float of the upper Kaw, the wildest section of the river between Junction City and Lawrence. Two days before our new start date, the rains let up. We had a tentative go.

Still, conditions were dicey. The rain had ended but the river kept rising. In Lawrence the Kaw was almost a half-mile wide, and all of the sandbars—our campsites—were submerged. But my biggest concern was Tuttle Creek Lake. On day two of the float we would pass the mouth of the Big Blue River. The flow would go from two thousand cubic feet per second to over eighteen thousand. A giant eddy lake had formed behind the mouth of the Big Blue. The Kaw flowed backward for almost a mile; we would have to navigate a formidable whirlpool.

Everyone was giving me advice. When I called the Junction City Police Department to let them know we'd be leaving our car in the park overnight, the matronly dispatcher said, "Honey, you boys be careful. If your boat gets caught in a whirlpool you'll never get out. We've lost a couple people down there over the years."

"How many years?" I asked.

"Twenty-eight."

An IT guy I knew who wore thigh-high leather moccasins and paid actual money to learn how to read a wild animal's emotions from its tracks told me, "I'm telling you, there is a lot of fear in those woods."

But I knew Alan and I would be capable on the river; I had hundreds of miles of day floats under my belt and he was used to kayaking the Mekong River near the Chinese border with Thailand. I called the night before our departure and asked him what he thought. How difficult would this float be with the Kaw doing its best imitation of a pissed off Mississippi?

"Duck soup," he said. High water didn't faze Alan. He'd come halfway around the world for this. Flood or no flood, we were going to launch our boat on the upper Kaw the next morning before sunrise.

Thursday morning was cold and rough as we drove to the end of two dirt ruts that bottomed out next to the banks of the Republican River in Junction City. A twenty-four-hour sentry posted on a lookout over the junction of the Republican and Smoky Hill Rivers guarded the main entrance to Fort Riley, the old home of Custer's 7th Cavalry and now headquarters of the Big Red One. The wars in Iraq and Afghanistan had turned the fort into something of a ghost town with so many troops deployed. As I changed into river boots and started to throw gear from the car onto the grass, a loud explosion somewhere out on the reserve scared up a flock of pigeons roosting under the bridge.

I was depressed and worried. Even here at the start the Kaw was a swollen torrent. I wasn't sure there would be sandbars for camping. I felt like throwing up. I'd eaten an omelet of fake eggs, roasted Anaheim peppers, and American cheese at 5:30 a.m. We had spent the night sleeping in the back of my car in the parking lot of the Goodnow House Museum in Manhattan. I wasn't sure whether the next loud blast was ordnance or my stomach.

We dragged all the stuff down to the river, and Alan got busy stashing everything in three large blue wet sacks. We carried two sleeping bags, a green dome tent that I bought in 1990 for a bike ride from Seattle to San Francisco, two hand-held Garmin GPS units, three paddles (green, red, and silver), a first aid kit, hand sanitizer, a clutch of sandalwood incense, a $3.99 lighter, one roll of toilet paper in a Ziploc bag, a pocketknife, a case of bottled water, two green life jackets, two blaze orange vests, roasted almonds, green apples, protein bars, cranberry raisins, no-sodium-added tuna in cans, one can opener, and a half-dozen bagels. Unlike

Lewis and Clark, who visited the Kaw twice, we carried no rations of alcohol. Fog stole our view of the junction from the put-in; visibility was less than twenty feet.

A Carolina wren scolded our activities. I don't know if it was my stomach, the fog, or the big cottonwood logs flowing past us in the high surf, but I felt woozy. Alan didn't say anything; he packed and repacked the boat, not worried about the river, I suspected, but about my resolve to get this thing started. I dug around in the packs for some Tums and spent way too long deciphering exactly how we would navigate the first twenty yards of the float from launch to the cement pillars under the bridge. Finally, Alan waded a little bit into the water, cleaned the mud off his boots and looked up at me: "Are we going to hang out here all day?"

I waded into the thin stand of sandbar willow and took my place in the stern as Alan pushed us out into the current. The canoe broke free of land, and I grabbed the tie rope and fastened it behind me. We were on the river. An island of willows and scouring rush appeared suddenly out of the fog. We paddled left, and the nose of the boat gently swung around. We had entered the current of the Smoky Hill, the ancient buffalo river. We were on the Kaw, Kaw-ward, Kawterized, Kawnivores! Two crows flew by and yelled back over their shoulders, "Kaw, Kaw!" It was a great feeling.

In its first twenty miles the Kansas River felt like a small prairie stream with a kingfisher on every logjam. Cottonwood, sycamore, and willow were the most common trees along the entire river, but in its first miles, willow dominated except where limestone camel humps came down and injected their prairie-capped red cedar and oak-hickory forests among the bottomland species.

Every few minutes we heard the blast of artillery from the fort, a vivid reminder of a war far away from the prairie. A few logs drifted past and one struck our boat, which called me to attention. Even if the river doesn't look treacherous, it can always be deceiving. You afford it the same kind of respect as a long lonely stretch of highway in the middle of the night. Stay awake! On the river *you* are your own worst enemy.

The water, usually knee-high, was well above six feet deep and the color of Earl Grey tea, or possibly Neosho-brown, the Osage name for the central Kansas river that means "Water-Like-the-Skin-of-a-Summer-Cow-Wapiti."

I was poor company those first few beautiful miles. Near Ogden, the serene crust of fog finally lifted. Orange prairie occasionally gave way to cultivated fields. We passed a cutbank with a row of corn on top that looked like skeletons ready to leap into the river with the next heavy rain. The channel varied in width between one hundred and three hundred feet and, despite the high water, if we didn't get serious about paddling we'd never make Manhattan by nightfall.

Sliding under the Ogden Bridge, we left Fort Riley for good. The town of Ogden was hidden behind the cottonwoods a mile or so away with its American flags and discount cigarette shops and liquor stores and cheap tire places. We didn't see or hear the Fort Riley elk herd (Alan: "Think they use them for target practice?"). Instead we watched the first bald eagle of the trip soar along a prairie swale.

I warmed up with the sun. Alan sang, "Midnight at the Oasis, sing your camel to bed. . . ." We stopped for lunch on a sandbar at the mouth of Clark's Creek in a triage of inlets mined with logjams. Sandbars on the Kaw have yielded a treasure trove of Pleistocene relics over the years: chocolate brown mammoth molars, giant camel femurs, saber-toothed tiger fangs, vertebrae from dire wolves, hooves of extinct horses. Alan asked, "Think we'll see a big beaver?" He meant *Castoroides ohioensis*, the "Giant Beaver," an eight-foot-long rodent that went extinct about ten thousand years ago.

I ate canned tuna with my fingers and combed the sand for relics, finding several flakes of chert worked on one edge by some ancient stone tool knapper. My stomach settled, but I had heat rash on my legs from rubbing the gunwales and my shoulderblades stung. Alan took photographs of the cottonwood grove above the high-water mark.

Back on the river we navigated some small submerged gravel bar riffles near Konza Prairie. The Kaw looked clean here. The hills came right down to the river. Freshwater mussel beds clung to limestone boulders. Pterodactyl-like great blue heron tracks decorated translucent sand knobs. Terns and gulls dotted the shores above their normal sandbar enclaves, which were largely under water. The Manhattan water tower at Warner Park loomed in the distance on river left but we still had almost ten miles to paddle. The natural communities seemed to play musical chairs; long flats were stripped bare except for cornstraw-yellow foxtails; cottonwood groves got thicker but nowhere near as dense as what we'd find further downstream; and oak-hickory forests grew down to meet the river where hillsides burrowed into the alluvial mud.

This section of the river was calm, peaceful, and beautiful—I should have been happy, but I couldn't stop thinking about what waited for us ahead. One mile past Manhattan the Big Blue barreled into the Kaw at eighteen thousand cubic feet per second. Even eight miles away the current slowed down as the hand of the Big Blue pushed the main channel—and my will to continue—back toward the Smoky

Hill. I told Alan I was a little freaked out about the Big Blue. He yawned—politely, mind you—but still, he yawned. I asked him if he'd noticed the whirlpools. There were more whirlpools in the last part of the float. Alan turned all the way around in the boat and said, "They're from your mind racing in circles. Relax."

I tried to focus on the river—one way or another the next day would take care of itself.

In golden late afternoon light we watched a man on a golf cart disappear into the forest on river left, the first human we'd seen all morning. A crazy cackling came from the tops of the trees. We stopped paddling and grabbed binoculars. After some loud drumming I heard it again, a hollow throaty laugh, unevenly paced, like a flicker gone mad or an Olympic ping-pong tournament sped up a hundred times. Definitely a pileated woodpecker, the largest woodpecker in the United States. The pileated is rare in Kansas; most lifelong residents never see one.

As we neared Manhattan, the tall bluffs of Konza Prairie came into view on river right, and the channel narrowed and deepened. Deep Creek Road brought traffic. Luscious scenery punctuated day one of the float but we never had any real silence, with artillery blasts, airplanes flying low, and automobile traffic. On the final bend I looked up to a mud flat above slack water and saw a flash of brown fur—a small slender mink slid into the river and disappeared, only the third I'd seen in Kansas, and in the exact spot where I had seen my first mink seven years earlier. Was it the same animal? American mink are common in Kansas, but nocturnal, so people don't usually see them.

As we came to the end of the day's float, my friend Ted Dace was waiting under the Highway 177 bridge. We'd covered twenty-three miles the first day—not bad. Alan and I dragged the canoe into a field of poison ivy hidden behind some shrubs—any thieves were at least going to suffer. We drove out to survey the Big Blue. The torrent was almost up to the bottom of the highway bridge. Ted said he'd never seen it so high. Giant logs bobbed in the roil. The energy was nothing if not explosive. It was even worse than I'd feared.

"Day two: Frazier's pissy mood lingers" (Ziegler's notebook).

We ate oats, honey, and raisins, and drank green tea in darkness—knees rubbed raw from yesterday's gunwales—neck, back, arms in mutiny—my will to continue rubbed raw as well. Half an hour before first light I told Alan I wanted to scout the Big Blue again, so we got in the car, drove to Linear Park, and scared off a pickup that brought last night's party over from Aggieville. No reassurances. The river was still epic. But unless it rained, it would get no worse. The ranger at Tuttle Creek had told me they wouldn't release more than eighteen thousand cubic feet per second because they had just stocked the Big Blue with trout. Any more water would wash the fall trout season downstream to springtime in Saint Louis.

We walked a levee spur toward the river to inspect the collusion firsthand. "Duck Soup," Alan reassured me. "Duck soup," I repeated.

Was he crazy? Was he looking at a different river than I was, one where the Big Blue didn't slam into the main channel at a thousand miles per hour, standing waves cresting as tall as a man, forcing the Kaw back into a giant whirlpool, like a big hydraulic washing machine? A few Canada geese rested on a small sand island while others swam circles on the eddy lines to form an infinity symbol. The goose island separated distinct left and right channels where the Kaw joined the Big Blue. Alan said, "We'll hold onto the left side of the river until we get next to the island. Right before we enter the current we'll point the boat to the middle of the river; we need to keep it straight, but we'll paddle hard so when we break the eddy line we'll be going faster than the current. We need to keep focused. We can't mess around with our cameras or talk on our cell phones; we have to paddle, but after we get past this mess we can let the river do some of the work for a change."

It would be hard digging against the backflow for almost two miles between K-177 and the mouth of the Big Blue, and on the final descent we'd have to bank in like the space shuttle reentering the atmosphere. Alan threw a walnut at a goose and missed. "Let's go," he said. Yes, Alan had floated the Mekong and Salween and would soon climb Kilimanjaro before the glacier melted. Duck soup. Maybe. But one man's duck soup is another man's Kilimanjaro. We got back in the car and drove off to meet our fate.

Back on the river again, I heard another pileated woodpecker laughing from the cottonwoods. I wondered how many people driving US Highway 24 inside Manhattan city limits knew they could walk one hundred feet from the road and see a woodpecker the size of a small poodle. Paddling against the current was easier than I expected but slow going; it took almost an hour before I could see the goose island ahead. I tried not to panic when I saw it—in fact, I tried not to think at all. Per strategy, we hugged river left. It seemed like I could feel each of my heartbeats pushing blood down into my arms and legs. I was as ready as I ever would be. We approached the Big Blue. On the other side of the deluge, a long field soaked in knee-high water marked the stop where Blue Earth Village once stood.

In 1719, seventy years before the Kansa built Blue Earth Village on the Big Blue, Bourgmont returned to France a minor hero, his desertions and dalliances forgiven—for the most part. A man with a bride in every port, he married a widow twelve years his junior when she got pregnant. He received a pseudo-title created just for him: the Knight of the Order of Saint Louis. But this pseudo-title was only that, pseudo. Bourgmont craved nobility. The French government used this carrot to convince him to return to America and forge an alliance with the Padoucahs. The tribe was certifiably badass; there was no telling what they might do to a French nobleman showing up in their village, government officers reasoned, so they might as well send Bourgmont. The reward, if he survived, was a promotion to Duc d'Orleans, a title normally reserved for French royalty.

Bourgmont left France and arrived on the Missouri in the summer of 1724, feeble with malaria. After several days' journey, his entourage arrived at the Kansa's Grand Village, where they would wait for a large shipment of supplies for the journey across the prairie. The tribe launched into a week of feasting and drinking, but the debauchery laid Bourgmont's men low. One after another, they came down with fever, and then the Indians started getting sick. Bourgmont bled five of the Kaws, who recovered. He needed to rest, but couldn't wiggle out of the constant partying and drinking that carried on in spite of the illness that crept through camp. With each passing day, the supplies failed to arrive and the binging continued. Tensions began to rise.

Finally, on or about the first day of July, Bourgmont received his shipments. He quickly finalized his route to the main Padoucah village. The Kansa insisted on accompanying him into the teeth of the wind—the homeland of their mortal enemy. The day before their scheduled departure, the leader of the Kansa offered his fourteen-year-old daughter to Bourgmont as a bride. Bourgmont wasn't known for refusing women, but even he had his standards and certainly wasn't in a position to take another wife. He fell over himself with politeness, explaining in French, in pigeon sign language, in his lame Missouri (which is related to Kansa) what a great honor it was, but that perhaps his son—who was half-Missouri—could come back later for the girl and marry her himself. Finally the Kansa leader acquiesced, saying Bourgmont was a chief after all; he could have as many or as few wives as he chose. Another calamity averted.

Bourgmont's overland journey to the village of the Padoucah commenced on a sweltering July morning in 1724, fully 130 years before the Kansas territory was opened to pioneer settlement, eighty years before the first eastern tribes were sent

to establish Indian Kansas, long before the Santa Fe and Oregon Trails, before
most of the rivers and streams had the names we know them by today, when Kansas was still a pristine grassland wilderness. If you don't have the timeline of Kansas settlement memorized, know that this event happened about as far to the left
side of that graph as you can get. It must have been a crazy scene.

Three hundred Kaw warriors, two Kaw leaders, three hundred Kaw women,
five hundred Kaw children, and at least three hundred Kaw dogs pulled fully
loaded travois spread out in a motley line across upland fields of neck-high big
bluestem, little bluestem, Indian grass, and a smorgasbord of blooming prairie flowers that left a medicinal fragrance in their wake. The French trappers in
Bourgmont's group liked to travel light, but the Native Americans brought everything and the kitchen sink. Since Kaw men didn't help carry *anything*, the caravan
made very slow progress. The women and little children fell way back in the line,
so the riders would move ahead a little, stop, smoke, and wait for them to catch
up. They traveled through future Atchison, Leavenworth, Jefferson, and Shawnee
Counties, crossing the Kansas River near Buffalo Mound. They saw meadows in
the Flint Hills that looked like paintings of buffalo, elk, and deer too numerous
to count.

But Bourgmont was sick. He spent forty-eight hours alternately throwing up,
riding, throwing up, riding. Fearing death, he finally had to take a few of his men
and head back to their camp one hundred miles back on the Missouri. The rest of
the caravan continued and eventually met the Padoucah somewhere near modern
Lyons, Kansas, although the exact location is unknown (scholars in fact don't even
agree on who the Padoucah were—whether the Comanche, the Pawnee, a separate
branch of the Apache, or a different group altogether that disease wiped out at
some later time).

Bourgmont's emissaries negotiated with the Padoucah in his absence. For a
peace offering they returned two captured slaves. When Kaw warriors suddenly
appeared over a hill, the Padoucah warriors grabbed their bows, but after a tense
couple of moments everybody fell into the spirit of the meetings. After three days
of feasting, the Padoucah leaders returned with the entourage to the Grand Village
des Canzes and met with Bourgmont, who hadn't deserted for once. Bourgmont
returned to finish negotiations at the main Padoucah village and on October 11,
1724, he crossed the Kansas River near Buffalo Mound on his way back from the
Padoucah homeland with a successful peace agreement.

The treaty Bourgmont brokered for the Kansa would be the only one that didn't bring them dispossession, thievery, and death. He gained the trust of the Kansa and their Siouan brothers, but after his return to France, the coureurs des bois continued to ply the tribe with liquor and spread disease among the Indians. The French built Fort Cavagnial on the Missouri near Leavenworth, but their days in the Kaw Valley, too, were numbered. America would soon claim the Kansa homeland after the Louisiana Purchase. The Kaws would abandon their Grand Village and move a hundred miles west to Blue Earth Village. This would provide a buffer against American influence in the Missouri territory, but it would take more than distance to save the Kansa from the calamity that soon arrived.

Happiness is for the brave.

As we approached the confluence of the Big Blue, we hugged river left per Alan's plans. The water was as placid as meditation, the backflow on river right. Alan swung the stern into the current and before I could get my paddle in for a second prying stroke we sailed down the middle of the river smooth as silk.

What a relief.

The braided western stream near Fort Riley had turned into a deep mover, and we cruised easily along in the swift current. A dozen irritated Canada geese launched in noisy protest as we paddled past Swamp Angel on river left at a solid four miles per hour.

The high water made islands of sandbars and hid the detritus of half-drowned refrigerators, Plymouth Satellites, tornado-crushed grain silos, and the usual river junk. Many species make good use of this for shelter, but the high water had things out of whack. Gigantic logs bobbed inside tight bends. Secret roils like champagne bubbles marked drowned sandbars where the quicksand belched air from below. The cottonwoods were getting taller as the water deepened, and hawks that looked like napping cats spaced themselves out every few hundred feet. The longer straights on the way to Saint George had an illusion of gradient, like looking down a flight of stairs, though I knew we couldn't have been losing more than a few feet of altitude per mile.

Our new goal was to keep the boat straight and let the river do the work for us. But even though the flow had quadrupled, we weren't going *that much* faster, only about one mile per hour, proof that the real force behind a large farm-country river is gravity, not gratuity. Keeping squarely in channel became trickier, the river harder to read. The channel playfully darted between slackwaters as it bounced off waterlogged banks. Erosion was more noticeable as the prairie began to give way to more and more cornfields.

After a quick lunch at the river park in Saint George, we floated between spans of an old bridge and for the first time in two days put some distance between ourselves and the nearest road. Quiet, at last. The ten miles to Wamego weren't the most scenic but at times the Flint Hills joined the panorama and we counted three more pileated woodpeckers, eight great blue herons, one osprey, one immature bald eagle, and one beaver. Later that evening, driving through Wamego past To-toz Tacoz, Scissorz of Oz, and a converted military missile silo that once held the largest illegal LSD lab in America, I realized that Alan and I would make the rest of the float. We had two days left before we got to Lawrence, two days that would take us into the heart of the Kansa's last homeland along the river.

The twenty-two miles from Wamego to Maple Hill form the final river segment in the Flint Hills and there is no more beautiful stretch along the Kaw. Hard mounds on river right cast cold shadows that made us draw up our jackets and don stocking caps in the predawn hours. Holsteins were scattered dreamily on the slumbering golden prairie two hundred feet above us. Twelve yellow-shafted flickers, one red-headed woodpecker, and four pileated woodpeckers worked on a single dead sycamore. Two of the pileateds flew across the river when they saw us, screaming like gibbons.

The world of cattle and corn and oil changes and auto plazas was probably somewhere not far beyond the cottonwoods, but it seemed a world away. Now we were of the river. The slow rhythmic mantra of J-strokes massaged the knots out of my shoulders. Alan and I were working as a team now; we both had our legs under us. Another day alone with river and sky and sun—what a gift.

Two miles down from the woodpecker tree I saw what looked like a small log floating near the shallows. The log bobbed up and down twice, then started crossing the river. I put my paddle down and pointed: "A swimming dog?" Once it was halfway across the channel, Alan sat up and said, "Paddle as hard as you can; it's a deer!"

I'd witnessed squirrels swimming across the Wakarusa River and once saw two beavers, knowing full well I was watching them, crawl up on a bank of ice along Mud Creek and mate, but I'd never seen a doe swim the Kaw. We almost spun the boat around trying to catch her. She maneuvered elegantly, paddling calmly with

Willow on sandbar, Wabaunsee County, Kansas.

her hooves, easily eluding us despite our best efforts. Finally, we eased up and I steadied the boat while Alan got some photos. She dragged herself out of the water and disappeared into a thicket of sandbar willow.

We didn't notice it, but while we chased the deer the wind had picked up. Even with the swift current in our favor, after we turned due north into a four-mile straight aimed directly into the teeth of the wind, we fought to make forward progress. We paddled toward Jeffrey Energy Center, a triple-stack coal-burning plant that looms like an evil mirage on the prairie. We had to hug the west bank. It took almost two hours to reach the Vermillion River at the top of the bend before we gratefully turned east into a lush wetland next to US Highway 24. The sandy alluvium was twenty feet high; Alan interpreted strata like a chiromancer reads palms, guessing which lines represented the big floods of 1844, 1903, 1951, and 1993. I looked for mammoth tusks. Large stands of scouring rush grew along the banks like Chinese bamboo gardens. Not really a rush, this member of the horsetail family has stems that contain silica if you ever need a backwoods manicure.

We needed a break, so Alan pointed to a landing on river left where we climbed up into a little floodplain forest. We were beat and there was a good place to lie in the sun, but since it was above the high-water mark, technically we were trespassing.

On cue, I heard the sputter of a three-wheeler get louder and louder, and soon a man in overalls and a baseball hat drove down to the edge of the river and looked down at our boat and then over at us.

Alan walked right up to the guy and introduced us, apologizing for borrowing his landing. He told us not to worry about it. "I just came down because a friend called and asked if I'd take a look for his boat," he said. "He tied it off at Belvue and hasn't seen it since the water came up." We promised to keep an eye out and took his cell number just in case we saw something. Alan told him about the deer swimming the river. The guy said, "You see some pretty cool stuff on the river. My daughters and I take our boat down to Maple Hill a couple times each summer. If there wasn't so much water you guys would have plenty of company on the sandbars. Today's the first day of duck season, but with all the flow nobody can get down to their blinds to set decoys.

"I've had a golden eagle here for three straight years," he continued. "It must have a nest nearby, but I've never found it. Once I saw it eating a dead deer there on that island. Four bald eagles were pacing around, giving it plenty of space. It was a lot bigger than them."

Back on the river we saw duck blinds. Some were substantial constructions of plywood and camouflage netting. One had cattails heaped up on the roof. We didn't find the johnboat.

Finally, on a sharp south bend, I noticed a singular hill alone in the distance: Buffalo Mound, Bourgmont's old landmark. We were close to where he crossed the river in 1724. The Maple Hill bridge was half a mile away. For three days we had been floating the Flint Hills and finally we'd made it to the end. It was more beautiful than I had imagined. Best of all, we hadn't seen another boat.

Calamitous change began for the Kansa when the United States took control of the future lands of Kansas and Missouri after the Louisiana Purchase. When Missouri entered the Union in 1821, a plan was hatched to extinguish all Indian claims in the state. By then, most of the Kansa had lived at the Blue Earth Village more than thirty years. The US government worked out a treaty with Kaw leader White Plume to acquire the bulk of the Kansa homeland for a new Kansas Indian Country, a group of reservations used to relocate thousands of Native Americans from tribes back east. White Plume was of mixed ancestry—part Kansa, part French. He once wrote, "I consider myself an American and my wife an American

woman—I want to take her home with me and have everything like white people."
His great-grandson Charles Curtis would become vice president of the United
States. Nonetheless, White Plume signed for the tribe, and the Kaw agreed to re-
strict themselves to a thirty-mile-wide reservation extending approximately from
Topeka west to the buffalo country.

As part of the treaty, the United States set aside twenty-three 640-acre plots to
the east of the reservation (north of Topeka east to the modern vicinity of Perry)
for mixed-blood members (who were "too French to be Indian and too Indian to
be French"). This began an internal rift between the full-bloods and mixed-bloods
that continued for over a century.

The deal also came with a supply of cattle, hogs, and chickens, and a "government farmer" to teach the tribe how to farm. The Kansa had coexisted with Euro-
peans and Americans for the better part of two hundred years, but this treaty was
a watershed. In retrospect it amounted to nothing less than cultural revolution.

The Kansas abandoned Blue Earth Village. White Plume took his people to a
new site east of the tracts set aside for people of mixed blood, but the main body
of the tribe remained farther west, with three traditionalist leaders in villages along
what became known as Mission Creek. It was there that the death moon rose.

Beneath US Highway 75 in Topeka, a water weir creates a low-head dam that paddlers must portage around. Because the river was so high, we chose to begin our
fourth and final day a few miles downstream from where we left off, skipping the
section between Maple Hill and the Seward Avenue boat ramp and the urban core
of Topeka. We had twenty-five miles to go before our trip would end in Lawrence.

An hour before dawn the thermometer read twenty-eight and the river was
completely fogged in. After we loaded the boat, I sat on the bank and drank green
tea, hoping the fog would lift. Sunrise was near, but the gathering light didn't dint the
gray murk that made this urban section of the river seem more remote than anything
we'd faced. I worried about a wing dike not too far downstream near the Tecumseh
Energy Center that might be more like a waterfall with the river still swollen from
Tuttle Creek's ongoing discharge. It would be nice to actually see where we were going. I was content to wait and drink more tea. As usual, Alan had other plans.

Soon we pushed off into the fog and edged the boat into a thin strip of daylight
on river right beneath a monoculture stand of redbud trees. The fog bank was a
slab of angel food cake almost twenty feet high.

Close to camp, Shawnee County, Kansas.

"Hey in there, dammit! Are you there, Topeka?" I yelled.

Topeka, which means roughly "good place to dig potatoes," apparently wasn't. All was silent though we were less than six hundred feet, as the flicker flies, from two strip clubs. Black orbs like blind spots loomed in the fog; I presumed they were logjams sitting on drowned sandbars, but I couldn't be sure. We stopped paddling as the river veered left and we became invisible in the cloak, suspended in space and time, closer it seemed to the ancient Kansa river villages than the modern Kansas capital. Our speed was a paltry two miles per hour since we couldn't safely paddle. The sun rose like a faint suspicion, like sunrise on Uranus, as we floated past the power plant, which remained invisible to us except for a brick building with a boat mooring that could be raised or lowered depending on the water level.

A quick pit stop on a sand island enunciated the confusion between worlds: A wet track six feet long traced where a beaver ambled from its shoreside willow buffet to river's edge. The deep lobes of an ATV crossed the trace as they came up from the water—either the island was connected to land under normal conditions or somebody rode semi-aquatic recreational vehicles in T-Town. An Evenflo diaper bag, one vintage porcelain toilet, and some ten-foot sections of four-inch pipe were tangled up in a logjam as big as a house.

When we pushed off again, the fog was lifting and we could see the shores. No more Topeka. We followed an eroded bend and worked around minefields of sycamore snags toward a deep bottomland forest, the thickest woods of the entire trip.

Between Tecumseh and Lecompton the Kaw straightens out. Cottonwood, sycamore, and willow are still the dominant trees, but the cottonwoods are taller, giving rise to an understory of American elm, hackberry, silver maple, and redbud. Grape and trumpet creeper vines made the woods an impenetrable jungle, at least for the twenty paces away from the high-water mark before cornfields took over. Kingfishers crossed the river nervously between willow perches. The wind grabbed our boat and didn't let go for hours. We had to paddle full bent to maintain our three miles per hour. A river road hugged the south bank, but other than the occasional car, the only sound was the dripping of wind rushing over leaves in the cottonwoods. I wanted to find a place to get out and start a fire to warm up, but we needed to paddle. At this pace we'd have trouble beating sunset.

We did briefly beach the boat on an island for bladder duty. Alan took the other side of the willow breaks and came back ten minutes later to report he had watched another deer swimming in the water, which now was deeper than twelve feet. At the last second the deer decided to swim back to shore rather than land on the island. She probably caught wind of us.

The rest of the morning was sheer athleticism. As we came up on the new Lecompton bridge, we saw four big guys crammed into a little johnboat at the mouth of Coon Creek, fishing poles and lines and legs and arms jutting out in a confusing tangle—it was hard to figure what belonged to who. One of the guys yelled, "You think we could fit any more people in this boat?" They probably were carrying nine hundred pounds of fishermen and another seventy pounds of beer. Farther down on a sand island below the mouth of the Delaware River, two guys were setting out mallard decoys. We passed Lecompton Rising Sun River ramp and ducked under the Lecompton bridge.

On a slight ridge to the right we could see the back of the old Lecompton Democratic headquarters, a small yellow limestone cabin built in the 1850s. Lecompton was a territorial capital of Kansas and for a while the center of national attention when pro-slavery sympathizers stuffed the ballot boxes and stole the territorial elections of 1858, establishing Kansas, for a while, as a pro-slavery state. The "Bogus Legislature" that resulted from this electoral farce held court in Lecompton, just upstream from their despised abolitionist opponents in Lawrence. The city of Denver was officially named in the Rowena Hotel, which was one of the finest hotels in the west. President Dwight Eisenhower's parents were married at Lane University, which closed in the early 1900s. On the left side of the river there once was another town, Rising Sun, where criminals were hanged from a tall sycamore by the river. The purveyor of the ferry there, a hollowed-out twenty-foot log, told his clients, "Don't be a skeery mister; she's as dependable as Old Glory and as dry as a Missourian's throat."

Lecompton's original name was Bald Eagle. In winter when the river freezes, the deep current below the town usually leaves an opening in the ice. I've seen thirty eagles perched in the cottonwoods along the north bank. The twelve miles between Lecompton and Lawrence are the most floated section of the Kansas River. In normal conditions, the first three miles are a braided stream with sandbars. I'd canoed this stretch dozens of times. Once we found a bald eagle nest, one of the first half-dozen built on the river in more than a century. In 1991 I found a lone specimen of tamarisk on a prominent sandbar, as far as I know the first known tamarisk plant in Douglas County. The flood of 1993 swept it away.

We floated past a limestone cliff with a small pocket cave that popped out on the other side by the Lecompton waterworks. Alan and I had discovered it years before walking the south bank of the river from Lawrence. Following a gravel road along oak-hickory bluffs, we started spooking beavers from their sunning spots. The home stretch was slow going with the wind in our faces, but I was in shape now. It was a sad shame this was the last day. I was probably good for Saint Louis at least, if not New Orleans. We stopped briefly again to warm up around a little fire. I ate my last can of tuna with a ciabatta roll and some granola.

Like several other notable creeks and rivers in eastern Kansas (Wakarusa, Mill Creek, Illinois Creek, Dragoon Creek, Marais des Cygnes), Mission Creek rises from the spring-fed prairies of Wabaunsee County, near Wildcat Hollow. Today it runs through the western fringes of Topeka. Clumps of suburbia have grown up through the cracks in the agricultural landscape that line the valley. A stallion with the personable name of Robert McGregor, raised on the banks of the creek at Prairie Dell Farm, became the "Monarch of Home Stretch" in the 1870s. Orleans Gentleman's Club enjoys free advertising in its roost above I-70 just south of the junction of Mission Creek and the Kaw River. Despite the modern humdrum, an epic struggle once took place in this valley. Mission Creek would be the Kansas's last stand on the Kaw.

Although the Americans considered White Plume "head chief," three traditionalist leaders held sway with the full-bloods. In 1830 they permanently abandoned Blue Earth Village in favor of three new communities along Mission Creek. About seven hunded people joined Lah-tah-lesh-yeh, or Fool Chief, at Chachhaa Hogeree (or "Fool Chief Village") on the north side of the Kaw several miles west of Soldier Creek. Fool Chief was a bad drunk; one of his own warriors eventually killed him in self-defense. Peh-gah-hosh-she, or American Chief, had traveled to Washington in his youth and met Thomas Jefferson. His village of about twenty lodges was located two miles from the mouth of the Kaw on Mission Creek, then called American Chief Creek. The most traditional of all the leaders was Kah-he-ge-wah-che-ha, or Hard Chief. About eight hundred people lived at Hard Chief Village on a high ridge of limestone above the floodplain south of the Kaw.

The Mission Creek villages received very little of the apportionments accorded by White Plume's treaty of 1825. Frederick Choteau operated a trading post at American Chief Village. Although he was a friend to the Indians, his livelihood consisted of supplying them goods, and he retained a Native American "medicine man" to collect bad debts by "wielding the power of life and death." Various missionaries attempted to convert the Kansa. William Johnson, who had a very amenable relationship with the Indians, opened a Mission School. The tribe politely sent a student or two every year (except for Hard Chief, who flat-out refused to send Indian children to church). Although Fool Chief professed to be a Methodist for a couple of years, the only person Johnson was able to convert to Christianity in Kaw Country was Daniel Morgan Boone, the government agriculturist and son of the famous explorer. Some Kansa believed the Methodists had violated a sacred tribal taboo by teaching Christianity in the villages, leading to the tragedy that soon unfolded.

Beginning in the late 1820s the emigrant tribes began to arrive in eastern Kansas. In a very short period of time the population of the old Kaw territory more than doubled. By 1830 the Kansa were almost completely dependent on European technologies and trade goods, which they obtained through the fur trade. For more than three hundred years they had lived on the abundant game of the Kaw River, and as late as 1828 Isaac McCoy wrote that the region had "Elk, Deer, and Bear plenty, and a few antelopes." But between 1820 and 1835, probably because of overpopulation and increased hunting pressure for trade items, the large game species of the Kaw Valley vanished. In 1830 the expedition of John Wyeth found little game near Fool Chief's village. By then bear and elk were probably gone. Reverend Johnson wrote in 1835 that the "deer have entirely disappeared."

At the same time the Kansa were waging a nearly constant war with their enemies, the Pawnee. Battle provided two things: an opportunity for young men to distinguish themselves and a way to acquire new horses. In an ongoing dance, the Kaw raided the Pawnee and in return the Pawnee raided the Kaw.

Without sufficient game, and unable to make their traditional winter journey to the Missouri River because the Delaware Tribe had relocated to those lands, the Kansa were forced to add a winter buffalo hunt in order to have enough food to survive the cold months. Previously they had only made the trip to the buffalo country in summer, when there was good grass for the horses. The winter hunt was successful for the first few years and the Choteau trading post enjoyed a boom in buffalo robes. But the winter trips took a toll on the tribe's supply of horses. There wasn't much nutrition in winter grass, and the buffalo country didn't have many cottonwood trees, which the horses grazed for bark. Every winter their herd dwindled. This created more incentive to raid the Pawnee for replacements.

September 1827 brought the first disaster at Mission Creek: smallpox. That month seventy Kansa died and almost two-thirds of the tribe were sickened. There hadn't been a widespread outbreak of smallpox among the Kansa since the 1750s. By springtime 180 people were dead, almost 15 percent of the population.

Conditions only deteriorated in the 1830s. Three hundred more Kansa died of smallpox between 1831 and 1833, and further outbreaks took place in 1838, 1839, and 1840. The Kansa population began to crash and never truly recovered. Johnson reported that the "awful cries of Indians around the dead sounded in our ears every day." He lost his own young daughter.

The epidemics threw the tribe into a frenzy. Many departed for the buffalo plains and abandoned their small fields, which had become important food sources. The Pawnee attacked them mercilessly. Those who remained prepared for war and organized revenge parties. In 1839, after several skirmishes, some of the Mission Creek Kansa found an unguarded Pawnee camp. They attacked the unsuspecting occupants—mostly old men, women, and children—with a pent-up fury, brutally killing sixty people. The Pawnee responded with a campaign of constant revenge. The Kansa would never again resume their annual buffalo hunts in the Smoky Hill country.

The final winters of the 1830s brought starvation. Johnson wrote that "400 or 500 starving Kansa are going to the white settlements to beg provision." The traveler Edwin Bryant wrote, "They roam in quest of such small game as now remains to keep themselves from absolute famine. . . . The Kansa are now starving and have turned pensioners of the United States, and beggars of the emigrants passing west, for clothing and food."

Finally in 1844, as the inhabitants of American Chief Village, Fool Chief Village, and Hard Chief Village struggled for survival along Mission Creek, the river itself struck the mortal blow. Twenty-seven inches of rain fell in May and June. At one point it rained for eighty straight hours. The river rose to historic levels. By almost every measure, the flood of 1844 was the most catastrophic in the history of the river.

Because it happened before settlement, there are few written records, so the data we have is the result of some fairly nuanced fluvial archeology. A thirty-eight-foot high-water mark visible on a piling that supported the Hannibal and St. Joseph railway bridge over the Missouri River remained until 1920. This was two feet higher than the peak of the 1951 flood, the highest crest ever recorded on the Missouri River at Kansas City. Farther up the Kaw the damage was even more intense. S. D. Flora, head of the US Weather Bureau in Topeka from 1917 to 1941, scoured documents and oral histories to reconstruct flood data for the upper Kaw. He estimated that the crests at Ogden and Topeka were six feet higher than in 1951. The flood rearranged a lot of merchandise. It ripped Turkey Creek, a small Kansas City stream, from its ancient mooring on the Missouri River and glued it onto the Kaw. It struck the Delaware Indian Tribe particularly hard, killing more than one hundred. There were reports of Oregon Trail travelers stranded along with bears on prairie mounds turned islands. The flood dissected a major bend below Lecompton, creating an oxbow lake that today is home to Lakeview, a country club where the children of doctors and judges learned to swim in the early twentieth century.

The river swelled to eight miles at the Kaw villages. It completely destroyed Fool Chief Village. Hard Chief and American Chief Villages, on higher ground, fared better, but the damage was done. The Mission Creek Treaty of 1846 moved the tribe south to a reservation near Council Grove. Although they would remain in the Kansas territory for another quarter-century, the Kansa never again lived along the river that bore their name. By the beginning of the twentieth century their population had plummeted to just 250. The tribe moved one last time to Indian Country in Oklahoma. In 1902, a bill supported by Charles Curtis, a one-eighth-blood member of the tribe, officially dissolved the Kansa as an entity recognized by the United States. By the end of the twentieth century, the Kansa language was among the most endangered on earth. On April 23, 2000, four months after the end of the millenium, William A. Mehojah, the last full-blooded Kaw, died in Omaha.

The last miles of the float were a tradeoff between the noisy Kansas Power & Light plant that lights Lawrence and the finest cottonwood forests of the journey. Just before sundown at Riverfront Park, the river fully mature at last, we took out 120 river miles from where we started in Junction City. Although still fifty miles shy of Lewis and Clark Point in Kansas City, we had successfully floated the upper Kaw, the most scenic and wild stretch of the river. Not wanting to give up our hard-won deceleration, we lingered at the park while sunset's dalliance lit up four panels of altocumulus. But the show soon ended, clouds and sky both drained from the effort, everything cooled to a dull blue, a painting done in reverse.

From a pristine wildlife sanctuary in the early nineteenth century to a polluted dumping ground in the earthy twentieth, the Kansas River is cleaner, but not clean enough, at the beginning of the twenty-first, thanks in part to Friends of the Kaw. One thing that no other Kansas stream has is an official "riverkeeper." It might be the coolest paid job in Kansas. Laura Calwell, director of Friends of the Kaw and the longest-tenured Kansas riverkeeper to date, helped protect the ecological integrity along the river by spending her days searching for rogue discharge pipes, fighting proposed dredging operations, finding money for river access ramps, and raising awareness of the Kaw in river communities. The Water Keeper Alliance, an international organization founded by Robert Kennedy, Jr., is a grassroots advocacy organization dedicated to preserving and protecting rivers and watersheds, in part, through its water keeper network.

Calwell told me the river's main threat used to be point source pollution: "The river used to be a lot dirtier in the early twentieth century. Point source pollution was horrible—dead cows, untreated sewage, that kind of stuff."

The turning point came with the Clean Water Act in 1972. Since then point source pollution is largely under control, but much more work remains before the river is as clean as in the days of Bourgmont. Calwell told me, "Non-point source pollution continues to be a big problem. The river is dirtiest just after a big storm because of agricultural and urban runoff. Atrazine, PCBs, and *E. coli* are three of our biggest problems. If you run more than three hundred head of cattle, KDHE

(Kansas Department of Health and Environment) monitors you, but smaller ranches don't have to comply. Some do a very good job, but we still have cows stomping around in creeks."

Calwell believes that an important step toward improved water quality is restoration of bottomland forests. A large riparian buffer filters runoff. The soil filters stormwater before it reaches the river. Runoff is an urban issue as well. New developments have to build retention ponds so that rainwater seeps slowly into the ground instead of running directly into creeks and, ultimately, the river. Calwell said, "There is grant money to build the stream buffers and establish retention ponds, but many people don't know it's there. Some of these are weekend ranchers who keep a few cattle near the river. We need to do everything we can to rebuild the bottomland forests. That's one of the keys to a cleaner Kaw."

Interestingly, restoration of the Kansas River got under way at about the same time state officials announced proposals for a Kaw Reservoir in Oklahoma (which, of course, is not on the Kansas River). Although the federal government dissolved the Kansa at the turn of the century, the tribe stayed together and elected new leaders, some of them full-bloods descended from ancestral leaders who lived in the Kansas River valley. The Kaw Reservoir would inundate a large portion of the tribe's original landholdings in Oklahoma, including Washunga Cemetery, the burial ground named after the leader who presided over their move to the new state. Opposition to the reservoir became a rallying point, and though the lake was eventually built, the Kansa were re-energized by their efforts. Today they are trying to save their language. Although no full-blooded Kansa remain, the Kaw Tribe of Oklahoma has almost thirty-five hundred members, a greater number than at any time in the last hundred years. Today it owns and runs Allegawaho Memorial Heritage Park in Council Grove, the first tribal holdings in Kansas since their exile to Oklahoma.

After Hard Chief left Mission Creek in 1846, the remains of his village, built on a virgin prairie, remained clearly evident for decades. In 1905, ruins of more than a dozen earth lodges were still plainly visible. It was not until the 1930s, when farmers plowed the prairie where the village had been, that the last readily discernable link to the Kansa presence along the river that bears their name was finally gone.

I asked Randy Theis, a Kansas State Historical Society archeologist who led a detailed survey in 1987, if he could see evidence of the earth lodges. "I couldn't," he told me. "We'd done some test digs and found charcoal and burned limestone—not a lot, though. But Tom Witty, being the great archeologist that he was, pointed to

Alan Ziegler paddling into the fog, Shawnee County, Kansas.

a place on a little rise and said he thought that was an earth mound. It didn't look like anything to me. He said we could prove it by poking down in the middle of the circle. Sure enough, we found the hearth. It was full of charcoal."

Kathleen Fox, who bought the land in the 1990s, donated Hard Chief Village to the Kansas Archeological Society in 2007, preserving the location of one of the most epic events in Kansas history. Plans aren't complete, but someday the association will likely make a portion open to the public. It's possible they will build a new earth lodge, which would be the first on the banks of the Kaw since the days of Hard Chief.

The Kansas River has always been a place between worlds, a seam binding landscapes, wildlife, and cultures. It has borne the scars of our misuse, but, ever resilient, might someday heal because of the good efforts of people in Kansas who value the river for what it is: the most well known of the last wild places of Kansas. Like in Tibetan mythology, where the self embarks on a journey at death—a journey shrouded in fog and uncertainty, between what has been and what will be—the river, like all of the last wild places of Kansas, enjoys neither rest nor a guaranteed future. Only a fragile magnificence.

Acknowledgments

Just after first light on President's Day, 2006, I pulled off the Kansas turnpike to watch a coyote stalk slowly toward the middle of a frozen pond. She was big and healthy with a salmon tinge to her coat, the same color as the clumps of little bluestem glistening with frost along the margin of the highway. I was somewhere between the last mobile home village south of Topeka and the eastern edge of the Flint Hills where I planned to spend the morning hiking a backcountry trail at Tallgrass Prairie National Preserve in Chase County.

The coyote seemed to know she was risking it; she inched forward tentatively, testing the thin ice one paw at a time before trusting it with her weight. Twice she slipped and scampered back a few steps, but both times steadied herself and continued. In the dim light of pre-dawn I couldn't see what she was after. Her pups were probably hiding in the willows along Frog Creek or nestled in their den somewhere along the Wakarusa River farther out in the prairie.

Something about that coyote and her ice pond was a catalyst for *The Last Wild Places of Kansas*; the idea came to me as soon as I pulled back onto the highway and began to drive, and by the end of my hike later in the afternoon, I had both the provisional title and a down payment on the resolve it would take to see this work through to completion.

In addition to my coyote muse, many people helped as I planned and researched, hit the road and did fieldwork, wrote, edited, and worked through final production.

Maria Eifler from KU Natural History Museum, Diane Johnson from Operation Wildlife, and William Busby from the Kansas Biological Survey patiently answered my questions about the southern flying squirrel. Biology teacher and flying squirrel whisperer Kelly Haggard took me on an athletic tour of flying squirrel habitat complete with falling ladders, black widow spiders, and mice that jumped out of squirrel boxes on our faces. He also gave me the idea to spread peanut butter

189

on oak trees to lure the secretive squirrels to my motion-triggered camera. Thanks Kelly, but I still don't have the money shot!

Matt Peek, research biologist at KDWP; Ryan Frohling, refuge manager at Marais des Cygnes National Wildlife Refuge; and Randy Nelson, manager of the Farlington Hatchery, helped aim me toward river otters in Kansas, although Lloyd Fox, who initially reintroduced them in the South Fork of the Cottonwood River, planted the seed in my mind years earlier. Bunnie Watkins from Perry Lake told me about her early otter sighting on the Delaware River. Marcus Jones spent an entire day tromping through otter creeks and teaching me to "smell" otter sign. Roger Boyd of Baker University gave me permission to set up motion cameras in Baker Wetlands and encouraged me as I looked for otters near Lawrence. Ann Gardner and Cory Smith of the *Lawrence Journal-World* helped me spread the word about local otters in the press.

Carlyle Hinshaw and Rebecca Hawkins of the Shawnee Tribe, historian Herb Shuey, and Melissa Fisher Isaacs, assistant curator at Johnson County Museum, provided information about White Feather Spring, and Dale Nimz and Jeff Page helped me research Black Bob and Black Bob Cave. Martha Long allowed me generous access to the cave and told me some great stories about its history. Ernesto and Lupe Arvizu shared their enthusiasm and theories on the Shawnee Prophet and his time at White Feather Spring.

Chris Meek and T. J. Hittle clued me in on the confusing laws about canoeing in Kansas. Terry Arthur, general counsel for Kansas Farm Bureau, helped me understand their side of the story. Roy S. Baker, Shari Perry, and Becky Bartley helped me create the landowner map for my performance art along the Marais des Cygnes.

Plant experts Caleb Morse and Shirley Braunlich helped turn me on to the Leavenworth Woods. Thanks, Shirley, for organizing so many great trips to local prairies and forests in search of "showy spring ephemerals." Ron Klataske from Audubon of Kansas invited me and the members of Jayhawk Audubon to tour the site of the black-footed ferret reintroduction. Larry and Bette Haverfield graciously hosted us on their land and made lunch for everybody. Bob and Charlene Larson similarly hosted me at their ranch and stayed up late around the campfire telling stories about the Red Hills. Kansas wild lands guru and biologist Stan Roth provided much fodder for my trips to the Red Hills. Chris, Kent, and Karen Shrack put me up at their cabin in the Gyp Hills. Phyllis and Dee Scherich met me at Schwarz Canyon, and Keith Yearout filled me in on activities at the Barber County

Z-Bar Ranch. Andy Chappell, wildlife biologist at the Cimarron National Grassland, told me everything he knew about the high plains black bears and some information I didn't want to know about fleas and plague in prairie dog populations.

Laura and Mike Calwell explained the role of Friends of the Kaw in helping promote recreation on the Kansas River. If you are interested in a group float, I highly encourage you to visit http://kansasriver.org. State archeologist Randy Theis told me about the Kansa villages along Mission Creek, and Kathleen Fox gave me permission to visit one.

On the publishing side, Kim Hogeland at University Press of Kansas acquired the book and made the project possible. Thank you, Kim! I'm fairly certain that the geographical center of the 2015 seventeen-year Kansas cicada hatch was located right outside of her office window—a sign, no doubt, that she made the right choice about this project. Thanks also to Kelly Chrisman Jacques, Rebecca Murray, and Michael Kehoe of the Press. Peer reviewers Rex Buchanan and Jim Shroyer gave me invaluable feedback during the fourth revision. Prolific author and professor David Dary provided some concise advice about Kansas books when I needed it most. Jessica Hensley helped me on some critical edits near the end. Bunny Smith scoured the last revision with eagle eyes.

I spent many evenings after work hammering out the first draft in the upstairs "Glass Onion" space above Yello Sub near the KU campus. Alas, campus Yello Sub—in its own way one of the last wild places of Kansas—is no more, but I owe the staff a debt of gratitude for letting me camp out with their Wi-Fi so many times in the early days of the book. At the opposite end of the timeline, Sachin and Asha Mithal let me crash at their beautiful pad in San Jose for five days as I finished the fourth edit of the book. Nothing beats western tanagers flitting about in the lemon trees to help surgically select words about the prairie.

Thanks also to my parents, William and Sara Frazier, my sister Jennifer Haight, and her kids Austin and April Haight.

My love for the wild places of Kansas comes from the thousands of trips out into the prairies, woods, streams, arroyos, rivers, and tick-infested thickets of our state. Alan Ziegler and Lee Bissinger joined me too many times to recount—but I still don't know who dropped the sleeping bag at Perry Trail and why I had to hike six miles through the snow to find it! Special thanks also to Alan's parents, Bob and Margaret Curry. Terry Slocum, Bob Nunley, William Baker, Bill Johnson, and others in the KU Geography Department helped make an honorary geographer out of me while I was studying computer science in grad school, and *Wild Earth*

Journal published some of my early writings on Kansas during that time. Both helped incubate concepts that appear in this book.

Kidwalkers Tim Hindman, Ann Marie Glodich, Jackie Hyland, George Thompson, Karen Matheis, Todd Kitchen, Keegan and Eleanor Kitchen, Seth Thompson-Glodich, and Sam and Lolly Hindman took weekly trips with me to wild places around Douglas County. I'm glad we hauled our children off the grid when they were young and hopefully some of it will rub off. Otherwise let's throw their electronic devices in the Wakarusa.

Lifelong friend Ted Dace not only encouraged me during my writing, but led memorable hikes into the prairies around Manhattan. We'll have to bake potatoes at Cinderella prairie again someday.

Jay Bredwell, who shares my birthday, read every word of every draft and hauled all over the state with me in search of wild places. I'm glad we saw the otter together at Baker Wetlands, but if we had finished last in the Gritty Fitty along the Kaw it might have been more memorable. As much as that coyote catalyzed the book's beginning, Jay catalyzed its completion.

More than any other person, however, my wife, Christina Frazier, was my single greatest critic, mirror, artistic collaborator, and creative partner during the writing of this book. On one of our first dates, while wearing a dress and thigh-high leather boots, she tiptoed up to a hopelessly lost northern saw-whet owl and urged it along until it picked up its pantaloons and flew off into the pitch night sky and hopefully back onto its migration path (though how I got her to drive way out in the country with me that night is a completely different tale). We've explored every corner of Kansas together; wild places are a part of our family story. Our daughter Chloe has her own penchant for June prairies and September pawpaws, and was essential to the fieldwork on river otters. I'm sorry you got covered with ticks on Ancient Trees Trail, but I'm glad we observed the customary two-year waiting period to tell your mother about it.

Finally, a deep *hapchang* to Gary Shea, who taught me most of my outdoors skills; donated camping equipment I still use; and taught me how to mend tents and make fried okra with cumin, sourdough bread, and homemade beer. Gary, I wish you were here to read this book; I'm sure you would have picked it apart, rolled your eyes, and then helped me make it better.

In 1992, Gary wrote a song inspired in part by Breidenthal Forest. There is no official recording, so I can't point you to an iTunes link, but I can hoist up a geo-challenge to anybody who hikes in those woods to find the exact location he wrote about. The lyrics, which I recall from memory (I played the song with him many times), convey well the spirit of *The Last Wild Places of Kansas*.

"ATSF & G"
by Gary Shea

Down by the tracks and out in the fields,
Behind the barn where the sun's repealed,
History is gathered in the grass.
Where the rust set in and the grade collapsed,
The old bridge beams are lying back to back,
J. D. was here in 1866.
A train was on the track,
Came down this grade,
Cut into a hill,
And vanished clean away.

But I don't care, I can still hear that train.

The old mill's burned,
Bridges washed away,
Soap factories and canneries decayed.
Trolley car and interurban rolled away.

But this is a fine old town,
And there's no going back,
Elkin's prairie's plowed,
Landmarks burn and crack.

But I don't care, I can still hear that train.
I can hear it now, I can hear it to this day.

Bibliography

Ancient Cross Timbers Consortium website, http://www.uark.edu/misc/xtimber/.

Anderson, M. Kat. "Canadian Wildginger." *US Department of Agriculture Plant Guide*, online publication, http://plants.usda.gov/plantguide/pdf/cs_asca.pdf.

Ashworth, William. *Ogallala Blue: Water and Life on the High Plains*. New York: W. W. Norton & Co., 2006.

Audubon, Maria R. *Audubon and His Journals*. New York: Scribner's Sons, 1897.

Barrell, Joseph. *The Red Hills of Kansas: Crossroads of Plant Migrations*. Rockford, IL: Natural Land Institute, 1975.

Barringer, Felicity. "In Kansas, a Line Is Drawn Around a Prairie Dog Town." *New York Times*, December 6, 2006.

Barry, Louise. *The Beginning of the West: Annals of the Kansas Gateway to the American West, 1540–1854*. Topeka: Kansas State Historical Society, 1972.

Bee, James W. *Mammals of Kansas*. Lawrence: University of Kansas Museum of Natural History, 1981.

Bergman, Charles. *Wild Echoes: Encounters with the Most Endangered Species in North America*. New York: McGraw-Hill, 1990.

Black-footed Ferret Recovery Program website, http://www.blackfootedferret.org.

Boyle, Steve. "North American River Otter (*Lontra canadensis*): A Technical Conservation Assessment." Report for USDA Forest Service, Rocky Mountain Region, 2006.

Brosius, Liz. "Red Hills Rocks and Minerals." Kansas State Extension Service, http://www.kgs.ku.edu/Extension/redhills/rocks.html.

Brown, Dee. *Bury My Heart at Wounded Knee: An Indian History of the American West*. New York: Rinehart & Winston, 1970.

Bruchac, Joseph. *Flying with the Eagle, Racing the Great Bear: Stories from Native North America*. Mahwah, NJ: Troll Communications, 1998.

Brunson, Ken, Phyllis Scherich, Chris Berens, and Carl D. Jarboe. *A Pocket Guide to Kansas Red Hills Wildflowers*. Wichita, KS: Great Plains Nature Center, 2013.

Buchanan, Rex, and James McCauley. *Roadside Kansas: A Traveler's Guide to its Geology and Landmarks*. 2nd ed., rev. and updated. Lawrence: University Press of Kansas, 2010.

Chapman, Thomas. "James Richard Mead." *Portrait and Biography Album of Sedgwick County Kansas*. Chicago: Chapman Brothers. 1888: 155–162.

Charvat, Don. *Kansas Canoe Trails Guide*. Belle Plaine, KS: Self-Published Pamphlet, 1976.

Cockrum, Lendell. *Mammals of Kansas*. Lawrence: University of Kansas Museum of Natural History, 1952.

Cokinos, Christopher. *Hope is the thing with feathers*. New York: Warner Books, 2001.

Collins, Joseph T., ed. *Natural Kansas*. Lawrence: University Press of Kansas, 1985.

Conard, Rebecca, and Susan Hess. "Tallgrass Prairie National Preserve Legislative History 1920–1966." Report for National Park Service, 1998.

Contoski, Victor. *Broken Treaties*. New York: New Rivers Press, 1973.

Dary, David. *The Buffalo Book*. Chicago: Sage Books, 1974.

———. *The Santa Fe Trail*. New York: Alfred A. Knopf, 2000.

Deatherage, Charles P. *Early History of Greater Kansas City, Missouri and Kansas: The Prophetic City at the Mouth of the Kaw*. Kansas City, MO: Interstate Publishing, 1927.

Dixon, Benjamin Y. "Furthering Their Own Demise: How Kansa Indian Death Customs Accelerated Their Depopulation." *Ethnohistory* 54, no. 3 (summer 2007).

Downer, Deborah. "The Spirit Spring of Waconda," in *Classic American Ghost Stories*, 47–55. Little Rock, AR: August House, 1990.

Dyche, Lewis. "A Kansas Beaver." *Transactions of the Kansas Academy of Science* 21 (December 1907): 165–167.

Edmondson, Jesse. "An Ancient Red Cedar Woodland in the Oklahoma Cross Timbers." Honors thesis, University of Arkansas, 2006.

Edmunds, David. *The Shawnee Prophet*. Lincoln: University of Nebraska Press, 1985.

Farrar, Anthony. "Natural Resources of Kansas." Emporia State University, http://www .emporia.edu/earthsci/amber/go336/farrar/#Gypsum.

Ferber, Edna. *Cimarron*. New York: Grosset & Dunlap, 1929.

Flora, S. D. "The Great Flood of 1844 along the Kansas and Marais Des Cygnes Rivers." *Kansas Historical Quarterly* 20 (1952–1953): 73.

Francaviglia, Richard V. *The Cast Iron Forest: A Natural and Cultural History of the North American Cross Timbers*. Austin: University of Texas Press, 2000.

Freeman, Craig C., William H. Busby, Kelly Kindscher, Caleb Morse, Jennifer Delisle, Vaughn Salisbury, and W. Dean Kettle. *A Natural Areas Inventory of the Ft. Leavenworth Military Reservation, Leavenworth County, Kansas*. Kansas Biological Survey, Open File Report 77, August 3, 1997.

Friends of the Kaw website, http://www.kansasriver.org.

Genzel, Bill. *Dust Bowl Descent*. Lincoln: University of Nebraska Press, 1984.

Great Plains Nature Center. "Eastern Spotted Skunk." http://www.gpnc.org/esskunk.htm.

Green, Charles R. "Historical Work in Osage County." *Transactions of the Kansas State Historical Society*, 1903–1904.

Gregg, Kate, ed. *The Road to Santa Fe: The Journal and Diaries of George Champlin Sibley.* Albuquerque: University of New Mexico Press, 1952.

Gruchow, Paul. *The Necessity of Empty Places.* New York: St. Martins Press, 1981.

Gutmann, Myron, and Geoff Cunfer. "A New Look at the Causes of the Dust Bowl." Charles L. Wood Agricultural Lecture Series, no. 99-1. Lubbock, TX: International Center for Arid and Semiarid Land Studies, Texas Tech University, 1999.

Hittle, Thomas J. "Obstacles to River Recreation in Kansas." *Planet Kansas.* Sierra Club, October/November 1999.

Houts, Mike. "Cougars in Kansas: Recolonization or Fiction?" Proceedings of the 20th Annual Biannual North American Prairie Conference, 2006.

Irving, Washington. *A Tour of the Prairies.* New York: John B. Alden, 1886.

Johnston, John H. "Nez Perce Indians spent 8 months at Fort." Leavenworth *Times Weekend*, April 10, 1988.

Jones, Marcus. "Otters Return." *Kansas Wildlife and Parks* 65, no. 5 (2008): 16–23.

Kamler, Jan, and L. Green. "Recent Occurrences of Black Bears in the Southwestern Great Plains." *The Southwestern Naturalist*, 48, no. 2: 303–306.

Kansas Farm Bureau. "Kansas Farm Bureau 2008 Resolutions Online Policy Book," www .kfb.org.

Kansas State Historical Society. "Cool Things. Waconda Spring Drawing," http://www .kshs.org/c0013/waconda.htm, 2008.

Kellogg, Remington. "The Mammals of Kansas with Notes on Their Distribution, Habits, Life Histories, and Economic Importance." Thesis, University of Kansas, 1916.

Kilgo, James. *Deep Enough for Ivory Bills.* Athens: University of Georgia Press, 1995.

Kindscher, Kelly, William H. Busby, Jennifer M. Delisle, and Craig C. Freeman. *A Natural Inventory of Douglas, Johnson, Leavenworth, Miami, and Wyandotte Counties in Northeast Kansas.* Kansas Biological Survey. Open File Report 124, September 1, 2005.

Klataske, Ron. "Mountain Lions Confirmed in Kansas in Recent Years." Audubon of Kansas website, http://www.audubonofkansas.org/MountainLions/mountainlions.html, September 2, 2007.

Madson, John. *Where the Sky Began.* San Francisco: Sierra Club Books, 1982.

Marshall, James. "Archeology at Hard Chief Village." *Kansas Anthropologist* 21(1): 57–89.

McCoy, Isaac. *History of Baptist Indian Missions.* Washington, DC: William M. Morrison, 1840.

McKinley, Daniel. "History of the Carolina Parakeet in its Southwestern Range." *Wilson Bulletin* 76, no. 1 (March 1964).

Meek v. Hays, 785 P.2d at 1356, 1362 (Kan.1990).

Miner, Craig, and William Unrau. *The End of Indian Kansas: A Study of Cultural Revolution, 1854–1871.* Lawrence: University Press of Kansas, 1977.

Mollhausen, Heinrich B., and Anthony Burzle (transl). "Over the Santa Fe Trail through Kansas in 1858." *Kansas Historical Quarterly* 16, no. 4 (November 1948): 337–380.

Murphy, Dave. *Paddling Kansas*. Boulder, CO: Trail Books, 2008.

Neihardt, John. *The Splendid Wayfaring: Jedediah Smith and the Ashley-Henry Men, 1822–1831*. Lincoln: University of Nebraska Press, 1970.

Norall, Frank. *Bourgmont, explorer of the Missouri, 1698–1725*. Lincoln: University of Nebraska Press, 1988.

Ostroff, Andrea. "Distribution and Mesohabitat Characteristics of River Otter in Eastern Kansas." Master's thesis, Emporia State University, Emporia, KS, 2001.

Parker, Martha, and Betty Laird. *Soil of our Souls: Histories of the Clinton Lake Area Communities*, 5th ed. Lawrence, KS: Parker-Laird Enterprises, 1994.

Pearce, Michael. "Deer population at Shawnee Mission Park causing problems." *Wichita Eagle*, November 26, 2008.

Peterson, Jeffrey M. "Science in Kansas: The Early Years, 1804–1875." *Kansas History* 10, no. 3 (1987).

Popper, Deborah, and Frank Popper. "The Great Plains: From Dust to Dust." *Planning Magazine*, December 1987.

Reid, William. 1995. "Growing pecans in Kansas." Kansas State University Experiment Station and Cooperative Extension Service, Manhattan, KS, Publication MF-1025.

Robertson, Jason. "Navigability Laws." *American Whitewater* 18 (2001), http://www.americanwhitewater.org.

Roy, Jerry C. *Shawnee Indians in Johnson County, Kansas*. Overland Park, KS: Shawnee Indian Mission, 1985.

Sawin, Robert, and Rex Buchanan. "Kansas Springs Inventory: Water Quality, Flow Rate, and Temperature Data." Kansas Geological Survey Open File Report 2002-46, November 2002.

Sibley, David. *The Sibley Guide to Birds*. New York: Alfred A. Knopf, 2000.

Sierra Club. "America's Great Outdoors: Haskell Baker Wetlands," http://www.sierraclub.org/greatoutdoors/kansas/index.asp.

Simmons, Donald. *Centennial History of Argentine, Kansas City, Kansas 1880–1980*, Kansas City, MO: Special Publication of Simmons Funeral Home, 1980.

Smith, Cory. "Otter spotted in wetlands waters." *Lawrence Journal-World*, March 5, 2008.

Smith, Huron H. 1933. "Ethnobotany of the Forest Potawatomi Indians." *Bulletin of the Public Museum of the City of Milwaukee* 7: 1–230.

Staab, Rodney. "Kansa Presence in the Upper Kansas Valley, 1848–1867." *Kansas Anthropologist* 16(1): 24–25.

Streeter, Floyd B. *The Kaw, Heart of a Nation*. The Rivers of America Series. New York: Farrar & Rhinehart, 1941.

Sun City website, http://www.rootsweb.ancestry.com/~ksbarber/suncity.htm.

Taylor, Dale. "Notes on a Recent Collection of a Black-footed Ferret." *Transactions of the Kansas Academy of Science* 64, no. 1 (spring 1961): 41.

Thompson, Craig. *Along the Kaw: A Journey down the Kansas River*. Self Published, 2012.

Tolme, Paul. "Toughing it Out in the Badlands: Black-footed Ferrets Battle for Survival in the Nation's Heartland." *Defenders Magazine*, Summer 2005.

Toplikar, Dave. "KU Butterfly Expert Reports Mountain Lion." *Lawrence Journal-World*, December 15, 2004.

Trowbridge, Charles C. *Shawnee Traditions*. New York: AMS Press, 1980.

United States Department of Agriculture. "State Marketing Profiles: Kansas in Brief." Report, 2003.

United States Department of Agriculture Forest Service. "The Sea of Grass." Brochure, 1999.

———. Draft Cimarron and Comanche National Grasslands Land Management Plan. December 2005.

Unrau, William. *The Kaw People*. The Indian Tribal Series. Phoenix, AZ: Indian Tribal Series, 1975.

———. *Indians of Kansas*. Topeka: Kansas State Historical Society, 1991.

Ward, Kathleen. "Starting in Kansas, Untouched Forest Is Oldest in the Eastern United States." Kansas State University Research and Extension Service, May 2005, http://www.oznet.ksu.edu/news/sty/2005/untouched_forest050405.htm.

Warren, Stephen. *The Shawnees and Their Neighbors, 1795–1870*. Champaign: University of Illinois Press, 2005.

Weston Missouri website, http://westonmo.com.

Whittier, John Greenleaf. "The Burial of Thomas Barber." In *Complete Poetical Works of John Greenleaf Whittier*. Whitefish, MT: Kessinger Publishing, July 2003.

Worchester, Beverley, ed. *The Nature of Kansas Lands*. Lawrence: University Press of Kansas, 2008.

Yost, Nellie. *Medicine Lodge: The Story of a Kansas Frontier Town*. Chicago: Sage Books/Swallow Press, 1970.

Young, J., and J. C. Beard. *Caves in Kansas*. Educational Series 9. Lawrence: Kansas Geological Survey, 1993.

Index